CREDITS

Design
Andy Collins and James Wyatt (leads),
Eytan Bernstein

Additional Design
Tavis Allison, Andy Clautice, Mike Donais,
Matthew Goetz, Stephen Schubert

Additional Contributions
Greg Bilsland, Michele Carter, Chris Champagne,
Greg Collins, Brady Dommermuth, Don Frazier,
Doug Goldstein, Daniel Helmick, Craig Krohn,
Shelly Mazzanoble, Dan Milano, Didier Monin, John Rogers,
Peter Schaefer, Reid Schmadeka, Matthew Sernett,
Chris Tulach, Wil Wheaton

Development
Stephen Radney-MacFarland (lead),
Peter Schaefer, Stephen Schubert

Editing
Andy Collins (lead), Jean Nelson, Bradley Will

Managing Editing
Torah Cottrill

Director of D&D R&D and Book Publishing
Bill Slavicsek

D&D Creative Manager
Christopher Perkins

D&D Design Manager
James Wyatt

D&D Development and Editing Manager
Andy Collins

D&D Senior Art Director
Jon Schindehette

Art Director
Jon Schindehette

Cover Illustration
Mike Krahulik

Graphic Designers
Keven Smith, Leon Cortez, Emi Tanji

Additional Graphic Design
Kate Irwin

Interior Illustrations
Kalman Andrasofszky, Steven (Stan!) Brown,
John Tyler Christopher, Michael Faille,
Empty Room Studios/ Peter Lazarski,
Victoria Maderna, Patrick Thomas Parnell,
Adam Phillips, Drew Pocza

Cartographer
Jason A. Engle

Publishing Production Specialist
Angelika Lokotz

Prepress Manager
Jefferson Dunlap

Imaging Technician
Carmen Cheung

Production Manager
Cynda Callaway

Game rules based on the original DUNGEONS & DRAGONS®
rules created by **E. Gary Gygax** and **Dave Arneson**,
and the later editions by **David "Zeb" Cook** (2nd
Edition); **Jonathan Tweet, Monte Cook, Skip Williams,
Richard Baker,** and **Peter Adkison** (3rd Edition); and
Rob Heinsoo, Andy Collins, and **James Wyatt** (4th Edition).

620-25382000-001
9 8 7 6 5 4 3 2 1
First Printing: May 2010
ISBN: 978-0-7869-5488-9

U.S., CANADA, ASIA, PACIFIC,
& LATIN AMERICA
Wizards of the Coast LLC
P.O. Box 707
Renton WA 98057-0707
+1-800-324-6496

EUROPEAN HEADQUARTERS
Hasbro UK Ltd
Caswell Way
Newport, Gwent NP9 0YH
GREAT BRITAIN
Please keep this address for your records

WIZARDS OF THE COAST, BELGIUM
Industrialaan 1
1702 Groot-Bijgaarden
Belgium
+32.070.233.277

VISIT OUR WEBSITE AT WWW.WIZARDS.COM/DND

DUNGEONS & DRAGONS®

PLAYER'S STRATEGY GUIDE

ROLEPLAYING GAME SUPPLEMENT

Andy Collins • Eytan Bernstein

CONTENTS

INTRODUCTION 4
Getting into Character 4

1: BUILDING YOUR CHARACTER . . .6
Know the Campaign 8
Understand the World. 8
Accept Limits .8
Solicit Recommendations 9
Immerse Your Character 9
Know the Other Players 9
Characterization Builder 10
Concepts Lead to Goals. 10
Playing It Forward. 10
Don't Fear the Cliche 11
Looking the Part 11
What's Your Motivation? 12

BUILDING A FOUNDATION 14
Choosing Your Class 14
What Class Are You?. 15
Choosing Your Race. 18
What Race Are You? 19
Setting Your Ability Scores. 23
Start at the Top 23
Secondary Ability Scores. 23
Filling Out the Rest. 23
Choosing Your Background 24
Background Benefits 24
Reimagining Existing Backgrounds . .24
Creating a New Background. 25
Using Backgrounds from the
Nentir Vale 26
What Alignment Are You? 30
Choosing Powers 31
Builds and Power Selection 31
At-Will Attack Powers 32
Encounter Attack Powers 33
Daily Attack Powers. 33
Utility Powers. 34
Choosing Skills 37
Skills of Avoidance 37
Skills of Knowledge 38
Skills of Observation 38
Skills of Persuasion 39
Miscellaneous Skills 39
Choosing Feats 40
Controller Feats 40
Defender Feats 40
Leader Feats 41
Striker Feats 41
Multiclass Feats 42
Consider Your Party 42
Simple Is Good 42
Level Up! 44
Decisions, Decisions. 44
Guidelines for Level Choices 45
Retraining 47
Replacing Powers 49
Paragon Paths 50
Narrowing the List 50

Evaluating the Choices. 52
Walking Your Path 53
Epic Destinies .54
Breaking All The Rules. 54
Recharging Powers 54
The End Is Near 54
Making Your Mark. 54
Advanced Options 56
Multiclassing and Hybrids. 56
Constructing Good Combos. 57
Adding Defender 58
Adding Leader 59
Adding Striker 59
Adding Controller 59
Unusual Races 59
Power-Swap Feats. 60
Skill Powers .61

HOW TO 62
. . . Make the Best Healer 62
. . . Make the Fastest Character 64
. . . Get the Best Initiative 66
. . . Make the Best Talker. 68
. . . Get the Best Armor Class. 70
. . . Never Miss 72
. . . Never Fail Saving Throws 74
. . . Have the Most Hit Points 76
. . . Deal Damage Forever 78
. . . Teleport Instead of Walk 80

2: BUILDING YOUR PARTY 82
Character Roles 84
Building a Large Party 84
Building a Small Party 86
Group Characterization 89
Linking Stories 89
Compatibility Test. 89
Why Are We Here?. 89
Party Optimization. 90
Defenders: Tank-Teaming 90
Strikers: Focusing Firepower. 90
Choosing the Right Leader 91
Character Redundancy 91
Skill Training. 92
Tactical Combinations 93
Have Patience 93
Sample Party: The Spellblades 94
Sample Party:
The Guardians of Eastfall. 96
Sample Party:
The Moonlit Watchers. 98
Sample Party: The Marked Ones 100

3: STRATEGY AND TACTICS. 102
Tactics 101 104
Role-Based Tactics 104
Focusing Fire. 105
Movement and Positioning. 107
Timing 108
Managing Your Resources. 109

Common Mistakes 112
Healing 113
Hit Points and Healing Surges 113
Using Healing Surges 113
Leader Healing Tactics 114
Healing from Other Classes 115
Maximizing Your Healing Surges. . . 116
Consumable Healing 117
Know Your Enemies. 119
Monster Roles 119
Using Your Powers. 122
Know Your Powers 122
Organize Your Powers 123
Customize Your Powers. 123
Tracking Effects. 124
What to Track, and How to Do It . . 124
Who Does the Work? 126
Troubleshooting 127
You Can't Hit 127
Not Enough Healing Surges 128
Combat Gets Boring. 128
Combat Lasts Too Long 129
Your Teammates Don't Use Tactics 129
Tactics in Action—Irontooth. 130
Tactics in Action—Storm Tower. 132

4: PLAYING THE GAME 134
Storytelling 136
Driving the Story. 136
Taking the Bait. 137
Creating Your Own Hooks 137
Narrating Powers 138
Being Part of the Party 140
Rising to the (Skill) Challenge 142
Knowing When to Rest. 145
Short Rests 145
Extended Rests 145
Seriously . . . Get Some Sleep. 146
The Campaign Journal 148
The Journal 148
Treasure and Rewards. 150
Acquiring Treasure 150
Dividing Treasure 154
Customizing Your Gear 156
Other Rewards. 157
Don't Be a Jerk 158
Hogging the Spotlight 158
Lack of Preparation. 158
Interruptions 158
Ignoring Your Team 158
Arguments 159

INTRODUCTION

EVERY PERSON who plays the DUNGEONS & DRAGONS® roleplaying game has his or her own reasons and rewards for playing the game. Some players revel in working alongside their friends to achieve goals. Others enjoy exploring the stories crafted by the Dungeon Master and players as the campaign unfolds. Still others appreciate the opportunity to transport themselves beyond their everyday lives to a world of fantasy and adventure.

If you're reading this book, it's likely that you enjoy playing effectively at the table—building an interesting and powerful character, using your powers efficiently and wisely, creating compelling storylines, and working well as part of a team. If that's true, congratulations! You've come to the right place.

On the other hand, you might be struggling with the number of options available to your character. If you have difficulty deciding between one feat and another, or if your party can't seem to overcome the challenges placed in front of you by the DM, relax. We're here to help.

In this book, you'll find tips, tactics, anecdotes, and explanations, all designed to help make your games better. This book helps you optimize your characters, provides tips for managing character resources, advises you on solving age-old gaming challenges, and assists you in creating and managing effective adventuring parties. You'll also find ideas for how to create cohesive parties, how to enhance the capabilities of allies (buffing) and how to hinder the effectiveness of enemies (debuffing), and how to adapt your party's strategies to take advantage of the strengths of different combinations of characters.

WHERE CAN 1 FIND THAT POWER?

This book references classes, powers, feats, and other elements of the game from a variety of sources. To find the latest versions of these game elements, consult the D&D Compendium at www.wizards.com/dnd.

GETTING INTO CHARACTER

"We spent last session really getting into our characters." That phrase can frighten some players, but it doesn't usually mean a whole session of amateur theater, in which the heroes sit around in a tavern interacting with nonplayer characters while the players trot out hammy accents and faux-medieval dialogue. It can mean constant edge-of-your-seat tension as you immerse yourself into the simulation of a deadly battle, or that shivery sense of wonder as you visualize the marvels that lie beyond the vault door that your character has just pried open. Getting into character is about reaching the point at which you are so strongly in tune with your character's emotions and goals that your experience of playing the game aligns with what really being in that situation might be like.

In other words, when you get into character, it feels like you're not just playing a game, you're living an adventure.

You start the cycle of getting into character by creating an interesting adventurer. The character needs to be interesting to you, so that you're drawn to seeing the world through that character's eyes. But don't forget

that your character also need to be interesting to the Dungeon Master and to the other players, so that they want to involve your character in exciting events.

The process continues at the gaming table, when you actively listen to the other players (and the DM) and remove potential distractions that might come between you and your character. As you begin to identify with your character, you'll naturally do things at the table to express your character's identity. Your voice might reflect genuine anxiety when you say, "Let's get out of here before we get killed," or glee when you say, "Everyone fill your pockets with as many gems as you can carry." Hearing that emotional involvement helps the other players get into character, too, making the scene more real and vibrant for the entire group. This cycle is the essence of roleplaying, and without it your game can easily slide into little more than repetitive turn-taking.

For some players, that's all they want from DUNGEONS & DRAGONS. That style of playing is perfectly fine—as long as you're having fun, no one can tell you that you're playing the game wrong. Even the most

diehard roleplayer sometimes just enjoys blowing off steam with a simple dungeon crawl devoid of story.

But a roleplaying game can offer so much more than that, and most players—even dyed-in-the-wool character optimizers—can't play without injecting a bit of personality into their characters. So before we dive into the heavy stuff, let's talk about three basic ways to get into character by roleplaying.

ROLEPLAYING IS ACTION

"Show, don't tell" is the first rule of good drama. You define your character by the actions you choose to take in play. If you lead the charge into battle, or if you are the one to go to for esoteric knowledge, you demonstrate the essence of your character's identity.

Deeds speak louder than words, so the actions you take—or don't take—shape the image that you and the other players have of your character. Don't just write "brave" somewhere in the margin of your character sheet, display your character's bravery by challenging the toughest monster in the room or agreeing to stand up against the nastiest tyrant in the land.

You'll know you've been successful when the other players at the table can describe your character's personality as easily as if your character were their own.

ROLEPLAYING IS CHOICE

You express who you are through the decisions you make. When an adventure gives you a choice, the consequences of your choice shape your adventurer's life story. Get into character and let your character's unique concerns and motivations guide your decision so that the result is true to who you want your character to become.

Don't depend on the adventure to present your character with life-altering choices. Help the Dungeon Master create meaningful decisions for you by clearly and consistently expressing what matters to your character, and take the initiative to set up your own choices. Think ahead of time about objectives your character might pursue, and look for ways to achieve those goals through minor quests, interactions with nonplayer characters, or coordination with the other players.

ROLEPLAYING IS OTHER PEOPLE

The process of building a character involves making the character vivid in your own imagination. But the difference between a character sheet and a character isn't really established until the character comes to life in the minds of everyone at the table. The greatest moments of roleplaying are group efforts. Come up with characterization hooks that your friends can latch onto, and build on the characterization hooks the other players throw out.

HOW TO ROLEPLAY

No matter what you read or hear, there is no one correct way to play D&D (or any other roleplaying game). Some groups have fun rolling dice, slaying monsters, and leveling up. Other players gain the most enjoyment from long conversations between their characters and the DM, even if the dice never get rolled. Both of these groups are roleplaying, even if the table activity seems very different from one group to the other.

Don't listen to anyone outside your group who tells you that you aren't playing the game correctly. Above all else, play the game the way that makes it the most fun for you and for everyone else sitting at the table.

BUILDING YOUR CHARACTER

THE PROCESS of character design is one of the most enjoyable parts of any DUNGEONS & DRAGONS game. Some players are driven by a character's story. They research names and come up with elaborate backgrounds. Other players thrill to a mechanically optimized character who blasts through challenges with ease.

Most of us fall somewhere between these two extremes. We want a well-designed character who also has an interesting and compelling background. This chapter is for players in the middle of the spectrum. It guides you through the various aspects of character building and advancement, from the basics of your race and class to planning your epic destiny. It includes the following sections.

* **Know the Campaign:** The importance of the Dungeon Master's authority over his or her game.

* **Characterization Builder:** Painting the big picture to guide your choices.

* **Building a Foundation:** Concrete advice for making decisions about your character's class, race, and background elements, from both a mechanics perspective and a story perspective. Also includes tips on selecting powers, skills, and feats that you will enjoy using and that will add the most to your party as a whole.

* **Level Up!:** What to think about when you gain a level, including retraining and replacement advice.

* **Paragon Paths:** Get the most from your paragon tier character.

* **Epic Destinies:** Plan your character's destiny.

* **Advanced Options:** Explore the possibilities of multiclassing, hybrid character rules, and other unusual options.

* **How To . . . :** Each of these entries explores how specific mechanical choices can build a specialized character who maximizes his or her talents in a specific area.

KALMAN ANDRASOFSZKY

There is no such thing as a perfect character, but you can build a character who is perfect for the game you'll be playing in. To do that, you need to learn about the campaign, and the best way to learn about a campaign is to talk to your Dungeon Master.

If the goal of a D&D game is to make inspiring music together, your character is your instrument. You'll feel out of place playing a xylophone if the rest of the group is playing punk rock, or an electric bass if the Dungeon Master plans to orchestrate a grand symphony. Approach the DM beforehand to find out what kind of campaign he or she plans to run and what kinds of characters would get the most out of it.

Sometimes, you find a DM whose preferences just don't match yours. This section also describes some warning signs that can signal later problems in the campaign. If you don't already know your DM's style, these signs can point out a game that you might want to avoid.

UNDERSTAND THE WORLD

Learning some details of the campaign setting chosen by the DM allows you to choose key world elements to attach to your character. When your character concept meshes with the themes and conflicts explored in the game, major events in the campaign can have meaningful repercussions for your character, and accomplishing the goals you set for your character is more likely to have an effect on the world around your character.

Campaign settings contain a multitude of themes, so talk to your Dungeon Master to understand where he or she wants to go with the game. For example, knowing that you'll be playing in Eberron isn't enough—you could be spending your time investigating shadowy crimes in the dark alleys of Sharn, or exploring the mysteries of the Draconic Prophecy across the entire continent of Khorvaire. However, if you know that the DM intends to focus on the dark continent of Xen'drik, you can choose a primal class and take wilderness-based backgrounds to feel at home in the jungle. Alternatively, you might choose for your character to be affiliated with a dragon-marked house likely to sponsor an expedition to Xen'drik, such as Orien, Lyrandar, or Cannith.

Even if you choose to design a character that goes against the grain of the campaign's themes, you should always ensure that you have a reason to participate in the action. You can expect an EBERRON game that centers on house politics to involve tense scenes of diplomatic negotiations. Roleplaying a loud-mouthed half-orc whose uncouth presence inevitably disrupts the hushed halls of power might tempt you to forego such activity. Instead, give yourself a compelling reason to explore those halls of power and influence by making your character a scion of House Thar-ashk, or a hard-boiled investigator from Sharn who is empowered to dig out the rotten secrets of the dragon-marked houses . . . whether they like it or not.

Warning Sign: This is the first and most obvious place at which you can learn that a campaign isn't for you. If you can't get excited about the campaign setting or the themes chosen by the DM, you might find yourself growing bored easily. Boredom leads to distractions or skipped sessions, which lead to your feeling uninvolved and uninspired even when you're present. These feelings can easily rub off onto other players, and can ruin an otherwise solid campaign.

Many DMs avoid this problem by discussing the setting and themes with their players before choosing a setting. Encourage your DM to do the same. Talking about what the players and the DM expect from the world your game takes place in lets everyone at the table feel excited and involved even before the first d20 hits the table.

ACCEPT LIMITS

Many Dungeon Masters place restrictions on character creation options as part of building their own unique campaign settings, even when a setting is a variation on an existing world. Before you become committed to building your character according to a particular concept, make sure that it doesn't conflict with any limitations on character creation established for this campaign.

Rather than bridling at such limitations, see them as opportunities to challenge your preconceptions about various character combinations. You might find that working within tight restrictions spurs your creativity. Trying a campaign in which the players agree to an extremely restricted set of options—such as all martial characters or all dwarves—can allow the players to explore elements other than race and class that make characters unique.

Sometimes, a restriction might be a matter of the flavor of a class or a race: "I don't want drow player characters in my game, because in my campaign they're always villainous." You and your Dungeon Master might both be happy if you use the mechanical elements of the option but alter the flavor to suit the campaign. Even if the DM doesn't want drow player characters, he might be amenable to a special shadow-infused eladrin with racial traits fundamentally identical to the drow.

If you don't feel comfortable working within the limits set by the DM, negotiate for the elements that matter to you about making your character. A good DM knows that keeping players happy makes for a fun game, so if you can make a reasonable case for changing the campaign restrictions to allow your preferred character type, he or she might bend on that point. Don't be rude or demean the DM's work; one of the joys a DM gets from the game is building a unique campaign world, just like players enjoy building unique characters.

Even if you don't have any issues with the limitations, talk to your Dungeon Master about the significance of the campaign restrictions he or she has established. Chances are you'll learn a lot more about the campaign than just which elements are restricted.

Warning Sign: A DM unwilling to negotiate or to help you understand why he or she has established limits on character options is likely to become a DM who isn't interested in letting your character perform unusual or unexpected actions in play. If you can't find a way to build a fun character within the DM's limitations, consider finding a different game.

SOLICIT RECOMMENDATIONS

Don't just guess about the kinds of characters that might be rewarding to play when you can ask the one person who's most likely to know. Your Dungeon Master probably has plenty of ideas about backgrounds, classes, and concepts perfect for the adventures to come.

Once you understand the DM's recommendations, look for ways to put your own spin on those ideas. If he or she recommends primal characters for a wilderness-based campaign but you are most interested in the fighter class, you could decide to play a fighter raised in a barbarian tribe. Even if you don't use any of the DM's specific suggestions, these conversations can give you insights into how to build a character who meshes with the campaign, as well as an idea of what to expect in the gaming sessions to come.

Warning Sign: If you feel that the DM is unwilling to allow you to personalize his or her recommendations, you might have run into one of those rare Dungeon Masters who seek to use the players and their characters as proxies, effectively running the adventure and playing it simultaneously. Unless you're happy being a watcher, such a game isn't likely to be much fun for you.

IMMERSE YOUR CHARACTER

The *Dungeon Master's Guide*® advises your DM on how to hook characters into an adventure by giving them motivations for getting involved in the action and caring about what's at stake. Make this job easier by providing sturdy handles for those hooks.

Use what you know about the campaign setting to create meaningful relationships between your character and various people, places, and organizations in the campaign. Craft one or more individual goals for your character, based on the themes your DM has described

to you. When you find ways to make adventuring personal, you gain more than XP and gold for fulfilling the quest, you also advance your character's story.

Many gamers make hooking their characters difficult by building orphans who aren't tied down to anything in the world and who care only about themselves. Successfully resolving a conflict that threatens the people or things your character loves is more satisfying than rescuing an anonymous NPC. Choose background elements that are close to your heart, and give your character motivations and personal issues that give him or her a stake in the outcome of the adventure.

Warning Sign: Inexperienced DMs often make the mistake of holding too tightly to the story reins of the campaign. They don't want players to define anything in the world, even their own characters' places in it. Assure the DM that you don't want to derail or diminish the importance of his or her story, you just want to feel more involved in it. Once the DM gets over his or her initial concern, you might find that you've helped your DM build a better game. However, if your DM is reluctant to incorporate details about your character's background into the setting of the campaign, you might find that your interest in the game falls off after a few sessions.

KNOW THE OTHER PLAYERS

Ultimately, your character spends more time interacting with the other player characters around the table than with the setting and its nonplayer characters. Talk to the other players about their character concepts and about how your characters all fit together. During character creation, establish roleplaying relationships within the party. Build a connection between your character and at least two other characters, such as a shared background, a common friend or mentor, or a mutual goal. These connections can be mildly contentious—a friendly rivalry over who's the best talker, or contrasting beliefs or personalities. Just don't let the conflict overshadow the teamwork necessary for fun and success.

These interparty relationships are especially important in a far-ranging campaign. When you know the game will center on a limited geographical region, establishing strong connections to the local people and places makes sense. But when you and your companions head off into the wilderness or the Underdark with only one another for company for the next several sessions, you can ensure rich roleplaying interactions by establishing multiple, overlapping relationships among the characters.

Warning Sign: If you can't interest any of the other players in building these links between characters, you might have found a table of prima donnas more interested in describing their own characters' greatness than in helping you achieve it yourself.

Everyone knows that the choices you make during character creation shape the experience of playing your character at the table. But some players think this applies only to your effectiveness in combat encounters and skill challenges. Every decision you make during character creation also influences your ability to get into character and, by extension, your friends' ability to do the same. Build a character who is fun to play and fun for your fellow players to interact with.

Characterization starts with a broad concept or image. Big ideas help your character stand out. They let you easily grasp the essence of your character's personality, and they help the DM and the other players at the table understand the context of the actions you take while in character. What's more, roleplaying a character who has an oversized personality is engaging and fun. During play you'll find more opportunities to express a basic passion for gold, grog, or glory than to pursue a more refined interest, such as flower arranging.

Paint your concept with a few bold strokes, rather than detailing every little personality quirk. If you give your character too many peculiarities, you'll find that keeping track of them is difficult and none of them come up enough to stick in anyone's mind. Instead, choose one particular detail, such as vanity regarding personal appearance, that you can emphasize in many different situations.

CONCEPTS LEAD TO GOALS

Think about your favorite characters from books, movies, or comics, and summarize each of these characters' essential concepts in a sentence or two. You'll find that the best ideas are simple, but they set up interestingly complicated ramifications when that basic concept is translated into action. As you develop your own character concept, focus on future goals.

Say your initial character idea is "My wizard escaped from the destruction of her father's keep with nothing more than his spellbook and the clothes on her back." This leaves your character's motivations and future directions vague. What's the importance of your past if it doesn't mean something about your future?

Include some aspect of your character's personal goals in that big picture. The same character might be described in this way, instead: "My wizard is driven by hatred for those who destroyed her father's keep, and by the fear that she will prove unworthy of his legacy by failing to master the spells in his spellbook."

This tells both you and the Dungeon Master right away what the character wants to do: seek revenge and unravel the clues found in the cryptic notes in her father's grimoire.

PLAYING IT FORWARD

A solid concept helps you stay true to your characterization goals during character creation and gameplay. As you make choices during character creation, think about which options make sense for your idea, and how you might explain your chosen options in light of your character concept. Why does your chosen class present the right method of achieving your goals? What significance does your starting feat have in light of your character concept? Do your powers need new names or flavor text to describe how you use them?

Imagine that the player of the wizard described earlier felt drawn to the Wintertouched feat. The player might decide that her character's father's keep was made of ice and that she suspects that the spells and rituals in his grimoire were taught to him by a gelugon. Furthermore, the player decides that her flaming sphere spell works by first stealing heat from the nearby area. When she casts the spell, she describes how everyone feels a chill in the air just before the flames burst into life. That's a detail that everyone will remember.

A simple, unified concept also helps other players get on board so they can play along. Once you have a sentence that boils down the essence of your character, don't be shy about sharing it. When you put your figure on the table and announce, "My dwarf ranger, Rakshukshak, is the world's foremost expert on all manner of beasts—or at least he thinks he is," you immediately offer the group fun ways to interact with your character. One player might remember to turn to you and ask your opinion on each new creature the party encounters, giving you an opportunity both to roleplay your character and to take advantage of your investment in monster-knowledge skills. Another player might pick up on the hint that you don't take Rakshukshak's mastery too seriously and set himself up as your rival, with each of you seeking to outdo the other by inventing unlikely bits of monster trivia for the edification of your fellow adventurers and the entertainment of the group.

Don't Fear the Cliché

When confronted with familiar races and classes, many players revert to stereotypes for those characters' actions. Rather than fearing this tendency or allowing it to straitjacket your creativity, embrace it and then tweak those stereotypes.

The good news about these built-in player expectations is that they help everyone get to super-awesome-let's-pretend time sooner. Without a familiar frame of reference, other players might struggle to understand who and what your character is.

As an example, take a look at the taglines provided at the start of each race's description in the *Player's Handbook*, as well as the "play this race if you want . . . " bullet points for each race. Do these statements embrace every potential member of the race equally? No—they set up in broad strokes what you can expect from a character of the race in question. Without that framework, a dragonborn just becomes a big scaly humanoid who can breathe fire. When you use preconceived notions as building blocks, you can spend less work establishing the baseline expectations of your character and more time on what makes you unique.

Embracing a stereotype need not limit your creativity or options. A seductive troubadour feels different from a fighting skald or a mysterious storyteller, but each character concept fits easily within the broad archetype of the bard class. Focus on one aspect of your class's archetype to exaggerate. Fighters are driven to prove themselves through conflict, so maybe yours is especially prone to rivalry. Then deepen your characterization by thinking about how the consequences of that aspect would have been reflected in your character's background. Does constant competition cause your fighter have to a tense relationship with a sibling? Is your fighter unwilling to talk about anything related to his or her most stinging defeat?

Once you establish that baseline element, you can create dramatic contrast by choosing a notable place to play against your archetype. A warlock fanatically devoted to carrying a treasured weapon is more memorable and interesting than a fighter who has the same obsession.

Looking the Part

Helping others visualize your character's appearance can also establish your identity. When you introduce your character to the other players, describe what he or she wears. When the time comes to spend your adventuring wealth, shop for particularly utilitarian or extraordinarily flamboyant clothing, or specify exactly how an item being created for you should look.

Visuals at the table can help, too. Basing your character concept on a favorite miniature can inspire your creativity and also constantly reminds others of what your character is all about. Draw a portrait or search the Internet for an image that depicts your character's style and add that to your character sheet. If you use nametags or table tents to identify yourself in the game, add your illustration there, as well.

Don't overlook your character's equipment as a tool for establishing appearance and characterization. Compared to other aspects of character building, your choice of equipment offers plenty of room for creativity and flexibility. This goes beyond the obvious decisions of weapons and armor: Come up with a couple of interesting possessions to wear or carry around, such as a distinctive gold-plated whistle or a shrunken head in a lead-lined box. Of course, you'd better have an explanation ready for when the other players ask you what's going on with that box! Be reasonable, and don't expect any significant game effect from these items unless you work something out with your DM beforehand.

THE MOTIVATIONS

Here's a brief rundown of the eight basic player motivations. See Chapter 1 in the *Dungeon Master's Guide* for more details.

Actor: You like to pretend to be your character, valuing your character's personality and motivations over mechanical elements.

Explorer: You want to experience the wonders of the game world, learning about the people, places, and history you encounter.

Instigator: You enjoy making things happen. You prefer action over planning, and sometimes make deliberately bad choices to see what happens.

Power gamer: You like to optimize your character, choosing the best mechanical elements to create a perfect build.

Slayer: You just love to kill monsters, and you prefer combat to any other situation.

Storyteller: You want to hear the ongoing story of the game. It's important that your character's background is significant to the game's narrative.

Thinker: You prefer to make careful choices, solving challenges and puzzles in an organized and methodical way.

Watcher: You like being part of the group, but you don't want to be the center of attention. You just want everyone to have fun.

WHAT'S YOUR MOTIVATION?

Every D&D player agrees that the game provides a unique kind of enjoyment and satisfaction unlike anything you get from other forms of entertainment. But different types of players are motivated to play by the different experiences they get out the game.

The *Dungeon Master's Guide* identifies and describes eight basic player motivation categories: actor, explorer, instigator, power gamer, slayer, storyteller, thinker, and watcher. Which one are you? Take this quiz and find out.

INSTRUCTIONS

For each question, choose the answer that best applies. If you can't decide between two options, select them both. Then, find your answers in the key below. Add up the number of answers you gave for each motivation to see how important that motivation is for you.

1. Deep in the Underdark, your party pursues a wizard who has betrayed you. Footprints lead one direction, but you hear something coming down the other tunnel. You say:

A. "Let's ambush whatever's coming, because we know that'll be a fight. We could waste hours of time in these passages without meeting a single foe."

B. "My lust for revenge burns like alchemist's fire. Each moment it remains unquenched, I suffer. If these footprints might belong to my enemy, I must follow."

C. "The approaching noise is probably a mindless predator drawn by our lights. Our contact in the mage's guild said the wizard had apprentices—if these footprints aren't his own, they might have been left by a student who could lead us to him."

D. "According to my map, this tunnel leads to the duergar city. I see nowhere else the wizard might be headed. Let's get there first and learn something about the city that we can use against him when he arrives."

2. Another player wants to set up an ambush in preparation for an upcoming combat encounter. Which argument is most persuasive?

A. With a surprise round, a good initiative check, and an action point, your rogue gets combat advantage with three attacks before the enemies get to move.

B. Surrounding the enemies prevents them from escaping and spreading word of your presence, which could prevent problems for you later.

C. It gives you a chance to describe how your character learned to set up camouflage blinds and decoys while growing up in the Fellreeve.

D. The friend who proposed the ambush hasn't gotten the party to follow her suggestions lately.

3. A social skill challenge with the prince of the Efreet broke down, and now the party has to fight their way out of the City of Brass. What explains the breakdown?

A. Nobody in the party is trained in Insight, even though you told the paladin to swap her Heal training for Insight last time you all leveled up.

B. Who cares? It's time to stop talking and start kicking efreet butt!

C. During the skill challenge, you learned that the prince opposes the faction that can aid your quest. Publicly making an enemy of him will help you befriend his rivals.

D. The party had all the information it needed from the prince, so you used his crown of flame to light your pipe.

4. During a session, the Dungeon Master notices you're writing something. You show her:

A. A map of the dungeon, with notes indicating the possible location of areas you've heard the inhabitants talk about.

B. A list of suspects responsible for the mysterious crime wave hitting the characters' home city.

C. A note to the DM describing how you want to plant a forged love letter from the goblin empress in one of your comrade's backpacks.

D. Funny things people said during the session, to be added to the campaign's quotation list.

5. Which of these behaviors from other players bugs you the most?

A. Talking out of character during intense role-playing moments.

B. Moving to a square that prevents your character from charging into a flanking position.

C. Putting you on the spot to make an important decision for the group.

D. Forgetting the name of the duke's chamberlain during a tense negotiation.

6. It really makes your day when you:
- A. Discover a hidden sublevel in a dungeon that other characters passed by without noticing.
- B. Hear the other players talking about a crazy situation you got them into months ago.
- C. Use what you've learned about the enemy to manipulate them into fighting each other instead of you.
- D. Roll back-to-back critical hits and drop an enemy before it takes a swing at you.

7. When you level up, how do you prefer to choose your new power?
- A. Visit the character optimization forum at the DUNGEONS & DRAGONS website to read discussions about builds for your class.
- B. Think about what best fits the things your character might have learned based on the last few sessions.
- C. Get advice from the DM or another player.
- D. Figure out the maximum damage that each one could do, and pick the biggest number.

8. Why might you choose to seek out an artifact?
- A. The potential for conflict between its goals and yours offers great roleplaying opportunities.
- B. It has a mind of its own, and following its impulses is sure to keep things interesting and unpredictable.
- C. Finding it requires a long, exciting process of researching buried secrets and interpreting clues.
- D. It is the last link to a forgotten world of the past, and it might know secrets of an ancient culture.

9. A dispute has arisen among your fellow players. What would most make you want to resolve it?
- A. People are starting to take it personally, and you want everyone to get along.
- B. The disagreement is taking time away from an exciting combat.
- C. Success in D&D depends on teamwork, and an unresolved argument makes cooperation more difficult.
- D. Your character has been through a lot with this party, and the dispute imperils those hard-won bonds of fellowship.

10. The most important feature of a dungeon is:
- A. A complex, nonlinear layout, with branching paths, hidden areas, and alternate routes.
- B. Puzzles, clever traps, and opportunities to gain a strategic advantage through good planning.
- C. Rooms full of chests to search and doors to open—preferably during combat!
- D. A rich history and intricate relationships among the dungeon's denizens.

SCORING KEY
Actor: 1B, 2C, 5A, 8A, 9D
Explorer: 1D, 4A, 6A, 8D, 10A
Instigator: 3D, 4C, 6B, 8B, 10C
Power gamer: 2A, 3A, 5B, 7A, 9C
Slayer: 1A, 3B, 6D, 7D, 9B
Storyteller: 1C, 3C, 5D, 7B, 10D
Thinker: 2B, 4B, 6C, 8C, 10B
Watcher: 2D, 4D, 5C, 7C, 9A

SCORING YOUR MOTIVATION

Add up the number of points you scored for each motivation.

4-5: This is a primary motivation for you. Share your motivation with your DM, so he or she knows the best ways to keep you engaged in the game.

2-3: This is a secondary motivation for you. You enjoy occasional events that satisfy this type of player, but you get bored without some variety in the DM's approach.

0-1: This is not your motivation. At best, you tolerate events designed for this type of player, but you're always itching to get back to what makes the game fun for you.

BUILDING A FOUNDATION

Some players begin the character creation process by thinking about their character's race, and others gravitate toward class choice first. At the risk of over-simplification, the former player tends to favor story over mechanics, and the latter often reverses those priorities. Since we have to start somewhere, this book handles class selection first, but you can easily jump back and forth between the sections depending on your preferences.

Regardless of which way you lean, you shouldn't make the two decisions independently of one another. Even though any race can pair effectively with any class, certain combinations offer significant advantages for your character.

This section guides you through the initial decisions that shape your character, including class, race, ability scores, and background. These selections influence all the later choices you make about character creation and advancement.

CHOOSING YOUR CLASS

Every player knows that a character's class has a larger effect than anything else on the other decisions made during character creation. Beyond mechanics and rules, though, your character's class also shapes a significant portion of his or her identity in the game. Your character's class influences where your character stands on the battlefield, which skills he or she brings to noncombat challenges, and how nonplayer characters think about and interact with your character.

With over two dozen classes to choose from, the combined scope and importance of this decision can be daunting. Opening up the D&D Character Builder for the first time when starting a new campaign can intimidate even experienced players. This section provides tips and guidance to help connect you with the ideal class.

Include the story of your class in your selection process. Treating a class as nothing more than features and a power list ignores valuable tools that can help you bring your character to life at the table. Anyone can tell the difference between a cleric and a warlord by the powers they use; strive to achieve that same individuality in your character's attitude, appearance, and actions by harnessing what makes your class unique from all others.

CHARACTER ROLES

Each class in DUNGEONS & DRAGONS falls into one of four basic character roles, described on page 16 of the *Player's Handbook*. This role describes, in broad terms, the class's basic function in battle. Your character's

role helps you (and the other players) know what to expect from your character, at least in general terms.

Don't confuse class and role. Your character's class clearly defines how you interact with various rules of the game: how many hit points you gain per level, what features you gain, which powers you can select, and so forth. With very few exceptions, your role doesn't have anything to do with the rules of the game. Instead, your character's role serves as a tool for understanding how you fit into your group.

Roles group the many classes of D&D into similar categories for easy comparison. Two different classes that have the same role, such as a fighter and a warden, aren't identical, but they have more in common with one another than with classes of other roles. Both of these defender classes share high defenses (particularly AC), good durability, decent melee attacks, and a talent for drawing enemy attacks toward themselves (and away from their allies).

Many players begin their decision on which class to play by first selecting a role. Sometimes that's because the player prefers the talents common to a particular role, but more often it's to help fill a gap and create a strong, well-rounded party. (See Chapter 2 for more on this topic.) Either way, knowing the roles can help you choose the class that's right for you.

The *Player's Handbook* provides basic information on each of the four roles, and anyone who's played the game has likely seen all four roles in action. But if you've watched only one or two examples of a character role in play (or if you weren't paying attention when the players identified which roles their characters filled), these hints might help you figure out which role you'd prefer for your next character.

Controller: If you play this role, expect to stand at the back of the party a lot. You don't want to get mixed up in melee: That's for your allies to worry about.

You don't deal as much damage—at least per target—as the strikers do, so if you measure your success by the damage result you call out on a hit, look elsewhere.

By spreading your damage across multiple targets, you don't get to deliver the killing attack quite as often on the big, tough enemies. Instead, you contribute more tactically by applying the perfect penalty or limiting condition on the monsters, restricting their ability to hurt you and your friends.

Of all the player motivations (see the quiz on page 12), thinkers fit best with controller classes. Played right, a controller can often turn the tide of a battle before it even gets dangerous. In a game with lots of minions, the slayer has great fun playing a controller.

Controller classes include the druid, invoker, psion, seeker, and wizard.

WHAT CLASS ARE YOU?

Have you ever wondered which of the D&D classes best fits your own preferences and talents? Take this quiz to find out which of the eight classes from the *Player's Handbook* matches you the best. The results might even suggest a class for your next adventurer.

INSTRUCTIONS

For each question, choose the answer that best applies. Then, find your answers in the key below. Add up the number of answers you gave for each class to see which class best fits your attitude.

1. What's your best quality?
   A. I'm the smartest one in the room.
   B. I know how to get out of trouble.
   C. I have a winning personality.
   D. I don't know how to quit.

2. Who would you trust to teach you?
   A. Only the greatest tactical minds of the kingdom.
   B. I deserve training from a mighty archmage.
   C. The elders of my temple can teach me all I need to know.
   D. Nobody. My talents will be self-taught.
   E. You don't want to know. Seriously.

3. Where do you like to stand in battle?
   A. Right in front of the enemy.
   B. Wherever I can keep an eye on my friends.
   C. Someplace dark, where the enemy can't see me.
   D. Surrounded by my protecting comrades.

4. What does your wardrobe remind people of?
   A. A college graduation.
   B. An appointment they have . . . somewhere else.
   C. A taxidermy shop.
   D. A scrapyard.

5. How do you like to fight evil?
   A. With a weapon in one hand and my holy symbol emblazoned on my armor.
   B. With the best weapon I can find.
   C. With the talents of my fine comrades.
   D. With fiery magic.

6. Which of these is your favorite deity?
   A. Pelor, the enemy of all that is evil.
   B. Kord, the lord of battle.
   C. Avandra, because she brings me luck on my travels.
   D. Corellon, patron of arcane magic.

7. What's your favorite moment in battle?
   A. Feeling enemy attacks bounce harmlessly off my armor.
   B. Dropping an enemy with a single strike.
   C. Blowing up a room full of goblins.
   D. Seeing an ally deliver the killing blow.

8. How hard is it for enemies to take you down?
   A. Everyone knows I'm pretty fragile, so I stay in the back.
   B. Why bother finding out?
   C. I'm not afraid of taking a hit or two.
   D. Not gonna happen.

9. Do your allies trust you?
   A. As long as I'm between them and the monster.
   B. Only when they can see me . . . which isn't all that often.
   C. No, but that's just because I accidentally blew them up a couple times.
   D. Trust me? I'm the one keeping them alive!

10. Are you a people person?
   A. Are you kidding? The main table at the local tavern is my home away from home!
   B. People look up to me, so it doesn't pay to build personal relationships.
   C. I'm good with people, but I've never quite fit in.
   D. I prefer solitude, whether in my study or walking in the woods.

SCORING KEY

Cleric: 1D, 2C, 3A, 4D, 5A, 5C, 6A, 7D, 8C, 9D, 10B
Fighter: 1D, 2A, 3A, 4D, 5A, 6A, 7A, 8D, 9A, 10C
Paladin: 1C, 1D, 2C, 3A, 4D, 5A, 6A, 7A, 8D, 9A, 10C
Ranger: 1B, 2D, 3D, 4C, 5B, 6C, 7B, 8B, 8C, 9B, 10D
Rogue: 1B, 1C, 2D, 3C, 4B, 5B, 6C, 7B, 8B, 9B, 10A
Warlock: 1B, 1C, 2D, 2E, 3C, 4B, 5D, 6D, 7B, 8B, 9B, 10C
Warlord: 1A, 1D, 2A, 3A, 4D, 5C, 6B, 7D, 8C, 9D, 10B
Wizard: 1A, 2B, 2D, 4A, 5D, 6D, 7C, 8A, 9C, 10D

SCORING YOUR CLASS AFFINITY

Add up the number of points you scored for each class.

8 or more: You're a natural fit for this class. I bet you've been playing one for a while, right?
5 to 7: You have a definite knack for this class. Even if it's not your highest-scoring class, you'd probably enjoy it.
2 to 4: You don't enjoy what this class offers. You should probably steer clear of it unless you're interested in a distinct change of pace.
0 or 1: This class is a terrible fit for you. If the group tries to pressure you into playing one, find a new table!

Defender: You stand at the center of the action. When played right, your defender takes more attacks than any two other characters combined, but that's just the way you like it.

Yes, you kill things with your sword, but don't try to keep up with the damage output of the strikers. By the end of any fight, you should instead be bragging about how much total damage you took, while accepting the grateful thanks of all those other squishy characters.

Many players new to 4th Edition D&D mistakenly assume that defender classes require no tactical decision-making. The choice of how to use your marking ability, which monsters to ignore and which to engage, and even which square to occupy all offer great puzzles for the defender to solve on the battlefield.

Players who have the instigator motivation like playing defenders because they can survive the risks they provoke. Slayers also like defenders because of the visceral enjoyment gained by taking the monsters' best hits without flinching. Thinkers love the defender's ability to lock down monsters and win combats through patience and high defenses.

Defender classes include the battlemind, fighter, paladin, swordmage, and warden.

Leader: Whether the other players at the table realize it or not, you're in charge of every battle. You decide who gets healed and who gets buffed. You influence the party's tactics with situational bonuses and extra actions. Every player at the table counts on you to be at the top of your game. If you can't see opportunities when they occur or foresee challenges before they happen, you'll all be in trouble.

An optimal leader understands that group success outweighs individual achievements. With every decision made during character creation, the leader thinks about how it improves the party and helps win battles. The leader gladly trades a little of his or her own personal glory to let another character pull off something fantastic.

The tactical responsibilities of a leader appeal to thinkers who see every combat as a puzzle to be

FORGETTING TO HEAL YOUR ALLIES

If you don't enjoy healing others, don't play a leader. If you worry that you might forget to dish out the healing, or if you become annoyed when another player asks you to spend actions for healing, don't play a leader. If you intend to spend all your healing on yourself, don't play a leader. If you hope to auction off your healing like Sotheby's or if you expect religious conversion, monetary payments, or player contributions for your healing service, don't play a leader.

If you need any of this advice, don't play a leader.

solved through the timely application of the right powers and positioning. The power gamer who understands that boosting the right ally is just like dealing damage him- or herself gravitates toward the leader role. Actors like playing leaders who also function as the party spokesperson (a common overlap, due to the large number of Charisma-focused leader classes).

Leader classes include the ardent, artificer, bard, cleric, runepriest, shaman, and warlord.

Striker: You kill monsters and slip away to fight elsewhere. You are the king of dealing damage to individual foes; nobody has a higher damage roll than you.

Some players describe strikers as self-centered. A more charitable description might be "focused on maximizing their personal achievement." Strikers don't concern themselves with helping other characters at the table, other than by dispatching all the monsters quickly. If you'd rather focus on tracking down and dropping that one annoying monster rather than worrying about what your allies are doing, the striker role is right for you.

Slayers and power gamers alike love making the DM's jaw drop by announcing how much damage their striker just dealt to the lead monster. Instigators appreciate the striker's ability to get out of trouble. Watchers like the simplicity of the striker: Go kill that monster, then move to the next one.

There are more striker classes than any other role, including the assassin, avenger, barbarian, monk, ranger, rogue, sorcerer, and warlock.

HIDDEN TALENTS

Your character's role, however, only begins to describe his or her talents on and off the battlefield. Even though a fighter, a paladin, and a swordmage might all assume similar responsibilities as part of an adventuring team, they achieve the role in different ways. These varying approaches make each class unique, and they often form the basis for a player's choice of which class to play in the game.

Skim through the hidden talents of the various classes given below to see which ones make you want to learn more. The parenthetical letter indicates the class's role: controller (C), defender (D), leader (L), or striker (S). Although this book can't provide detailed analyses of every class, you can visit the Wizards Community D&D forums to learn more.

Ardent (L): Your Ardent Mantle class feature helps your entire party in social skill challenges.

Artificer (L): You manage your party's resources to maximize both survival and destructive power.

Assassin (S): You're the sneakiest of all characters; your patient stealth is rewarded with enemy death. Anything you hold becomes a deadly weapon.

Avenger (S): You hit more often than any character in the game. You can lock down a single enemy as well as a defender can.

Barbarian (S): You're the toughest striker in the game. Your rage powers let you adapt to the needs of a particular battle with frenzied energy.

Bard (L): You can shape your character to fit any party need.

Battlemind (D): You are the most versatile of defenders, with many at-will options that punish enemies for ignoring you, enhance your survivability, or control your immediate vicinity.

Cleric (L): You're the best healer in the game, but you also excel at reducing your enemies' ability to dish out damage.

Druid (C): You can shift easily between distant battlefield control and up-close-and-personal melee carnage.

Fighter (D): You can achieve great control over your immediate surroundings. Nobody is harder to run away from than you.

Invoker (C): Not only can you rain fiery destruction down on your enemies without endangering your nearby allies, such powers can aid your allies as well.

Monk (S): You're great at fighting mobs of minions. Like the assassin, you can turn any object into a weapon.

Paladin (D): You have the best healing in the game outside the leader classes. You're also the most self-sacrificing of the defender classes, putting your own safety on the line to rescue allies from danger.

Psion (C): You have more options at your fingertips every round than any other controller, and your psionic augmentation allows you to adjust power effects on the fly.

Ranger (S): Perhaps the simplest class to play effectively. You can quickly react to enemy actions, even when it isn't your turn.

Rogue (S): You're the most versatile striker, with answers for nearly any situation in or out of combat. You gain great benefits from strong tactical play.

Runepriest (L): Of all leaders, you're the best in melee combat, with good armor and frequent bonuses to damage rolls.

Seeker (C): Your powers have tremendous range, and you have great single-target powers for a controller.

Shaman (L): Your powers offer tremendous opportunities for tactical mastery.

Sorcerer (S): You combine the high damage of the striker with the multitarget attacks of the controller.

Swordmage (D): You're very mobile, and unlike other defenders you're good at fighting distant enemies. You can protect your allies even from across the battlefield.

Warden (D): You're incredibly tough and durable, and the best at shaking off harmful conditions. Your guardian form powers let you customize your defensive prowess for key battles.

Warlock (S): You frustrate your enemies with deception, teleportation, and nasty control powers.

Warlord (L): You make your allies look great by giving them extra movement and attacks. Your fighter hits enemies with his sword, but you hit enemies with your fighter.

Wizard (C): Your spellbook, ritual selection, and cantrips provide the widest range of problem-solving options of any character.

TELL US ABOUT YOUR CHARACTER

I am a huge fan of playing characters that are fun to role-play, even if they aren't optimized. As a result, I often base my characters on TV shows and movies (Doc Holliday from *Tombstone* for my sickly halfling rogue, or the Dude from *The Big Lebowski* for my gnome bard). One of my most memorable characters was Zwardheb the dragonborn paladin, whom I based on Ben Edwards's classic superhero, the Tick.

Zwardheb was an incredibly strong, virtually indestructible moron. I tanked his Wisdom (not the best stat for a paladin to tank) and Intelligence to bump up his Constitution, Strength, and Charisma. His Dexterity, and thus his Reflex, remained at base levels, but this wasn't a character that got out of the way of things. I made him an avenging paladin of Bahamut, the only build that allowed me to dodge his crippling Wisdom, and gave him feats to enhance his unstoppable juggernaut of justice persona.

I would never recommend this build for a paladin. His low Wisdom modifier made half the class's powers unusable. However, that let me focus on powers more appropriate for his character. *Divine challenge* gave me

plenty of excuses to cry out Tick-inspired threats of justice at my enemies. I loved charging headlong into the fray, depending on lots of hit points to keep me alive, screaming "Never swim against the mighty tide of justice!" as I went. That my character's lack of Intelligence and Wisdom got us into the situation in the first place was beside the point.

In the end, mighty Zwardheb did indeed fall as he held a bridge against a rampaging horde of bugbears. Even his stratospheric hit points could not survive 15d10 falling damage. But he died holding the line against a tide of evil, which seems appropriate. Zwardheb would have met his end in no other way. As the oft-clueless paladin would say: "The insomnia of evil is no match for the mighty *sleep spell of justice!*"

REID SCHMADEKA works in Organized Play at Wizards of the Coast as corporate programs manager. Luckily, the job is more exciting than it sounds. He is an avid D&D player, and he enjoys daggers, moonlit sneak attacks, and long tumbles on the beach.

CHOOSING YOUR RACE

Ask a player to describe his or her character: Odds are that he or she uses both race and class in the first sentence. Why? Compared to your selections of powers and feats, your race makes only a marginal contribution to your list of mechanical options. Instinctively, however, players recognize the importance that the choice of race has on a character's identity. Race influences a wide variety of aspects, such as a character's accent, speech patterns, clothing, backstory, and feat and paragon path prerequisites. Even a character's name often owes a debt to his or her race: Someone named Tordek Stonewalker isn't likely to be an elf.

Just as your class choice often operates as shorthand for the party role you plan to assume, your race can act as a signal to other players about the personality you intend to depict through your character. Sure, you could play an ale-swilling half-elf who has a plaited beard and a predilection for living in caves, but if it walks like a dwarf and quacks like a dwarf....

Before committing to a particular race, learn about any restrictions or alterations your DM has applied to the races present in his or her campaign setting. Even if elves are mechanically identical to the race depicted in the *Player's Handbook*, the fact that they live as slaves to hobgoblin warlords might influence your decision to play an elf rogue.

Beyond the story you want to tell with your character, a race's mechanical traits affect your choice of

continued on page 21

MATCHING PRIMARY ABILITY SCORES

Class	Primary Ability	Matching Races
Ardent	Charisma	Changeling, dragonborn, drow, gnome, half-elf, halfling, human, kalashtar, shardmind, tiefling
Artificer	Intelligence	Changeling, deva, eladrin, genasi, githzerai, gnome, human, shadar-kai, shardmind, tiefling
Assassin	Dexterity	Changeling, drow, eladrin, elf, githzerai, gnoll, halfling, half-orc, human, razorclaw shifter, revenant, shadar-kai, wilden
Avenger	Wisdom	Deva, dwarf, elf, githzerai, human, kalashtar, longtooth shifter, minotaur, razorclaw shifter, shardmind, wilden
Barbarian	Strength	Dragonborn, genasi, goliath, half-orc, human, longtooth shifter, minotaur, warforged
Bard	Charisma	Changeling, dragonborn, drow, gnome, half-elf, halfling, human, kalashtar, shardmind, tiefling
Battlemind	Constitution	Dwarf, half-elf, gnoll, goliath, human, minotaur, revenant, warforged, wilden
Cleric	Strength	Dragonborn, genasi, goliath, half-orc, human, longtooth shifter, minotaur, warforged
Cleric	Wisdom	Deva, dwarf, elf, githzerai, human, kalashtar, longtooth shifter, minotaur, razorclaw shifter, shardmind, wilden
Druid	Wisdom	Deva, dwarf, elf, githzerai, human, kalashtar, longtooth shifter, minotaur, razorclaw shifter, shardmind, wilden
Fighter	Strength	Dragonborn, genasi, goliath, half-orc, human, longtooth shifter, minotaur, warforged
Invoker	Wisdom	Deva, dwarf, elf, githzerai, human, kalashtar, longtooth shifter, minotaur, razorclaw shifter, shardmind, wilden
Monk	Dexterity	Changeling, drow, eladrin, elf, githzerai, gnoll, halfling, half-orc, human, razorclaw shifter, revenant, shadar-kai, wilden
Paladin	Charisma	Changeling, dragonborn, drow, gnome, half-elf, halfling, human, kalashtar, shardmind, tiefling
Paladin	Strength	Dragonborn, genasi, goliath, half-orc, human, longtooth shifter, minotaur, warforged
Psion	Intelligence	Changeling, deva, eladrin, genasi, githzerai, gnome, human, shadar-kai, shardmind, tiefling
Ranger	Dexterity	Changeling, drow, eladrin, elf, githzerai, gnoll, halfling, half-orc, human, razorclaw shifter, revenant, shadar-kai, wilden
Ranger	Strength	Dragonborn, genasi, goliath, half-orc, human, longtooth shifter, minotaur, warforged
Rogue	Dexterity	Changeling, drow, eladrin, elf, githzerai, gnoll, halfling, half-orc, human, razorclaw shifter, revenant, shadar-kai, wilden
Runepriest	Strength	Dragonborn, genasi, goliath, half-orc, human, longtooth shifter, minotaur, warforged
Seeker	Wisdom	Deva, dwarf, elf, githzerai, human, kalashtar, longtooth shifter, minotaur, razorclaw shifter, shardmind, wilden
Shaman	Wisdom	Deva, dwarf, elf, githzerai, human, kalashtar, longtooth shifter, minotaur, razorclaw shifter, shardmind, wilden
Sorcerer	Charisma	Changeling, dragonborn, drow, gnome, half-elf, halfling, human, kalashtar, shardmind, tiefling
Warden	Strength	Dragonborn, genasi, goliath, half-orc, human, longtooth shifter, minotaur, warforged
Warlock	Charisma	Changeling, dragonborn, drow, gnome, half-elf, halfling, human, kalashtar, shardmind, tiefling
Warlock	Constitution	Dwarf, half-elf, gnoll, goliath, human, minotaur, revenant, warforged, wilden
Warlord	Strength	Dragonborn, genasi, goliath, half-orc, human, longtooth shifter, minotaur, warforged
Wizard	Intelligence	Changeling, deva, eladrin, genasi, githzerai, gnome, human, shadar-kai, shardmind, tiefling

WHAT RACE ARE YOU?

Many players have an affinity for particular aspects of the D&D races, whether it's the pluckiness of a halfling or the gruff temperament of a dwarf.

Take this quiz to learn which of the eight races in the *Player's Handbook* has the most in common with your own personality and style.

INSTRUCTIONS

For each question, choose the answer that best applies. Then, find your answers in the key below. Add up the number of answers you gave for each race to see which one is the best match.

1. What is your most distinguishing physical feature?
- A. My short stature.
- B. My ears.
- C. My teeth.
- D. Actually, I look like lots of people.

2. What do people remember about you?
- A. I know everything.
- B. Everybody likes me.
- C. I never get sick.
- D. Fastest hands in the kingdom!
- E. My big muscles.
- F. You can't put one over on me.
- G. I'm good at everything.

3. Which trait is most important to you?
- A. Loyalty to friends.
- B. Self-sufficiency.
- C. Versatility.
- D. Luck.

4. What do you do when you're in a tight spot?
- A. I slip away to fight another day.
- B. I talk my way out of trouble.
- C. I stand my ground no matter what.
- D. I make my enemies regret the day they were born.

5. What is your favorite color?
- A. Gold, the color of wealth!
- B. Red, the color of blood and fire!
- C. Green, the color of nature!
- D. Silver, the color of a fine blade!

6. What does it take to become your friend?
- A. Hard-earned trust.
- B. Anyone who stands beside me in battle is my friend.
- C. A kind and joyous heart.
- D. I can get along with anyone.

7. How do you feel about the past?
- A. I miss the old days.
- B. Remembering the past helps shape the present.
- C. Nostalgia is overrated; I live for today.
- D. The best is yet to come . . . and I'm going to help make it happen!

8. What's the last letter of your name?
- A. A
- B. R
- C. S
- D. N
- E. Something else.

9. How's your family life?
- A. I respect my ancestors above all.
- B. I enjoy spending time with my great-great-grandparents.
- C. I live on my own, taking care of myself.
- D. Let me introduce you to all my cousins!

10. Where do you feel most at home?
- A. A noisy tavern.
- B. A dark alley.
- C. A raucous battlefield.
- D. The peaceful wilderness.

SCORING KEY

Dragonborn: 1C, 2B, 2E, 3A, 4D, 5B, 5D, 6B, 7A, 8A, 8B, 8D, 9A, 10C

Dwarf: 1A, 2C, 2F, 3B, 4C, 5A, 6B, 7B, 8B, 8D, 9A, 10A, 10C

Eladrin: 1B, 2A, 1D, 3A, 4A, 5C, 6A, 7B, 8A, 8D, 9B, 10D

Elf: 1B, 2D, 2F, 3D, 4D, 5C, 6C, 7C, 8A, 9B, 10D

Half-elf: 1B, 1D, 2B, 2C, 2G, 3C, 4B, 5C, 6D, 7D, 8D, 8E, 9C, 10A

Halfling: 1A, 2B, 2D, 3D, 4A, 5A, 5C, 6D, 7C, 8D, 8E, 9D, 10A, 10D

Human: 1D, 2G, 3C, 4C, 5A, 5D, 6D, 7D, 8E, 9C, 10A

Tiefling: 1C, 2A, 2B, 3B, 4B, 5B, 6A, 7A, 8A, 8C, 8E, 9C, 10B

SCORING YOUR RACE AFFINITY

Add up the number of points you scored for each race.

8 or more: I think we just learned about one of your past lives!

5 to 7: You have a lot in common with this race, even if you're not quite a paragon of its attributes.

2 to 4: You can probably get along with folks of this race, even if your tastes differ in many areas.

0 or 1: You would probably not be happy playing a character of this race.

MATCHING PRIMARY AND SECONDARY ABILITY SCORES

Class	Build	Ability Scores	Matching Races
Ardent	Enlightened	Cha, Wis	Kalashtar
Ardent	Euphoric	Cha, Con	Half-elf
Artificer	Battlesmith	Int, Con	None
Artificer	Tinkerer	Int, Wis	Deva, githzerai, shardmind
Artificer	Warrior Forge	Int, Wis	Deva, githzerai, shardmind
Assassin	Bleak Disciple	Dex, Con	Revenant
Assassin	Night Stalker	Dex, Cha	Changeling, drow, halfling
Avenger	Commanding	Wis, Int	Deva, githzerai, shardmind
Avenger	Isolating	Wis, Int	Deva, githzerai, shardmind
Avenger	Pursuing	Wis, Dex	Elf, githzerai, razorclaw shifter
Barbarian	Rageblood	Str, Con	Goliath, minotaur, warforged
Barbarian	Thaneborn	Str, Cha	Dragonborn
Barbarian	Thunderborn	Str, Con	Goliath, minotaur, warforged
Barbarian	Whirling	Str, Dex	Half-orc
Bard	Cunning	Cha, Int	Changeling, gnome, shadowmind, tiefling
Bard	Prescient	Cha, Wis	Kalashtar
Bard	Valorous	Cha, Con	Half-elf
Battlemind	Quick	Con, Cha	Half-elf
Battlemind	Resilient	Con, Wis	Dwarf, wilden
Cleric	Battle	Str, Wis	Longtooth shifter, minotaur
Cleric	Devoted	Wis, Cha	Kalashtar
Cleric	Shielding	Wis, Cha	Kalashtar
Druid	Guardian	Wis, Con	Dwarf, wilden
Druid	Predator	Wis, Dex	Elf, githzerai, razorclaw shifter, wilden
Fighter	Battlerager	Str, Con	Goliath, minotaur, warforged
Fighter	Brawling	Str, Dex	Half-orc
Fighter	Great Weapon	Str, Con	Goliath, minotaur, warforged
Fighter	Guardian	Str, Wis	Longtooth shifter, minotaur
Fighter	Tempest	Str, Dex	Half-orc
Invoker	Malediction	Wis, Con	Dwarf, wilden
Invoker	Preserving	Wis, Int	Deva, githzerai, shardmind
Invoker	Wrathful	Wis, Con	Dwarf, wilden
Monk	Centered Breath	Dex, Wis	Elf, githzerai, razorclaw shifter, wilden
Monk	Stone Fist	Dex, Str	Half-orc
Paladin	Ardent	Str, Wis	Longtooth shifter, minotaur
Paladin	Avenging	Str, Cha	Dragonborn
Paladin	Protecting	Cha, Str	Dragonborn
Paladin	Virtuous	Cha, Wis	Kalashtar
Psion	Telekinetic	Int, Wis	Deva, githzerai, shardmind
Psion	Telepathic	Int, Cha	Changeling, gnome, shardmind, tiefling
Ranger	Archer	Dex, Wis	Elf, githzerai, razorclaw shifter, wilden
Ranger	Beastmaster	Str, Dex	Half-orc
Ranger	Hunter	Dex, Wis	Elf, githzerai, razorclaw shifter, wilden
Ranger	Marauder	Str, Wis	Longtooth shifter
Ranger	Two-Blade	Str, Dex	Half-orc
Rogue	Aerialist	Dex, Cha	Changeling, drow, halfling
Rogue	Brawny	Dex, Str	Half-orc
Rogue	Cutthroat	Dex, Cha	Changeling, drow, halfling
Rogue	Shadowy	Dex, Int	Changeling, eladrin, shadar-kai
Rogue	Trickster	Dex, Cha	Changeling, drow, halfling
Runepriest	Defiant	Str, Wis	Longtooth shifter, minotaur
Runepriest	Wrathful	Str, Con	Goliath, minotaur, warforged
Seeker	Protecting	Wis, Str	Longtooth shifter, minotaur
Seeker	Vengeful	Wis, Dex	Elf, githzerai, razorclaw shifter, wilden
Shaman	Bear	Wis, Con	Dwarf, wilden
Shaman	Eagle	Wis, Dex	Elf, githzerai, razorclaw shifter, wilden
Shaman	Panther	Wis, Int	Deva, githzerai, shardmind
Shaman	World Speaker	Wis, Con	Dwarf, wilden
Sorcerer	Chaos	Cha, Dex	Changeling, drow, halfling
Sorcerer	Cosmic	Cha, Str	Dragonborn
Sorcerer	Dragon	Cha, Str	Dragonborn
Sorcerer	Storm	Cha, Dex	Changeling, drow, halfling
Swordmage	Assault	Int, Str	Genasi
Swordmage	Ensnaring	Int, Con	—
Swordmage	Shielding	Int, Con	—

CHAPTER 1 | *Building Your Character*

Class	Build	Ability Scores	Matching Races
Warden	Earth	Str, Con	Goliath, minotaur, warforged
Warden	Life	Str, Wis	Longtooth shifter, minotaur
Warden	Storm	Str, Con	Goliath, minotaur, warforged
Warden	Wild	Str, Wis	Longtooth shifter, minotaur
Warlock	Dark Pact	Cha, Int	Changeling, gnome, shardmind, tiefling
Warlock	Fey Pact	Cha, Int	Changeling, gnome, shardmind, tiefling
Warlock	Infernal Pact	Con, Int	—
Warlock	Star Pact	Cha, Con	Half-elf
Warlock	Vestige Pact	Con, Int	—
Warlord	Bravura	Str, Cha	Dragonborn
Warlord	Insightful	Str, Wis	Longtooth shifter, minotaur
Warlord	Inspiring	Str, Cha	Dragonborn
Warlord	Resourceful	Str, Cha or Int	Dragonborn, genasi
Warlord	Skirmishing	Str, Int	Genasi
Warlord	Tactical	Str, Int	Genasi
Wizard	Control	Int, Wis	Deva, githzerai, shardmind
Wizard	Illusionist	Int, Cha	Changeling, gnome, shardmind, tiefling
Wizard	Summoner	Int, Con	—
Wizard	War	Int, Dex	Changeling, eladrin, shadar-kai

continued from page 18

your character's race. Every race has a variety of traits that differentiate it from other races. However, these fall into a limited range of categories. When selecting your race, consider how each race's traits—ability score bonuses, racial powers, skill bonuses, and other miscellaneous racial traits—interact with your preferred class (or, if you're choosing race first, how they might guide your later class selection).

ABILITY SCORE BONUSES

Every class has a primary ability score that it uses for its attack powers. To maximize the accuracy and damage dealt by your powers, consult the Matching Primary Ability Scores table and select a race that has an ability score bonus that matches your preferred class's primary ability score.

A few classes have two primary ability scores influencing their attack powers. These classes appear twice in the table, with a different list of matching races for each line.

In addition to a primary ability score, most classes have secondary ability scores that affect their powers and class features. Matching one of your race's ability score bonuses to a secondary ability score of your class makes you more effective.

The Matching Primary and Secondary Ability Scores table lists these combinations based on racial ability score bonuses. The first column lists the classes in alphabetical order. The second column lists the builds of each class (or in the case of warlocks, the pacts), and the third column lists the ability scores for that build (primary, then secondary). The fourth column lists the races that match each build (those that have bonuses in both the ability scores listed).

The table includes all races that have received full treatment as player character races. It does not include races not fully designed as player characters, such as goblins or githyanki, even if those races appear in the D&D Character Builder.

ADAM PHILLIPS

Racial Powers

Although your ability score bonuses contribute significantly to optimally matching your race and class, your racial power helps make your character unique. An eladrin rogue who uses *fey step* to teleport into (or out of) battle feels very different from the changeling rogue who gets close to a target by posing as a trusted ally.

Think about how your character might use the racial powers of the various races you're considering. Some powers, such as *elven accuracy*, contribute equally well to just about any class, but others work best with a subset of classes. For example, both the halfling and the drow offer useful ability score bonuses for the trickster rogue build, making them seem equally optimal. However, the drow's ability to gain combat advantage through the use of racial powers meshes well with the rogue's Sneak Attack class feature.

Skill Bonuses

To maximize the benefit of racial skill bonuses, match them up with a class that includes those skills on its class skill list, then select them as trained skills.

For example, the halfling's bonuses to Acrobatics and Thievery match up well to the rogue's skill list. A halfling chaos sorcerer doesn't get much benefit from those skill bonuses, since he's unlikely to use the skills very often.

Other Traits

In addition to the basic categories shared by nearly every race, each race offers a variety of miscellaneous traits. Don't assume that these traits can't have an impact on your choice of class and build.

For example, the dwarf's speed of 5 squares makes the race a suboptimal choice for any class that relies on frequent movement (such as the avenger or the ranger), but it's not a drawback for a heavily armored character because of the dwarf's Encumbered Speed racial trait. When you also consider the benefits of Dwarven Resilience and Stand Your Ground, the dwarf starts looking like a solid choice for a melee-based defender class, even if the race's ability score bonuses don't quite match up.

PLAYING AGAINST EXPECTATIONS

As a player, don't feel forced to choose a race because of its compatibility with classes or because of tradition. Regardless of the class you choose, few racial traits prove useless. In fact, playing against type often makes for the most interesting and memorable characters. Here are a few examples of how you can make unusual choices work, both mechanically and flavorfully.

Baern Fireshaper, Dwarf Wizard: Traditionally, most players don't associate dwarves with arcane magic. The stereotypical magic-hating dwarf often actively disdains the wielders of such powers. Furthermore, many dwarf racial traits—such as Dwarven Weapon Proficiency and Encumbered Speed—match up poorly with the needs of the typical arcanist.

On the other hand, dwarves value tradition, so why not prize the wizardly practices passed down through generations? Dwarves have a strong elemental heritage, which suggests potential links to fiery arcane spells. And Dwarven Resilience gives the normally fragile wizard a nice dose of survivability.

If you're ready to play an ale-guzzling, beard-scratching, curse-shouting spell-slinger, ignore those firm suggestions of "Eladrin!" from the other players and bring Baern Fireshaper to the table for the next campaign.

Tryn Woodwalker, Halfling Barbarian: Although brave and stout of heart, halflings are also cheerful and known for their love of luxury. They wander the edges of civilization, rarely far from the river, road, or inn. They don't commonly manifest the savage blood thirst and primal anger that drives the barbarian, and they lack the physical power associated with this class.

But not all halflings pick the pockets of the locals and enjoy creature comforts. Perhaps you belong to a tribe of savage, primal-spirit-worshiping halflings living deep in the wilderness. In the dense underbrush of the woods or jungle, speed and agility can be more important than size and strength. Your racial bonuses to Dexterity and Charisma lend themselves to either the thaneborn the or the whirling barbarian builds, and your *second chance* racial power is just as valuable as a pile of extra hit points.

So when one of your comrades snickers about your "cute little barbarian," kick him where it hurts, then laugh as you easily dodge his clumsy counterattack. Let's see a half-orc pull off that trick!

Nadarr the Cruel, Dragonborn Rogue: Proud and noble, the dragonborn value honor above all else. Their culture views acts of theft, lying, swaggering, shadowing, sniping, and manipulating as dishonorable, rather than simply as means to an end. They prefer to fight from a position of strength, not a place of secrecy.

A smart rogue can take advantage of that reputation to gain an edge. Maybe your dragonborn grew up apart from others of his or her people. You still appreciate history, but you like it for the gritty survival lessons it teaches, not for its glorious tales of battlefield renown. You use your physical and social prowess to bend others to your will—your bonus to Intimidate checks comes in handy in back-alley negotiations, and your Dragonborn Fury means you're toughest when backed into a corner. Make sure to give yourself at least a 12 Constitution to gain some benefit for Draconic Heritage and *dragon breath*.

Sure, you can expect some odd looks at your six-foot-six, 280-pound rogue slipping quietly through the shadows, but you'll get the last laugh. Let the halflings and drow rely on trickery—after all, who's going to expect someone as big as you to steal their coin purse?

If any character-building decision has a longer history of in-depth dissection, optimization arguments, and outright dissension between storytellers and power gamers than assigning your character's ability scores, we'd be surprised. Since the earliest days of DUNGEONS & DRAGONS, the task of generating those six numbers might well have caused more crumpled character sheets than mind flayers and medusas put together.

The *Player's Handbook* describes three methods of generating your ability scores. This book focuses on Method 2 (customizing scores). Method 1 (standard array) is fundamentally the same as Method 2. The standard array represents a solid, middle-of-the-road set of ability score allotments, which you could easily generate using the customizing method.

Technically speaking, Method 3 (rolling scores) can also generate a similar array of ability scores, though you're just as likely to get a range of numbers above or below the standard array. We don't recommend rolling ability scores unless everyone in your group acknowledges that some characters will be better than others from Day 1. Most players prefer everyone to start on a level playing field. If you do use this method, you can use the guidance here to assign the scores effectively.

START AT THE TOP

Start by assigning your highest score to your primary ability score. Assuming you have a racial bonus to your class's primary ability score, this should be a 16, 17, or 18 (before assigning the bonus). If you don't have a racial bonus to that ability score, think long and hard about shelling out the points for an 18. Sure, you can play a fighter with 14 Strength, as long as you enjoy missing on a lot of attacks.

Using Method 2 as a guide, this costs you 9, 12, or 16 points from the 22 you have to spend.

SECONDARY ABILITY SCORES

Every class has at least one other ability score that influences its features and powers. In most cases, you don't need this score to be as high as your primary ability score. A 12, a 13, or a 14 (before racial ability bonus, if any) is usually good enough.

If this secondary ability score contributes to a different defense than your primary ability score, lean toward a higher secondary score. Even if the class-based payoff is minimal, you'll appreciate the extra point or two of defense it grants you.

Some classes might tempt you into setting two secondary ability scores roughly equal to one another.

Unless your racial bonuses line up particularly well—or if your primary and secondary scores are all in different defense pairs—this is usually a mistake.

Assigning this ability score likely costs you 2 to 5 of your remaining 9 to 13 points.

FILLING OUT THE REST

At this point, you might have anywhere from 4 to 11 points left to assign to your remaining four ability scores. You could just split them up evenly, but D&D tends to reward specialization over generalization, so avoid doing this.

Instead, pick out an ability score into which you can afford to put 0 points. This is often the other half of a defense pair you've already assigned; for instance, rogues can usually afford an 8 Intelligence because their high Dexterity already helps their AC and Reflex.

Even though you probably haven't chosen skills yet, think about the key ability scores you might need later. Don't put that 8 in Wisdom if you expect to be the party's high-Perception scout.

Now you're left with three 10s and some points to spend. Assign a 12, a 13, or a 14 to a defense pair that doesn't already have a better score. If you need help in two defense pairs, you probably can't do better than a 12 or a 13 in one of them.

If you can afford it, put a 12 or a 13 into an ability score to help out one of your skills. For example, if you want to be an athletic rogue, a 12 or higher in Strength helps your climbing and jumping.

ODD OR EVEN?

At first glance, setting an ability score as an odd number seems like a waste. A 12 and a 13 both result in a +1 ability modifier, so why bother spending the resources on the 13? Well, here's why.

Prerequisites: Many feats have ability score prerequisites, and these are always odd numbers. Thirteen is the most common ability score prerequisite used at the heroic tier, but some feats require a score of 15. These prerequisites increase at higher tiers; some epic feats require a score or 21 in a particular ability.

You probably don't know yet whether you need to meet a feat prerequisite. Be prepared to revisit one or two of your ability score assignments later on in character creation.

Ability Increases: Starting at 4th level, you get to improve your ability scores a point at a time. Setting your fighter's starting Strength to 17 rather than 16 doesn't make much difference during levels 1 to 3, but when you hit 4th level you'll notice that 18.

The FORGOTTEN REALMS® Player's Guide introduced the concept of backgrounds, a pairing of story information with small mechanical benefits that relate to a character's upbringing. These earliest backgrounds derived from the region in which the character was born, but later supplements (particularly Player's Handbook 2) expanded the concept to include a wide variety of other notable story elements of the character's history before becoming an adventurer, such as a remarkable event of the character's birth or the character's former nonheroic occupation.

Think of background elements as seeds for growing the story of your character's identity. Although a few elements can't hope to describe the entirety of your character's background, they can certainly spur your creativity by suggesting story hooks, and they can inspire your roleplaying by having you think about who your character is and where he or she is from.

For story purposes, you can select as many background elements as you want. If you want for your human character to have been born among elves in a forest during an ominous storm, grown up poor as a farmer before turning to crime, and only then taken up life as an adventurer, that's fine. But after a certain point, the proliferation of background elements becomes cumbersome and counterproductive to building a coherent story. We advise choosing three to five elements from which to build your character's background.

As you choose background elements, imagine how they work together to tell the story of your character's preadventuring life. Come up with at least one way that the background element contributed to your past, and how it might play a part in your future. Don't bother with choosing background elements just to fill blanks on a character sheet; this is an opportunity for storytelling, not a required chore. If one of your background elements doesn't suggest a significant life event, personality quirk, story hook, or other roleplaying opportunity, it might not be worth your time to choose it.

BACKGROUND BENEFITS

Regardless of how many background elements you choose, you only select one mechanical benefit. The most common background benefits offer a +2 bonus to checks with a particular skill, an extra class skill, or an extra language known, though some benefits—particularly the regional benefits found in the FORGOTTEN REALMS Player's Guide—offer some other unusual mechanical options.

For most players, the skill bonus is the simplest and best mechanical benefit to choose. If you select the skill bonus, you get the highest benefit by matching it to a class skill that you plan to select as a trained skill (just as with the skill bonuses granted by your race).

On the other hand, your background also offers the opportunity to pick up a skill outside your class's normal list of options. This can prove particularly useful if your party lacks access to certain skills. (Thievery is a common example of a useful skill that no character chooses as a trained skill, since it appears on so few class skill lists.) Just make sure you can afford to spend the skill training on this option; it doesn't do you any good otherwise. For an extra benefit, match up this newly gained skill with one of the skill bonuses from your race. (See why it helps to make these three decisions at the same time?)

If you play in a game in which languages come into play frequently—and if you followed "Know the Campaign" at the beginning of this chapter, you should know the Dungeon Master's opinion on this—consider selecting the extra language instead. The difference between rolling a 16 or an 18 on a skill check can pale in comparison with the difference between cogently explaining to the angry ogres why they shouldn't kill you and having them pick their teeth with your bones after the brawl.

REIMAGINING EXISTING BACKGROUNDS

What if you can't find a published background that matches your vision of the character you want to play? The regional backgrounds published in various campaign settings might seem like a poor fit for the homebrew campaign your DM has crafted, or maybe you just have an unusual combination of race, class, and other character elements that defies the puzzle-piece approach to existing background elements.

With your DM's permission, you can tweak existing backgrounds to better fit the campaign and your character concept. Backgrounds are intended to be about story first and mechanics second. The mechanical benefits are really just a small bribe for those players who would otherwise show up at the table without a character backstory. You know who we're talking about, right?

Here are two examples of published backgrounds that have been reimagined for characters whose backstories don't quite match the backgrounds' original intent. The first case presents a situation in which the player likes the mechanical benefit but doesn't want the associated story material, and the second presents an appealing story hook that just needs a new flavor.

Arcane Experimenter: Reading the FORGOTTEN REALMS *Player's Guide*, you come across the description of the Akanûl region: "Akanûl is a land defined by extreme geography, eldritch beasts, and genasi. A new nation formed in the devastated and warped lands between Chessenta and Chondath, Akanûl has overcome great adversity and is now a name to be respected and feared." You don't care so much about that part—your DM has already told you that you're playing in Eberron, not the Forgotten Realms, and you don't plan to play a genasi—but the regional benefit excites you: "You gain resist 2 cold, resist 2

WHERE DID YOU LEARN TO PICK LOCKS?

WHELOON.

AH. LOCAL THIEVES' GUILD?

MACRAME CLUB, ACTUALLY.

MIKE FAILLE

fire, and resist 2 thunder (or your existing resistance to these damage types increases by 2)." Not only do you like the idea of resisting some damage, you can already imagine a character known to all the locals as enjoying a strange, supernatural immunity to environmental hazards.

Instead of hailing from the unusual land of Akanûl, you decide that the regional benefit comes from magical research carried out during your wizard character's apprenticeship. Your wizard's bold creativity and dumb luck turned failed experiments into energy-resistant skin rather than burning your character alive.

Your DM recognizes that the regional benefit granted by this background is on the powerful side—particularly when compared to the more generic background elements published in other supplements—but he's willing to compromise. Since none of the other players are using the potent regional benefits, he suggests dropping one of the three resistances. You agree to relinquish the thunder resistance, and both of you end up happy with the character.

Psionic Refugee: While creating your battlemind, you stumble across the Arcane Refugee background from *Arcane Power*. You like playing lone wanderers, and the idea of playing a character permanently scarred by a mysterious conflagration that destroyed your home appeals to you. Though the background is aimed at a wielder of arcane magic, you see no reason why you couldn't reimagine the catastrophe—and the ensuing studies you began in secret—as psionic instead.

Since this background is pretty simple, your DM doesn't have any concern about the new flavor you've added. In fact, you've even given her an interesting story hook for a later adventure: figuring out what psionic cataclysm set you on your path.

CREATING A NEW BACKGROUND

Some players take great pains to write elaborate, even labyrinthine backstories for their characters, describing a life so unusual that no writer could ever have foreseen it and written an appropriate background element. Alternatively, your DM might present his or her own completely original setting for a campaign, making existing regional or geographic backgrounds obsolete. Whatever the reason, the best answer might be to craft your own background elements, including the mechanical benefits they grant.

Before you go to the trouble of designing your own background elements, see if you can build the background you want by using or reimagining existing elements. Waterdeep and Greyhawk City certainly aren't interchangeable, but as bustling, cosmopolitan gatherings of many races it's easy to imagine them sharing the same regional benefit: all you have to do is replace the Waterdeep flavor with appropriately Gygaxian descriptions and you're set.

But if that doesn't work, don't throw away your unique backstory just to fit into some author's pre-fabricated background structure: Build your own background element by combining a compelling story hook with a minor but useful mechanical benefit. (Because you get only one mechanical benefit from your character's background, you only have to design one benefit, no matter how many new background elements you write.)

For most players, starting with the story helps fuel the creative fires. Your story might be simple: "My human ranger grew up on a pig farm a few miles from Greyhawk." Or it might be bizarre: "My genasi wizard's parents lived in Sigil and belonged to the Society of Sensation, so I had all sorts of unusual experiences growing up. By the time I was 12, I had traveled to three different planes, I had died twice, and I had an extra arm for a whole year."

Don't forget to include your DM in these story con-coctions. Chances are, he or she has put a lot more thought into the campaign setting than you have, so why not take advantage of that expertise? D&D is a shared story experience, but most DMs feel a certain level of stewardship over their campaign settings, and before you introduce an unexpected element, it's only fair to see that the DM is okay with your idea.

Some players see the background's mechanical benefit as the crucial character-building hook they need. Maybe you really want an excuse for your fighter to be trained in Thievery, or you think it'd be cool for your dwarf cleric to speak Primordial. Again, touch base with your DM, particularly if you come up with a mechanical benefit that doesn't resemble one that already exists in another background.

Here are two examples of new backgrounds that a player might propose to his or her Dungeon Master:

Mercenary Negotiator: You want your half-elf fighter to have expertise in languages, but none of the background elements you find grant more than one extra language.

In chatting with your DM, you describe your char-acter as part of a family that served as guides and bodyguards along a trade route between somewhat unfriendly human, dwarf, and elf settlements. Mer-chants traveling along the route needed mediators to negotiate border passage and protect against brig-ands, and fluency in many languages was crucial.

Growing up surrounded by different languages, your character developed fluency in Dwarven and Goblin. As a mechanical benefit, it doesn't exactly threaten the game's balance, even though other

background elements typically grant only one extra language. Still, it's weaker than the Linguist feat (which grants three new languages), so the second language feels right for a new background's mechani-cal benefit. Your DM agrees.

Immortal Scion: You want to create a tiefling character descended from immortals. You decide that your character is descended from a star-crossed love affair between an angel and a succubus. Your parents were exiled from the Astral Sea for their actions, and you were born in the City of Brass. Soon afterward, both parents were assassinated by unknown killers, and you were spirited out of the city. Humans ignorant of your past raised you to adulthood, but through your dreams you recall shreds of memory of your youth.

You want your mechanical benefit to represent the vitality granted by your immortal heritage. You devise the idea that each time your character reaches a milestone, he regains a healing surge.

Your Dungeon Master likes the story angle—she already has ideas about how your parents' murderers might reappear later in the campaign—but she balks at your mechanical benefit. "That seems awfully good," she says, "much better than the benefits the other characters are getting from their backgrounds." You counter by pointing out that it's not as good as the two extra healing surges granted by the Durable feat (unless you hit at least three milestones in a single day). She agrees to let you try it out, but requests the right to reevaluate it after a few sessions.

USING BACKGROUNDS FROM THE NENTIR VALE

Precariously situated on the borderland between civilization and chaos, the Nentir Vale region—intro-duced in the *Dungeon Master's Guide* and explored in several other supplements and adventures since then—teems with possibilities for action and intrigue. Since it's familiar to most readers, we'll use it as an example of how to insert your chosen background elements into an established campaign setting. Follow the efforts of Ben (dragonborn fighter), Paul (half-elf ranger), Louisa (half-elf druid), Jerry (human cleric), and Sarah (tiefling warlock) as they begin to integrate their backgrounds into the setting.

Notice how some players choose elements that don't quite fit the setting. Everybody likes to be unique, and selecting a background element that marks you as a bit of an outsider can provide that feeling without completely ignoring the DM's lov-ingly crafted world. In each case, however, the player has made an effort to tie some aspect of his or her unusual background to the Nentir Vale.

As you read this section, imagine both sides of the conversation between the players and the Dungeon

Master that resulted in the conclusions below. Where might the DM have balked at a player's background idea? What challenges might the players have experienced trying to understand the key themes of the setting? Thinking about these questions helps you understand how to talk to your DM about the backgrounds you choose.

Unless noted otherwise, all background elements mentioned here appear in *Player's Handbook 2*.

Location, Location, Location: The most straightforward way to connect the setting and your character's story is to select a geographical element reflecting your character's birthplace or native environment.

Ben's fighter, hailing from the Cairngorm Peaks (background: mountains), instinctively distrusts the lowlanders occupying the rest of the vale.

Paul decides that his ranger grew up in sun-seared badlands, far from the Nentir Vale (background: desert). He never stops complaining about the cold, not to mention the difficulty of guarding against ambush in the dense thickets common to the vale.

Know Your Place: The game assumes that most characters enjoy a modest but comfortable place in society, but why not buck that assumption by choosing a different economic standing?

Sarah describes her tiefling as a direct descendant of one of the ancient rulers of Bael Turath, still retaining a measure of aristocracy despite the long years (background: noble). She has come to the Nentir Vale following rumors of tiefling ruins in the Witchlight Fens, and looks to her comrades to help her reestablish her family's position.

Your Last Job: Most characters aren't born as adventurers. What did you do before you starting delving into dungeons, and how does your previous work influence your approach to adventuring?

Louisa decides that her druid helped raise livestock before hearing the call of the primal spirits (background: farmer). Until recently, she lived with her family on a farm across the Nentir River from the town of Fallcrest.

Jerry's character studied religious lore at the Temple of Erathis for years before becoming a fullfledged cleric (background: scholar). He still believes that the best way to solve any problem is to think it through before acting.

On the other hand, Paul declares that his ranger didn't just leave the desert to flee the heat: He was an escaped convict (background: criminal) running from local authorities. He claims that he's not wanted in Fallcrest, but he keeps looking over his shoulder, anyway.

Accept Your Heritage: Many races offer unique background elements that help set them apart from other people. Don't just write "dragonborn" on your

character sheet when you can acknowledge your identity by selecting a dragonborn racial background element.

While living in the Cairngorm Peaks, Ben's fighter discovered an old cave bearing Draconic runes. He believes the cave dates back to the time of Arkhosia, and he wants to learn more about his people's past (background: brush with the past).

Embrace a Theme: It's one thing to pick up the name of a person or a place when crafting your background. Linking your story to one of the key themes of the campaign setting provides an even more valuable tool for players and DMs alike to build a compelling experience for everyone.

Sarah's warlock hasn't yet revealed her secret to her allies: She works as an agent for a mysterious group of arcanists claiming to work for the public good (background: arcane agent, from *Arcane Power*).

TELL US ABOUT YOUR CHARACTER

There's a disconnect in how we tell stories and how we play stories. Effective stories require a single strong viewpoint character. Most successful multiple-character stories actually split the narrative to accommodate these different viewpoint characters. For instance, in the gold standard of heroic fantasy mythology, *The Lord of the Rings*, Tolkien splits up the Fellowship for at least two-thirds of the story. In television—the media structure most similar to a roleplaying campaign—we actively call out these storylines as "A, B, and C stories" when breaking an episode. Many times in the story development process, when things seem muddled, we can track the problem back to the choice of a weak viewpoint character.

When we play stories, however, we each play our own viewpoint character. Good groups often align their characters' goals over time, and good DMs spend a fair bit of their time juggling those characters' motivations. But there are always conflicts, and though divergent goals can create fun moments, they only work when some overriding goal unites the party.

I take my character out of that part of the game. His job is to enable other characters. I'm the hired help, the ticked-off native guide, or the gunny sergeant. I get to deliver the most important line in all of storytelling: "So, let me get this straight. . . ."

I play the sidekick. You should give it a try.

Ironically, playing a sidekick requires as much if not more prep than usual. Because your character's motivations are largely independent of the campaign's ongoing storyline, you must engage in world-building just like the DM. What your sidekick character needs is a great, exciting Act Zero.

Act Zero is not backstory. Backstory is poorly named, because it's rarely story: It just rehashes where your character grew up or who he was before he started adventuring. In contrast, Act Zero is film slang for "the story that happened before." It requires all the trappings of a proper narrative, including intent, difficulties, resolutions, and complications. Your goal is to create a story starring your sidekick character that overlaps the story the other characters are playing in the campaign.

Let me lay out a character in the campaign I'm playing now: the human ranger, Jan Kormick. The setting is a magical Venetian society. The intricate relationships of the main city's families are a crucial part of the campaign Each of the other characters either comes from or works for one of these aristo families. Jan, however, comes from a miserably corrupt border city. He's just their guide, their sidekick.

In a series of short scenes, each just a few paragraphs long, I lay out the big moments in Jan's life up to the point of the campaign's opening session. I use other people's viewpoints in this section of the character development. Forcing myself to view my own character only through actions and dialogue—the way the other players will interact with him—helps sharpen his voice.

We begin our Act Zero with a scene featuring an assassination attempt on the would-be king of this border city, told through the target's eyes. The accidental death of a serving girl during that attempt is filtered through politics and characters the DM never needed to create (but can now draw upon for the campaign if he wants). Jan Kormick is that girl's younger brother, and his murderous response sets him on his path. He wants vengeance, but he cannot have it. Yet.

The second scene is from the viewpoint of a magical university's headmaster dealing with an amusingly troublesome student smuggling smokes and liquor into this private academy. The headmaster likes young Jan Kormick, even though he knows the boy is not long for this place.

In the third scene, a smuggler humors an inept agent of the king as the young man tries to unravel the crime ring working out of the man's caravan. Too late, the smuggler discovers Jan Kormick is a bit more than he appears, and it all ends in blood.

In the fourth scene, paladins have finally come to this backwater cesspool of corruption. The lead officer is not having a very good time of it, until a helpful man arrives to . . . well, cheat and game the system. Jan Kormick understands that getting to the influential people who killed his sister requires him to bring rule of law to his country, by any means necessary.

And in the last brief write-up in my Act Zero, we meet the king again, laying his plans for total political dominance of the peninsula. During the meeting he cuts one of his agents, Jan Kormick, loose to run an errand. That errand: acting as a guide for a group of influential nobles in a neighboring country. . . .

There we go. Jan's goal is to establish a just government in his home country to avenge his sister. That can never be accomplished within the span of the campaign; the campaign isn't even set in that country. But we know how he deals with institutions and rules. We know how he solves problems, his capacity for violence, what he finds funny or fair. We've heard him talk to people from different social classes. We know his attitudes, his voice, and his actions. Jan will evolve, but he comes to the campaign a fully developed character who'll contribute to the tale the group tells together.

JOHN ROGERS is a film and television writer. He created the show Leverage, the story of a party of 10th-level rogues who take on corporate bad guys.

Her secret reason for coming to Fallcrest? Infiltrating the Seven-Pillared Hall, underneath Thunderspire Mountain, to learn more about the rival organization known as the Mages of Saruun.

Something Special: Backgrounds are more than just a collection of places and occupations. Sure, even a farm boy can turn out to have an exciting backstory (just ask that kid who used to bulls-eye womp rats in his T-16), but that's because his player remembered to include "Secret Child of Dark Overlord" as one of his background elements.

As mentioned earlier, each of your background elements should add something important to your character's history. Adding something fantastic or supernatural to the mix can provide an extra jolt of creativity that moves your background from mundane to magnificent.

Louisa's half-elf druid was raised by human farmers, but she's not their child: They discovered her on the edge of a nearby forest (background: found in the wild, from *Primal Power*). Does that forest hide the secret that eventually manifested in her as primal power? (Of course it does!)

When Jerry's cleric was born, High Priest Dirina Mornbrow of the temple of Erathis proclaimed that his birth had been foretold by tales handed down many generations (background: prophecy). It was only natural that the character study religion under Dirina and become a cleric of Erathis himself.

TELL US ABOUT YOUR CHARACTER

I enjoy D&D most when my character survives. More to the point, I have the most fun when my character ends the fight without a scratch. Yet when 4th Edition was ready, I thought I would broaden my horizons a bit, playing a really good defender. For once I'd take the wallops. I decided to play Bartho, a dumb human fighter of the mold of Groo the Wanderer or Brom Bones.

Of course, I still didn't like taking damage. So I hunted through the system for ways to ramp up my defenses and my hit points. Now Bartho routinely draws half a dozen foes to his side and stands unconcerned amid their rain of blows. He walks past lesser foes, heedless of their attacks. And once, he leapt for a chain and missed, missed the platform beneath it, and fell over a hundred feet to land face first on stone. Then Bartho used an action point to stand up and say to bystanders, "Whoa! Did you see that? I mean . . . whoosh, and then bang!"

I've been playing Bartho since before 4th Edition was released, and I'm still having a blast. With every level, I look for a new way to make Bartho more impenetrable or to give him a means of bouncing back from attacks. Bartho is surviving—sixteen levels and he hasn't died yet—and he's being a great defender. Bartho sucks up a ton of attacks and renders them worthless . . . unless it's an attack against Will. But hey, that keeps things interesting.

MATT SERNETT is a writer and game designer for Wizards of the Coast who splits his time between DUNGEONS & DRAGONS and Magic: The Gathering. His recent credits include Player's Handbook Races: Tieflings, The Plane Above: Secrets of the Astral Sea, and Magic the Gathering: Zendikar. When he's not making monsters or building worlds, he's watching bad fantasy movies you don't realize exist and shouldn't bother to learn about.

ADAM PHILLIPS

WHAT ALIGNMENT ARE YOU?

Every D&D character has an alignment, from lawful good to chaotic evil, indicating his or her dedication to a set of moral principles. This quiz can help you decide which of the five alignments from the *Player's Handbook* best describes your character.

INSTRUCTIONS

For each question, choose the answer that best applies. Then, find your answers in the key below. Add up the number of answers you gave for each alignment to see how closely your character matches it.

1. Which of the following qualities do you value most in your allies?
  A. Loyalty
  B. Kindness
  C. Passivity
  D. Ambition
  E. Brutality

2. When is lying acceptable?
  A. Never. Truth is always the best answer.
  B. Small lies are okay if they help people feel better about themselves.
  C. Each situation is different and warrants its own considerations.
  D. It's fine if no one finds out about it.
  E. Whenever it gets me what I want.

3. Which of the following "sins" is the most despicable?
  A. Treason. The state puts its trust in its citizens and expects the same in return.
  B. Murder. No one has the right to take the life of an innocent.
  C. I don't believe in sins. They impose a structured worldview that I do not espouse.
  D. Weakness. It is a symptom of the collapse of society.
  E. Selflessness. If you can't look out for yourself, what good are you?

4. Children are . . .
  A. Tomorrow's heroes and leaders. We must protect them above all else.
  B. Our future and our responsibility. It brings joy to my heart to help them grow and flourish.
  C. What keep humanity in balance. Without children, the process of life, death, and rebirth would be disrupted.
  D. A necessary evil. They should be seen, but not heard.
  E. Always getting in my way. They're useless, unless one of 'em carries candy that I'd like to have.

5. Killing is . . .
  A. Something best left to the decisions of our leaders.
  B. Only appropriate to protect those at risk.
  C. Something I would do to protect myself.
  D. Appropriate for me to get what I want.
  E. Good fun.

6. You see a dozen goblins harassing an innocent family in a carriage. What do you do?
  A. No matter how many goblins are there, I do whatever I must to protect the family.
  B. I try to lure the goblins away so the family can escape.
  C. That's a lot of goblins. I go find the city guard so that they can help the family.
  D. I wait for the goblins to finish, and then search the carriage for leftover loot. Unless I think I can take the goblins afterward and get all the treasure for myself, of course.
  E. I offer the goblins my torch to light the carriage on fire.

7. Which of these statements would your fellow adventurers most likely say about you?
  A. "Vargach always does the right thing, even when it's dangerous."
  B. "Boldrik stands up for the little guy."
  C. "Adrin prefers to mind his own business."
  D. "Tasker likes to swipe coin purses from drunken merchants."
  E. "Brinjac is wanted for theft, murder, and treason in three kingdoms and seven city-states."

SCORING KEY

A: Lawful good
B: Good
C: Unaligned
D: Evil
E: Chaotic evil

SCORING YOUR ALIGNMENT

Add up the number of points you scored for each alignment.

6 -7: You are a paragon of this alignment.
4-6: You have a strong affinity for this alignment, but you might occasionally waver in your moral principles.
3 or less: You don't have much affinity for any particular moral perspective. You're probably unaligned (in that you haven't committed yourself to any particular set of morals).

More than any other decisions you make, your selection of powers differentiates you from other characters of your class or role. Even two paladins of the same race can play very differently at the table, depending on their list of powers. This section gives you pointers—and warnings—to help you choose powers to create the best character you can.

"Best" doesn't mean only "mathematically strongest"; consider factors other than just the amount of damage dealt. You can choose the most devastating powers in the game, but if they don't contribute to a fun character, you'll quickly lose interest in playing your unstoppable engine of destruction.

Do you like making lots of attack rolls on your turn? Look for multitarget powers, particularly large blasts and bursts. These powers probably don't deal as much damage (per target) as your single-target powers, but they increase the chance that you'll at least hit something.

Do you like staying active when it isn't your turn? Pick up powers that use immediate or opportunity actions, or that have an effect on your enemies' turns (such as certain auras). For some players, nothing brings more joy than killing a monster on its own turn, and these powers give you that ability.

Do you enjoy running all over the battlefield? Select powers that offer extra movement, particularly teleportation, and watch your character pinball between enemies.

The powers you pick help tell the story of your character, not just in dungeon battles, but also in the climactic encounter that your campaign will build toward for months or years. Will it end with a brutal shove that sends the villain flying 20 feet and into a pit of lava? With a crushing blow that destroys an eldritch machine used to raise hordes of undead? Or with an icy wall summoned to enclose a horde of enemies inside their own nefarious death trap? Choosing the right powers can help write the stories that bards tell the common folk—and that you tell your friends—long after the campaign is over. How will your character be remembered?

Some players see the Character Advancement table on page 29 of the *Player's Handbook* and falsely assume that because all characters gain powers at the same rate, they are somehow identical to one another. This simple conclusion overlooks the vast range of power options possessed by each class. Just because a fighter and a wizard both choose a new encounter attack power at 3rd level doesn't make those choices interchangeable—it just means that players have a familiar structure upon which to compare the various classes' abilities.

BUILDS AND POWER SELECTION

Each class includes two or more recommended paths of power selection, called builds. The build you choose to follow can help direct your power selections throughout your career.

Some classes, such as the paladin or the cleric, provide strong guidance through their builds. For example, a battle cleric who has a high Strength score should stick to attack powers based on Strength; otherwise, the character takes a big hit on accuracy.

Other classes fall at the opposite end of the spectrum. The two builds of fighters in the *Player's Handbook* don't have a lot of specific build-supporting powers, so following a build doesn't mean as much for that class.

Most classes fall somewhere in the middle of these two extremes. Look for these two clues to find powers that match your preferred build.

Class Feature: Many powers—particularly encounter attack powers—include a subheading listing a particular class feature. In most cases, this class feature is linked to a particular build, which means the power is ideal for that build. The 3rd-level rogue power *topple over* gives a character who has the Brutal Scoundrel class feature—a feature suggested for the brawny rogue build—a bonus to the attack roll.

Powers that list your build's class feature are almost always solid choices. Conversely, you can usually ignore powers that list a class feature you don't have; though the power functions even without the extra benefit, you should only voluntarily choose a low-potency option if it strongly fits your character's image.

Secondary Ability Score: Some powers include a secondary ability score as part of the damage roll or otherwise use this score to calculate the power's effect. *Trickster's blade* (another 3rd-level rogue power), for example, allows the rogue to temporarily add his or her Charisma modifier to AC, making it a good match for the trickster build. (Okay, the power name was probably a tip-off as well, but they're not always that easy.)

For best effect, select these powers only when your secondary ability score is 14 or higher (16 or higher is preferable).

In addition to these two obvious clues, be aware of powers that match your build's preferred tactics. The trickster rogue is good at darting in and out of combat, gaining a bonus to AC against opportunity attacks. Any power that grants free movement—say, *leaping dodge*—works well with this build, even if the power doesn't clearly mention your class feature or secondary ability score.

AT-WILL ATTACK POWERS

Of the many powers you choose during your character's career, none will come up more often than your at-will attack powers. You use these powers in nearly every fight, and they can guide the decisions you make when choosing every other power you get. Beyond that, your at-will powers help define your character, becoming an important part of your identity. Honestly, who would Jim Darkmagic be without *Jim's magic missile*? In other words, picking the right at-will powers is important. (No pressure!)

Most characters start play with two at-will attack powers. (At this point, the players of human characters are smiling happily.) To pick a good pair of powers, remember one key thought: variety. Since you'll always be able to use either power, make sure the choices feel different. It's much more important that one of your at-will attack powers is useful in any given round than that both of them are equally useful all the time.

One way to keep variety in mind is to categorize your choices as either offensive or defensive attacks. Most classes have at least one at-will attack power of each of these categories. The examples below, for instance, come from the fighter, rogue, and ranger classes.

Offensive attack powers typically have high accuracy, deal extra damage, grant an ally an attack bonus or a damage bonus, or reduce the enemy's defenses. They allow you to accelerate combat by killing the monsters faster. *Cleave*, *sly flourish*, and *twin strike* are all offensive attack powers.

Defensive attack powers, on the other hand, might apply a penalty to an enemy's attack roll or damage roll, allow you to control the enemy's movement or offensive options, let you escape a dangerous position, or grant you or your ally temporary hit points or a bonus to defenses. These powers draw out a combat by increasing the characters' survivability. *Tide of iron*, *riposte strike*, and *nimble strike* are examples of defensive attack powers. (*Riposte strike* looks like an offensive attack power because of the extra damage it can deal, but it's really about limiting the enemy's options by telling it to attack someone else.)

By choosing one power from each of the two categories, you can ensure that you're always capable of contributing in the way the party needs you to in this round, either by containing a stray monster for a few rounds or helping sweep up the trash after the fight is already in the bag.

You can take two powers of the same type as long as you remember the maxim of variety. A wizard with *magic missile* and *scorching burst* (both primarily offensive options) can decide which power to use based on the situation, since one is a long-range, single-target power and the other is a burst. Compare that to a fighter with both *reaping strike* and *sure strike*. Both attacks have single targets, and both improve your chances of dealing at least some damage. They serve the same purpose, and although each might be better than the other in some circumstances, that small difference isn't worth the commitment of your only two at-will powers.

Another difference between at-will attacks, albeit a difference mainly seen by leader classes, is whether they are self-sufficient or require another character for them to be really useful. At least one of your at-wills should function well by itself. You never know when you might end up isolated with a monster, and you want to have more than harsh words—or *commander's strike*—to fend it off.

Beyond pure functionality, your at-will attacks also contribute to the long-term development of your character. The wizard with both *magic missile* and *scorching burst* clearly has a slant toward dealing extra damage. Because you use your at-will powers so often, they influence you to spend resources, such as feats and magic items, on strengthening that facet of your character. This, in turn, can make similar powers more effective. In only a few levels, this wizard becomes very different from one who wields *ray of frost* and *illusory ambush*. Make your selections carefully, and be sure that the at-will powers you pick lead your character in a direction you want to go.

Encounter Attack Powers

If at-will powers are the skeleton of your character's combat capabilities, then encounter powers are the muscles. Not only are they more potent than your at-will attacks, but they also diversify the tactics at your disposal.

Don't overlook the importance of differentiating your encounter powers from your at-wills. If a given encounter power doesn't do something significantly different from your at-will powers, it probably isn't worth adding it to your repertoire. *Fearsome smite* deals a few more points of damage than *enfeebling strike*, but the powers are so similar that you're better off using one of your valuable encounter power choices to pick up something that has a wholly different effect, such as the high-accuracy *piercing smite* or the high-damage *radiant smite*.

But even though your encounter powers shouldn't step on the toes of your at-will powers, your encounter powers can follow a similar theme without significant drawbacks. You only get to use each of them once in a fight—and your at-will powers already cover a good range of options—so you can feel comfortable with encounter powers that cover a more limited variety of tricks. Picking encounter powers with strong similarities, such as area burst attacks that can be used as part of a charge, maximizes the benefit of other choices you make. The more powers you have that deal lightning or thunder damage, the more useful your Raging Storm feat becomes.

This doesn't mean that variety in encounter powers is useless. No matter how much you enjoy delivering bursts of fire or acid across the battlefield, some combats require different tactics. If your encounter powers are one-note, you might find yourself falling back on at-will powers—and giving up the extra punch of encounter powers—early in the fight. Controllers, in particular, often need to adapt their tactics based on the kind and number of foes they face. Enemies might start far away and in great numbers, but soon enough they stand amid your allies, and their numbers dwindle as the fight comes to a

close. If you choose powers that direct and exploit that flow, you'll be more effective. An invoker might open with *chains of Carceri* while his party members get into formation, then drop *baleful eye of judgment* when the enemies engage, and finally use *compel attention* to help finish off the lead monster after its minions have been taken out. For characters like this, whether they're actual controllers or just filling in the role on the side, diversity is the name of the game.

Don't overspecialize in encounter powers. You should expect to use your encounter powers in every combat. There's no reward for finishing an encounter with unused encounter powers—they're all coming back after a short rest, anyway. If an occasional fight goes by without *frostburn* being useful, that's okay. But if you spend an entire session without using it, you should consider replacing it with a different power. Chances are that what looked good at first turns out to require a combination of circumstances that, for whatever reason, just isn't common enough.

Finally, when choosing encounter powers, don't be blinded by extra weapon damage dice. A 3[W] power might look three times as good as a 1[W] power, but all the other modifiers that add to damage make the variation in damage dice less significant, particularly at higher levels. This is even more true with low-damage weapons—the dagger-wielding rogue gets a mere 2.5 extra damage for each [W], which makes the secondary aspects of the power—accuracy, number of targets, and conditions applied—much more important.

Daily Attack Powers

Your daily attack powers represent the pinnacle of your training and practice. These special techniques show your true power to friend and foe alike, and those who survive battle with you remember you for these attacks.

Obviously, your daily attack powers are your big guns, delivering the largest bang in combat. But treating them as upgunned encounter powers ignores three significant differences between daily attack powers and all other powers.

Reliability: With few exceptions, a daily power is guaranteed to have an effect. Some deal half damage to the target on a miss, which makes them good at finishing off hard-to-hit enemies. Still others include an Effect line, which applies even when you miss. If you're one of those players who always rolls 1s on key attack rolls, pick up some of these powers.

An odd subset of this category includes the powers that have the reliable keyword. In one way, this keyword is a misnomer, since you can't "rely" on the power to have any effect whatsoever. Sure, missing all the targets means you don't use up the power, allowing you to try again later, but you've still spent the action required to activate the power and gained

absolutely nothing. Saving your reliable power until the exact moment you desperately need it probably is not a good idea. Instead, use it at an early opportunity to ensure you'll have the time to land a hit . . . eventually. Also, don't load up on reliable powers—one or two is plenty.

Duration: Effects generated by at-will and encounter attack powers usually last no longer than a round. But daily attack powers apply conditions or effects that last multiple rounds, sometimes even until the end of the encounter. Daily powers with long durations beg to be used earlier in the combat. Why save the enemy attack penalty from *splintering shot* until the end of the fight? In practice, however, you might find it challenging to decide whether a particular fight merits the early use of one of these daily powers. Our advice: Better to use the power now and possibly regret it later than to finish the day having never found exactly the right time for it (or worse yet, for your character to take his or her daily powers to an early grave).

Some long-duration daily attack powers have an action cost to sustain or reuse them. Pay attention to these costs and think about how they might limit your options later in combat. The "sustain minor" cost of *curse of the dark dream* might seem minuscule, but warlocks also use minor actions to curse new targets. In some rounds, you might have to forego cursing a target (and give up the extra damage you'd deal that round) to sustain the spell you cast earlier.

Specialization: You choose at-will powers with the idea that one or the other will come in handy in every round, and you select encounter powers expecting that few fights could go by without providing

a good opportunity to use each of them. But your daily powers only need to be appropriate once in any given day of adventuring. In most situations, a ranged attack with a range of only 1 square isn't very useful. But when you just can't get away from an enemy, you'll be happy that you have *close quarters shot* in your back pocket.

UTILITY POWERS

Utility powers come in a wide range of flavors: temporary combat boosters, defensive enhancements, skill bonuses, and healing, among others. With such a variety of options, it's no wonder that some players become overwhelmed by them. Other players dismiss the entire category, reasoning that utilities can't be as important as attacks. But when chosen correctly, utility powers can dramatically increase your character's effectiveness both in and out of combat. Some characters—particularly leaders—can even become known better for their utility powers than for their attack powers.

In some ways, choosing utility powers relies on methods very similar to those you used when selecting your attack powers. An at-will utility power, for example, should prove useful over and over again. (There aren't very many at-will utility powers, so many characters won't face this decision.) If you choose an encounter utility power, you should be able to imagine using it in nearly every fight. You can afford to specialize when choosing a daily utility power—it only has to come in handy once per day—and such powers are typically very potent or very long-lasting.

However, since these categories of utility powers appear side by side–rather than separated by frequency of use–you can adjust your selection to best fit your style of play. Do you like having a wealth of options available every round? Focus on at-will and encounter utility powers. On the other hand, if you'd rather make a big splash with your utilities–or if you just don't want to keep track of all those power cards round after round, battle after battle–stick to the dailies.

Beyond a power's usage, its effect in play should also guide your selection. Despite the difficulty of categorizing such a broad range of powers, we've created a list of five basic groupings of utility powers to help you determine which powers best fit your style.

Offense: Although utility powers, by definition, lack the ability to deal damage or significantly influence enemies, plenty of them can still contribute to your character's (or your allies') offensive output. Many players find such utility powers the easiest to use and understand, since their effect is generally straightforward. *Dark one's own luck* allows you to reroll an attack roll (or a skill check, an ability check, or a saving throw, but I think we can be honest with each other about when you'll use it, don't you?). The ranger's *master of the hunt* grants you a bonus to damage rolls, and the paladin's *wrath of the gods* does the same for you and your allies alike. When in doubt, you can't go wrong by choosing a power like one of these.

Defense: Perhaps the most common category of utility powers includes those that provide defensive bonuses to the user or to his or her allies. For controllers and strikers, these powers provide self-protection. For example, the rogue's *slippery mind* and the wizard's *shield* both give self-preservation a high priority. Choose these powers if you often find your character off by himself or herself, or if your party's teamwork lacks some polish.

Movement: Tactically minded players gravitate toward utility powers that grant them or their allies extra movement. These players know that the combat advantage gained by smart positioning can make the difference between dropping a bloodied foe and giving it one more round of attacks. Not only that, but moving around the battlefield is fun: It creates cinematic action and keeps combat from becoming static.

Healing: It doesn't take a tactical genius to know that having hit points is good. Whether a utility power allows the target to spend healing surges, restores hit points, or grants damage mitigation such as temporary hit points or damage resistance, no party can ever have too many healing powers. Healing is like increasing your defenses, except you can use it after the fact and for only the attacks that hit you, so nothing gets wasted. Every character should strongly consider having at least one healing power. If you don't get healing powers from your class features, look to your utility powers.

Out of Combat: A small selection of utility powers, such as *beguiling tongue*, have little or no effect in a typical combat encounter. Choose these powers based on your expectations of the campaign, derived from your discussions with the Dungeon Master. Looking forward to long dungeon crawls? The light from *holy lantern* might be useful. Expecting tense negotiations with city nobility? The bonus to Diplomacy checks from *astral speech* might be more beneficial than the AC boost from *sacred circle*.

When evaluating utility powers that add to skill checks, go for options that improve skills you're already pretty good at, rather than trying to boost a low skill modifier. In most cases, the character making a skill check is the one who has the highest modifier, so increasing your Diplomacy check from +3 to +7 isn't worthwhile if another character already has +8 or higher.

UM... LITTLE HEALING HERE.

TELL US ABOUT YOUR CHARACTER

Tabitha Sparkles is a 29-year-old tiefling wizard who has a penchant for animal rights and blowing things up.

She's tall and lean and boasts a bitchin' pair of biceps, which she likes to show off by wearing sleeveless robes. She has purple-black hair and gold eyes that turn scarlet at the slightest raise in her blood pressure. She tends to look brooding and irritated, which might be due to the weight of her horns but more likely just reflects her truly brooding and irritated nature.

Most importantly, she is the antithesis of my first D&D character, Astrid Bellagio: a cheerful, beautiful sorceress with exquisite taste in shoes and wracked with guilt whenever she had to hit any creature resembling an animal. I played Astrid when I wrote *Confessions of a Part-Time Sorceress* and I made it my mission to keep her alive until I had finished the book. I owed her at least that, right? I'm happy to report Astrid safely retired from adventuring and now teaches sorcery at a charm school in Eberron. My quest to keep her alive resulted in the poor sorceress always stuck behind a pillar, in another room, with her hands over her ears shouting, "Is it over yet?" Good thing she had so many long-range powers.

I loved Astrid—maybe too much—but I knew the next character would be different. I actually wanted to play D&D!

When it came time to roll up Tabitha, I intentionally made her unlovable. (Maybe that's a bit harsh; how about "hard to love"?) No way was I getting attached to this one! That determination lasted all of six minutes.

What I love most about playing Tabitha is actually playing her. She instigates, gets targeted by enemies, and takes damage. She even gets knocked unconscious once in a while. It's exhilarating trying to figure out how to get her out of the latest mess. ("Can we get a cleric in aisle 2?")

Tabitha likes to tell people she was raised by dancing bears. The reality is she has two conniving, selfish, ego-tistical, maniacal gazillionaires for parents. They made their fortune in fur trading. Tabitha often awoke in the middle the night to the howls of innocent animals being slaughtered. Deer, dogs, cats, goats—it didn't matter. Her parents took the fur of anything with fur and turned it into a "stylish" accessory for human nobles. An animal lover, Tabitha fervidly opposed her father's line of work. She tried to rescue animals, sometimes right out of her father's slaughterhouse, so that she could treat them as beloved pets. But her efforts didn't matter. Her father always found out and made her return them.

Tabby was accepted at a renowned magic academy on a plane far away. Her parents refused to pay the tuition, believing instead that a female's place was "minding the home and not out in the wild, getting into bar brawls and blowing things up." Tabitha was unfazed, since she would never have taken a dime of her family's blood money. Instead, she put herself through Aldwyn's Academy for Wizardry by working in a sketchy—but lucrative—traveling burlesque show.

There, she met the good-hearted show bear Oso de la Fez. She knew this was her one chance to make up for all those animals she wasn't able to save. No more would Oso be subjected to an indentured life of performing on shaky rubber balls and minuscule bicycles while drunken patrons threw peanut shells and insults at him. Oso dreamed of a life of adventure as a wizard's familiar. And Tabitha was committed to giving it to him. She answered an ad from an exarch who agreed to grant Oso powers above and beyond their wildest dreams in exchange for a favor to be named later and a small piece of Tabitha's soul. Big deal, she thought. Souls are for wusses.

Currently, Tabitha and Oso belong to the adventuring group known as the Wyld Stallyns. Tabby still remembers Oso's first day in combat, when a shadar-kai bit the dust thanks to the extra damage Oso's powers dealt. Everything went swimmingly until one hot day in the desert, when Tabby summoned her beloved ex-show bear to mark a hag; Oso instead marked her, and redirected Tabby's *scorching burst* to hit the party! So the exarch had come a callin' after all. Tabby took Oso out with a *magic missile*.

Today, Oso's allowed to travel with the group as long as Tabitha promises to keep him in passive mode. But we all know what promises mean to a tiefling. Will Tabitha resign her beloved Oso to a passive life? Will Oso ever return as the badass familiar he longed to be? Will Tabitha risk her party's safety and successes to give Oso his dreams back? Yeah . . . probably. And that's why I love her.

SHELLY MAZZANOBLE proclaimed herself D&D's Player-in-Chief in 2009, and strives to bring justice to players everywhere by reining in the monster-loving maniacs in R&D. The other 99 percent of the time, she diligently works on the D&D Brand Team helping to promote the products created by those monster-loving maniacs in R&D. In her spare time, she enjoys fashioning armor for D&D minis out of candy wrappers and being bullied by her bipolar cat, Zelda.

CHAPTER 1 | *Building Your Character*

CHOOSING SKILLS

Most players think of skills as something to use outside a combat encounter. This observation has some basis in truth; most battles don't include a significant number of skill uses, and elaborate skill challenges typically occur at times when swords and spells aren't flashing.

An optimized character, however, knows the value of the right skill choices both inside and outside combat. Whether making an Arcana check to remember a monster's key vulnerability in the heat of a fight or rolling the Diplomacy check that will spell the difference between gaining the duke's favor and spending time in the city's prison, smart players don't ignore the importance of skill checks.

Skill checks fall into one of two categories. Either they allow the best character to attempt the check on behalf of the entire party, or they require multiple characters—sometimes even the whole party—to succeed. In general, the first type of check tends toward the higher end of the difficulty scale (using the moderate or hard DCs given in the *Dungeon Master's Guide*). Checks of the second kind are more often easy checks.

SKILL CHECK MODIFIERS BY LEVEL

Character	— Skill Check Modifier —		
Level	Low	Medium	High
1-3	+0 to +3	+4 to +8	+9 or higher
4-6	+2 to +5	+6 to +10	+11 or higher
7-9	+3 to +6	+8 to +12	+13 or higher
10-12	+5 to +8	+10 to +14	+15 or higher
13-15	+6 to +9	+12 to +16	+17 or higher
16-18	+8 to +11	+14 to +18	+19 or higher
19-21	+9 to +12	+16 to +20	+21 or higher
22-24	+11 to +14	+18 to +22	+23 or higher
25-27	+12 to +15	+20 to +24	+25 or higher
28-30	+14 to +17	+22 to +26	+27 or higher

The sections below refer to character skill modifiers as low, medium, or high. These correspond to the easy, moderate, and hard skill check DCs described in the *Dungeon Master's Guide*. A character who has a low skill modifier can expect to succeed on an easy check more often than not. The same is true of a character who has a medium skill modifier and a moderate check, and a character who has a high skill modifier and a hard check. For example, a 1st-level eladrin wizard who has an Arcana check modifier of +11 has a high skill modifier, since he or she needs to roll only a natural 4 or higher to succeed on a hard (DC 15) Arcana check.

At 1st level, a low skill check modifier falls between +0 and +3. If your check modifier is between +4 and +8, it's a medium modifier. A skill check modifier of +9 or higher at 1st level is

considered high. The Skill Check Modifiers by Level table details the target skill modifiers across all thirty levels.

SKILLS OF AVOIDANCE

Acrobatics and Athletics are crucial skills for melee combatants, particularly those who rely on mobility. And before you chime in about how solid and immobile your dwarf fighter is, remember that he or she still has to get to the monsters.

One common aspect for Acrobatics and Athletics checks is that when an encounter calls for one, everyone in the party is generally expected to attempt it. Climbing or jumping down from a wall, leaping a chasm, or swimming a river are all tasks that can't just be overcome by a single character's successful check. Thus, it pays for every character to keep his or her modifiers in these two skills to at least a low level.

Everyone knows you can use Athletics to jump over a pit, but players often forget that this skill is just as useful when jumping over hazardous or difficult terrain. If you can reliably hit DC 10 on your Athletics checks, single squares of this kind of terrain no longer concern you.

These two skills also frequently form the basis of exciting stunts, such as swinging on a chandelier. Expect to need a high skill modifier to succeed reliably on such cinematic action moves, particularly if you expect to gain an edge in combat by pulling them off. On the other hand, if you explain to your DM that it's just part of your character's style and you don't expect a combat benefit, he or she might agree to reduce the DCs for these flamboyant moves to moderate.

It might seem odd to group Thievery with Acrobatics and Athletics, but, like those skills, it comes in most handy when used to bypass or neutralize a difficulty. In the case of Thievery, such difficulties typically include locked doors and deadly traps. Without a good Thievery check, the only recourse to such problems typically involves time and noise spent breaking down a door, or, worse yet, taking a lot of damage by walking into the trap. Make sure that someone in your party is trained in Thievery and carries a set of thieves' tools. It doesn't have to be the rogue. Artificers, assassins, and warlocks all have Thievery on their skill lists, and any eladrin can pick it up with the Eladrin Education racial trait.

Although Endurance doesn't typically lend itself to avoiding physical difficulties, its most common use in checks and challenges involves withstanding some nasty environmental effect without taking damage or suffering a condition. That's a lot like successfully leaping across a crevasse or bypassing a trap, so we've grouped it here. Like Acrobatics and Athletics, Endurance checks are often required of everyone in an encounter featuring such an environmental effect, so it pays to keep everyone's modifier high to at least a medium level.

SKILLS OF KNOWLEDGE

Six of the seventeen skills are primarily concerned with gathering or remembering information. Five of these skills—Arcana, Dungeoneering, History, Nature, and Religion—fall into a category described in the *Player's Handbook* as knowledge skills. Characters use these skills most often to recollect a useful piece of information about their current situation, whether that involves a puzzle, a plot twist, or the monster charging across the battlefield.

As soon as your turn comes up in battle, ask the Dungeon Master if you can use any of your knowledge skills to learn about your enemies. Even knowing a monster's name, type, and keywords can provide clues useful in combat—the fire keyword, for example, is a good tip-off as to the type of damage

TOUGHNESS OR DURABLE?

Players looking to build resilient characters often ask whether Durable or Toughness is the right feat to choose. Though the right answer might be "both," which should you take when you can't afford both? To answer that question, figure out how many hit points each feat is worth over the course of a day.

Toughness grants 5 extra hit points to a heroic tier character. It also increases your healing surge value by an average of 1 point. A character who spends eight healing surges per day, then, effectively gains 13 extra hit points from Toughness. During the paragon tier, that number more than doubles (10 from the feat, +2 or +3 per surge, for a minimum of 26 to 34 extra hit points). By 21st level, you can expect for Toughness to provide you with roughly 50 extra hit points per day.

On the other hand, Durable grants no extra hit points, but the two extra healing surges are worth roughly 10-12 hit points at 1st level (assuming starting hit points of about 20 to 25). This value increases by slightly more than 2 points per level as your total hit points (and by extension your healing surge value) increase. By 11th level, each healing surge is worth 18-22 points, so Durable provides about another 40 hit points per day. At 21st level, the feat's worth over 60 hit points each day.

In the end, the right choice probably depends on your style of campaign. If your battles tend toward the long and brutal side, Toughness might help keep you alive. But if your group likes to last through lots of encounters, Durable can give you the staying power to take on one more fight.

a monster deals and the resistance it has—but an exceptional success can reveal its powers and even its vulnerabilities. If you plan to use this technique, alert your DM beforehand, so that he or she can have the pertinent information handy; a grumpy DM is less likely to reward you for your canny play.

Some players mistakenly believe that the knowledge skills should be loaded up into a single character. Not only is this mechanically challenging—three use Intelligence, and two use Wisdom—it risks putting all your fact-finding eggs into one basket. Sure, the brainy eladrin or human wizard can easily cover all five bases, but most classes have access to at least one of these skills, so why not spread out the knowledge? If you have the oppportunity—and if you know that your DM likes to reward knowledge checks—you can even consider doubling up on a couple of key knowledge skills, just to ensure you remember all the important facts.

Although not technically a knowledge skill, Streetwise comes in handy when facing a conundrum of any sort. It can even cover for weak spots in your knowledge skills, as long as you have time to ask around. Some Dungeon Masters also use Streetwise to handle a subset of social interactions, particularly long clue-gathering missions abstracted over many individual meetings.

If you go to the trouble of training in one or more of these skills, try to get your modifier high enough to handle hard DCs.

SKILLS OF OBSERVATION

This category includes only two skills, but they're the ones that players hear DMs ask for most often. Rarely does an encounter go by without the request to "roll Perception checks," so you're forgiven for thinking it's the most important skill in the game.

Truthfully, though, the payoff for multiple characters rolling well on the same Perception check is rarely worth the expense of multiple characters training in the skill. Once the ranger or the rogue has aced the check, your second-highest result probably doesn't help. Besides, a cleric or another Wisdom-based character is almost as good at Perception without training as the trained rogue. That said, make sure somebody maximizes his or her Perception skill and can hit the hard DCs, or you can expect to learn about surprise rounds the hard way.

The other observation skill, Insight, presents a similar but less crucial challenge. Again, a successful check can provide a significant advantage (or avoid a significant drawback), though calls for Insight checks occur less often than those for Perception. Like Perception, having one character who can succeed on hard checks is probably enough—but it is also pretty necessary.

Ask your Dungeon Master what benefit, if any, successful Insight or Perception checks might have during a typical combat. Some DMs might let you use these skills to recognize useful information, such as which monster is in charge or when a creature needs to recharge a power before using it again.

Skills of Persuasion

Three skills handle most social interactions in the game: Bluff, Diplomacy, and Intimidate. Unless your DM enjoys putting characters on the spot, you can probably afford a single specialist in each of these skills. As with the knowledge skills, consider spreading these out among multiple characters. If you decide to train in Bluff, ask another player to pick up Intimidate. These specialists should be able to reliably succeed on hard checks.

On the other hand, if you expect a campaign high in social interaction, each character should be able to succeed on medium checks with at least one of the interaction skills.

Miscellaneous Skills

The last two skills don't fit neatly into any other category. That doesn't mean you can ignore them. When used properly, either of these two skills adds almost as much benefit as a utility power.

Characters who have a leader in the party often overlook the value of the Heal skill, believing it unnecessary for survival. However, skill training in Heal can grant extra saving throws, stabilize the dying, or even allow an ally to spend a healing surge outside his or her turn. Any one of these effects can turn the tide of a battle, and you get them all as effectively at-will powers.

Unlike most other skills, the important DCs for the Heal skill are fixed at 10 or 15. That means that at higher levels, you can afford to retrain your Heal skill into another skill while still reliably hitting the target DC.

The other valuable but underutilized skill, Stealth, received a crucial update in *Player's Handbook 2* that more clearly defined how to use it to hide from enemies. Put simply, if an enemy can't see you at the end of your move action, you can attempt a Stealth check to hide from that enemy. Once you're hidden, you stay hidden with any kind of cover or concealment (other than another creature) until you attack. (Okay, it's a little more complicated than that, but if that's all you remember, you're in good shape.) Move around a corner, hide, and then move back up to the corner on your next turn and snipe your enemy.

A rogue gains the greatest benefit from being hidden (by dealing Sneak Attack damage), but every character appreciates combat advantage. Rangers, warlocks, wizards, and any other character who can afford to stay away from the fray should seriously consider training in and using Stealth whenever possible. Against many kinds of monsters, you need only hit moderate DCs to hide, but a specialist in sneaking should aim for the hard DCs.

PATRICK THOMAS PARNELL

A careful selection of feats can strengthen your character's theme as well as heighten his or her efficiency in battle. Unfortunately, many players become overwhelmed by the broad range of feats available, particularly when using the D&D Compendium or the D&D Character Builder.

The secret is to have a plan and stick to it. Decide what you want to do with your feats and find the options that best fit that plan. Want to become the master of the craghammer? Don't half-commit to specialization—go all-out. Plan on multiclassing? Go for those feats as early as you can, and come back for the other ones later. Do you want to use feats to boost your offensive firepower? Don't waste time looking at defensive boosts.

Knowing that you need a plan only gets you halfway there. This section presents guidance on how to come up with that feat-selection plan for your character.

Establish Your Identity

Your first few feats often represent integral and iconic aspects of your character. They help define you in the eyes of the other players and the Dungeon Master, so choose feats that have a notable, significant effect on your character's look and feel.

For example, if you expect to wield an unusual weapon, such as a fullblade or a drow long knife, take that Weapon Proficiency feat right away. Some races have iconic weapons available or that can be improved through feats, such as Eladrin Soldier or Dwarven Weapon Training. Even simple and martial weapons have feat options that define your style, from Reaping Blade for your longsword user to Crippling Crush for hammer-wielding wardens. This type of feat selection establishes your character's identity, and it also helps the Dungeon Master know what kind of loot to include for your character.

Other good early feat choices are those that fit your class, build, or preferred tactics. Does your brawny rogue like leaping into the fray at the start of an encounter? Aggressive Assault rewards that behavior and ensures that the other players won't forget your style. A tiefling sorcerer who enjoys burning her enemies can't go wrong with Hellfire Blood.

Controller Feats

Feats that add to damage give you more punch than most other characters, because you often deal damage to more than one target at a time. Astral Fire, Burning Blizzard, Dark Fury, and Raging Storm are good options if at least half your powers' damage types match the feat, although taking more than one of these feats risks diluting your feat effectiveness. Destructive Wizardry makes your burst and blast spells particularly deadly. When you can afford a second implement, Dual Implement Spellcaster becomes a great choice.

Extending the duration of a control effect is almost as good as an extra attack against the target. Choose feats that apply penalties to the saving throws made against the conditions that your powers apply, such as Dominating Mind, Armor of Burning Wrath, Trickster's Fortune, or the paragon tier feat Spell Focus.

Finally, look for feats that let you target more opponents. Enlarge Spell is a great first choice, turning your wizard's humble scorching burst into a 5-by-5 square of fiery, minion-killing destruction. Resounding Thunder is reasonable if you focus on thunder powers, and Invoked Devastation provides something for all invokers to look forward to selecting when they hit epic tier.

Defender Feats

As the defender, your job is simple: Take as much punishment as possible without dropping. To stay in the fight longer, look for feats that add to your hit points (such as Toughness) or your defenses (such as Armor Proficiency, Armor Specialization, or Improved Swordmage Warding).

If you select feats that improve your AC, creatures you've marked become more likely to ignore you in preference for your easier-to-hit allies. That makes the efficiency of your retaliation—from the accuracy of your fighter's Combat Challenge attack to the damage dealt by your paladin's Divine Challenge—even more crucial. Mighty Challenge helps your paladin keep the enemies focused on you.

Mark of Warding is an excellent feat for defenders, because it can increase your defenses while encouraging enemies to attack you by improving your mark. If you take Mark of Warding, consider reevaluating your powers to maximize their compatibility with this feat.

Avoid the temptation to overspend on feats that improve your offense. Unless the party has another durable melee combatant, you should focus on defense and survivability rather than damage-dealing.

LEADER FEATS

As a leader, your character likely serves as the party's primary source of healing, extra saving throws, and offensive and defensive boosts. Embrace that role by selecting feats that pass out even more of these benefits.

If you can afford to forego offensive output against bloodied foes, grab Pacifist Healer to supercharge your cleric's healing powers. By 6th level or so, Healer's Implement becomes a worthwhile choice for your cleric, adding your implement's enhancement bonus to your healing powers. Warlords looking to improve their healing ability should select Improved Inspiring Word immediately (as long as your Charisma is 14 or higher). Supreme Inspiration doesn't show up until epic tier, but it's nice to look forward to doubling the effectiveness of *inspiring word*. Improved Majestic Word (bard) and Strengthening Spirit (shaman) each grant temporary hit points rather than true healing, but in the thick of a fight, temporary hit points are just as good as the real thing.

An extra saving throw can turn the tide of a losing fight by bringing a character who is dazed or immobilized back into the fray. The best feat for granting extra saving throws is Mark of Healing, which grants a saving throw to the target of each healing power you use. For warlords, Saving Inspiration is the next-best option (and Inspired Recovery is another solid choice). Shamans have Rejuvenating Spirit, which fills a similar niche, and bards have Majestic Rescue (though it doesn't appear until the paragon tier). Shared Perseverance improves the saving throws granted by your powers. Paladins and wardens, although not true leaders, also have plenty of feat options that allow them to pass out extra saving throws, such as Touch of Salvation and Lifespirit Vigor.

Once you've covered healing and saving throws, look for feats that give your powers better defensive protection for allies. Defensive Healing Word and Shielding Word both grant a bonus to the target's defenses, and the bonuses stack with each other. Prescient Fortification improves the already useful defensive benefit of your bard's Virtue of Prescience feature. Shielding Spirit protects allies adjacent to your shaman's spirit companion.

STRIKER FEATS

As a striker, you depend on accuracy to help you pull your weight. With a preponderance of high-damage, single-target attacks, just one bad roll can spell the difference between dropping a bloodied enemy and feeling useless.

Grab Weapon Expertise, Implement Expertise, or Versatile Expertise right away. If you're human, consider Action Surge and save those daily powers for when you spend an action point. Nimble Blade is a must for a rogue, but it's also a good choice for a dagger-wielding sorcerer who picks up Distant Advantage. Arcane Spellfury, Primal Fury, and Reckless Curse all offer attack bonuses, as well.

Rerolling an attack roll is another form of improved accuracy. Arcane strikers should consider Spellseer Familiar. The Darren Gambler feat—perhaps reflavored to fit an appropriate region in your DM's campaign—gives you an edge on rerolls.

Once you're satisfied with your accuracy, pick up a couple of feats that let you get out of trouble. Ghostwalker Style works for rangers and rogues. Reckless Scramble turns your rogue's short power-granted shift into a longer move. Improved Misty Step extends your warlock's pact-based teleportation.

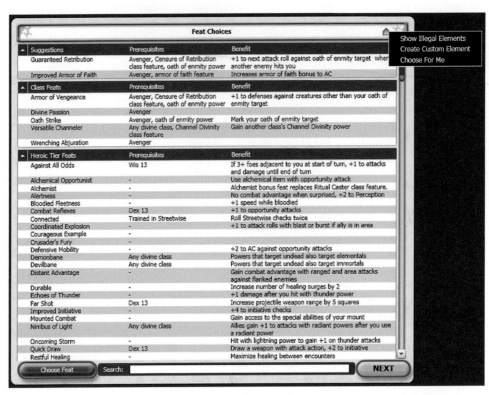

RACIAL FEATS

Don't forget to peruse the race-specific feats available to your character. In many cases, racial feats offer options superior to nonracial feats. For example, in the heroic tier, Dwarven Weapon Training grants a higher bonus to damage rolls than Weapon Focus.

Other racial feats enhance your racial power, which, as a useful encounter power, is likely to come up in every fight. Elven Precision makes it more likely that a rerolled attack will hit, making it popular with those low-roll-prone players. (You know who we're talking about.) With a broad selection of racial feats available, you can quickly stack up extra benefits to and effects on your racial power. A quick perusal of the D&D Compendium shows almost two dozen feats that add a benefit to the use of *fey step* or allow you to use *fey step* in a different manner than normal. It's unlikely that you'd be able to pick up more than a half-dozen of these feats, but even a few can make the moment when you teleport in every encounter a memorable event.

MULTICLASS FEATS

The various multiclass feats let you branch out from your character's normal range of choices. Not only do they add mechanical options, they also open up new story angles to explore.

See "Advanced Options," page 56, for more guidance on multiclassing.

CONSIDER YOUR PARTY

As with any optimization decision, consider the party as a whole when making feat choices. For example, a party with two leaders has more healing to go around, so specializing in leader feats is less necessary. Instead, you might choose feats that emphasize a secondary role (such as defender), depending on the gaps your party might have.

See Chapter 2 for tips on party building.

SIMPLE IS GOOD

If you can't decide on another plan, choose feats with simple, useful benefits that you can apply to your character and then forget about. This frees up your mind to worry about more important options in battle, such as where to move and what power to use.

Great but simple feats include any of the Armor Proficiency feats (in D&D, you can never be too rich or too well armored), Toughness (which not only increases your starting hit points by 20 to 25 percent, but also indirectly bumps up your healing surge value), Improved Initiative (great for defenders, to help them establish the battle lines, and for controllers, to deliver a key burst before the enemy has time to scatter), Weapon Focus (who doesn't like dealing extra damage?), and Weapon Expertise and its cousins, Versatile Expertise and Implement Expertise (who doesn't like hitting?).

TELL US ABOUT YOUR CHARACTER

I swear, I wasn't always the bad guy. But sometimes you just gotta step up and fill a hole.

I put a lot of effort into Gerhart Draken, my human wizard in my first "full-on" 4th Edition campaign. Not just by pouring over the *Player's Handbook* to divine my character's ultimate "career path," but also by creating an interesting, engaging background that would provide my DM with plenty of grist for his story mill. Cool stuff like "he was training to become a cleric, then his sister mysteriously disappeared, and after searching for her in vain, decided to take his sister's place at the arcane academy to retrace her footsteps and carry on in her memory." He never gave up searching for her, and maybe that made him a little crazy, but I never could've anticipated how that would play itself out over the course of the next year or so.

My role in the group started out pretty normally. I was a team player, dropping *scorching bursts* on (mostly) enemies, rolling *flaming spheres* into the paths of (usually) our foes, and generally making things go boom in the name of party cohesion and the advancement of our goals. Then something happened. I became the "instigator," and it all went downhill from there.

On one visit to an important town in the region, I got my paladin buddy Valenae and myself locked up by saying something stupid to an important priestess of a very influential temple. I was infuriated that they'd lock us away just for a little regressive behavior on my part, and of course I wanted out. When the guards took my impetuous wizard and his honor-bound elf paladin adventuring companion away to await judgment, they put us in separate cells, locking our equipment away in a nearby storage area, but leaving us with most of our other gear, including my ritual book. While Valenae steamed over her predicament, not sure why she'd bothered to stick up for such a brash young fool, Gerhart started plotting his escape. Of course, there would be no negotiating with the high priestess who had locked us up: I'd show her that a real wizard is not to be trifled with! I had a *dimension door* spell, and I meant to use it.

Since I needed to take an extended rest to get it back, I prepared myself for a nice little nap, confident that the arcane formula would once again be within my grasp when I awoke. As I bedded down in my cozy cell, a faint scratching sound made it difficult for me to get settled in for my slumber. It came from down the hall, inside a room sealed by a thick iron door with no windows and a giant lock barring entry by mundane means. I sensed opportunity here, and I knew right then that my DM, Greg Bilsland, would regret my next question.

"Okay, I still have my ritual book with me, right?" I asked Greg.

"Ah, sure," Greg said. "Are you going to cast something from it right now?"

"Oh, no. I'll just bed down for the night. I want to get my *dimension door* back."

I had a Knock ritual in the book, a gnawing curiosity, and a plan.

When I awoke from my rest, flush with the knowledge of the *dimension door* spell to teleport me out of my cell, I began a new round of questioning for Greg, determined to "enhance the story" of his meticulously crafted campaign.

"That big iron door with the scratching coming from the other side, it's got a good solid lock on it?"

Greg responded, "Yeah. It would be very tough to pick it open."

"Well, I have a Knock ritual. I'd like to give it a shot."

"You . . . want to open the door?"

"Yup. How hard do I think it'll be?"

"Pretty tough. Probably something like a DC 30 Arcana check."

"That is tough. But I'll give it a go."

As I began the ritual, Valenae watched on in abject horror. She wanted no part of this, but she was honor-bound to protect her fellow adventurers. It must be tough to have such scruples.

I threw a d20, and rolled a whopping 34 on my check. Greg informed us that the lock popped off as though picked by a master thief, and from behind the open cell door, the source of the scratching emerged. A wicked bat-winged humanoid creature strode forth into the room, gave me a hissing acknowledgement for freeing it from its prison, and proceeded down the hall, intent on punishing its captors. I had freed a berbalang.

"All right Valenae, while the temple guards are distracted, let's get out of here," I said, preparing to cast my *dimension door* to teleport out of the room.

"But it's killing them! We have to help put down the evil you've released!" She seemed a bit angry. But I was being so clever!

That was the beginning of some interesting times for Gerhart. Angels attacked us for my transgressions, old foes surfaced demanding recompense for my meddling, and ultimately, during the campaign finale, I left my entire party to be thrown into oblivion while I escaped to complete our last mission (which involved rescuing my sister). Ah, the memories!

What did I learn from all the chaos I spread over the course of many months? I found out that Gerhart was a hell of a lot of fun to play, and that sometimes it's great to play the DM's foil or take unwise risks to help tell the story of your game. Don't put it all on the DM's shoulders. Get out there and mess things up once in a while. Just do it in the name of fun.

CHRIS TULACH works for Wizards of the Coast as the Dungeons & Dragons organized play guy, developing D&D play programs responsible for the demise of characters worldwide. Chris lives in the orthodox geek way, constantly attempting to find gaming inspiration for his life experiences.

Attaining a new level is exciting because it opens up many choices, and having a wealth of meaningful decisions makes D&D–or any game–fun. Since one of an expert player's skills is making good choices, it's only natural that the *Player's Strategy Guide* has tips for this momentous occasion in your adventuring career.

You have two kinds of decisions to make when you go up a level. First, you can select new options depending on the level you've just attained, including powers, feats, ability score bonuses, or even such important choices as your paragon path or epic destiny (which are covered under separate sections later in this chapter).

Second, you can discard a previously chosen power or feat and replace it with something else (this is called retraining). Sometimes this helps correct a bad choice you made earlier in your adventurer's career. (It's okay, even expert players do this.) In other cases, the game uses forced obsolescence to inspire retraining: New encounter and daily powers, for instance, eventually force out lower-level powers, and some paragon- and epic tier feats provide all the benefit of a lower-level feat and more. But as an expert player, you'll learn when to retrain into better options, even when it hurts a bit to turn your back on an old favorite.

DECISIONS, DECISIONS

Whether you're picking up a new option or replacing an old one, the advice below helps guide you to good decisions.

REFLECT AND REVIEW

Like a birthday or New Year's Eve, leveling up is a great time to reflect on the adventures you've had since the last time this occasion rolled around. First, consider the moments you enjoyed most, especially when your character really shone. What could you choose now that would help those golden moments occur again? If your paladin extolled the virtues of sacrifice while taking a hit that was meant for an ally, keep an eye out for more immediate interrupt powers that have the martyrdom theme—both at your new level and as replacements for older selections.

Next, think about missed opportunities, when you were frustrated by being unable to rise to a situation. Such occurrences are not once-in-a-lifetime events, so use your newly gained choices to better prepare you for the next time. Do you still gripe about when the outcome of that battle hinged on your elf ranger's bow shot—when, as you picked up the dice to reroll, you declared that missing was not an option—and even the reroll from *elven accuracy* let you down? That thought can help guide you toward the Elven Precision feat.

OUT WITH THE OLD

As you look back, reconstruct your thoughts about the decisions you made at past levels. Are your selections working out as well as you'd hoped? Predicting the future is difficult, but now you have data about the challenges you've confronted. Reconsider your previous decisions in the light of recent information. Retraining is the obvious, but not the only, choice when things haven't turned out as you thought. If you were excited to choose *sweeping blow* for your fighter but you didn't use it much, you might not have to give up that precious power. Instead, look for options that help you get into the middle of the battle, and don't forget to talk to your party's controller about using his or her new level choices to funnel enemies into your close-burst attack.

THINK AHEAD

Once you have a short list of possible selections, consider how you might use them over the course of the next level. If a feat or a power is useful only in a specific situation, will that situation come up often enough to make the choice worthwhile? A selection too similar to one you already have might be redundant. Having one encounter power that spreads a little damage across a wide area is awesome, but a second one will be less useful because you will have already wiped out the minions that presented such a fine target for your first attack.

WE'RE IN IT TOGETHER

Your character doesn't fight alone, and you shouldn't make all of your decisions about your character's abilities alone, either. Discuss leveling up with the Dungeon Master and the other players. Reminiscing about the campaign's progress is a great opportunity to retell favorite gaming stories. Creating more fun and friendship around the table should be one of your goals as an expert player, and this group rehearsal also serves a practical function. Other players will remember moments you might have forgotten, or see events from a perspective that might suggest other ways you could develop your character's abilities.

This is also a good time for your group to reevaluate party tactics. Just as you collaborated to optimize your party at character creation, discuss how the players' new choices will work together. Do your selections enable a new plan of attack for your group, or plug a hole in one of your existing tactics? Review your marching order and contingency plans in the light of your new abilities. Even if nothing much has changed, rehearsing your group strategies once per level ensures that when the pressure is on, each member of the party knows how to react quickly, efficiently, and in coordination.

GUIDELINES FOR LEVEL CHOICES

When analyzing all the options facing you each time you level up, it's easy to become paralyzed by the fear that you won't make the right choice. Fortunately, it's almost impossible to make a choice that's completely wrong. No matter what your class or build, you have a lot of good choices every time you level up. Your personal preferences for weapons, combat tactics, and

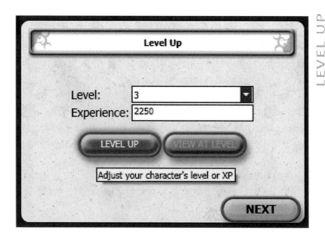

play style, plus the specific campaign environment and group dynamics in your game, can make choices that don't appeal to another player who has a similar character the perfect ones for you.

But even though different players are drawn to different selections at each level, a few universal guidelines can help your decision-making. See which of these categories best describe your character's needs, and explore the options described.

COMBAT PERFORMANCE

If you're having trouble breaking the skulls you aim at, try picking up Weapon Expertise, Versatile Expertise, or Implement Expertise. Particularly in the paragon and epic tiers (or if your DM doesn't give out many magic weapons and implements), monster defenses can start outpacing your bonus to attack rolls, making these feats very useful. Check your attack bonuses against the guidelines in Chapter 3 to see how you stack up against the game's expectations. If you're falling behind by more than a point or two, you can look forward to some frustrating combats unless you act to close the gap.

If these feats doesn't solve your accuracy problem, investigate options that improve accuracy in particular situations, such as Nimble Blade, or take Weapon Proficiency with a superior weapon with a higher proficiency bonus. Also, some powers are innately more accurate, either because they allow multiple attack rolls, allow you to use your weapon against a defense other than AC, or include a bonus to the attack roll. And adding a better weapon or implement wouldn't hurt, either.

GLASS JAW

If you find yourself serving as a punching bag for monsters—and if you're a defender, that's your job—improve your ability to suck it up by taking Toughness or Improved Second Wind, or by asking your leader to grab another healing power.

Chapter 3 also describes the defense scores expected of characters. Your defenses are likely to vary from these values by a few points, but check to be sure that one of your defense scores isn't leaving you vulnerable to certain kinds of attacks. You should be bolstering that weak Will, for example, if you're tired of mind blasts ripping through your skull.

Increase your AC with the appropriate Armor Proficiency or Armor Specialization feats, or your other defenses with Great Fortitude, Iron Will, and Lightning Reflexes (and, later, with their epic tier versions appearing in *Player's Handbook 2* and the D&D Compendium).

If all else fails, Durable gives you the extra healing surges to last a bit longer in the day.

Versatility

Strike a balance between being a one-trick pony and a jack of all trades but master of none. Specializing your build so that your character becomes a blaster extraordinaire is one thing, but being the sorcerer with nothing but single-target fire spells, or completely foregoing any defensive precautions in favor of more destruction, sets you and your group up for disappointment.

Everyone expects your fighter to own the melee, so why not surprise your enemies by grabbing a feat, a power, or an item that gives you a viable ranged attack? Even if you can only use it occasionally, you'll be happy to have it when the only foe left on the battlefield is flying just out of your reach. Similarly, characters focusing on ranged attacks, such as warlocks, wizards, and archer rangers, don't give up much potency by choosing an encounter or even a daily power that gives them something they can use up close and personal.

Noncombat Options

Think about expanding the range of your character's options beyond the combat encounter. Choose Ritual Caster to gain a magic toolkit for solving problems, or Linguist to better communicate with monsters and nonplayer characters. Tired of sitting on the sidelines during skill challenges? Jack of All Trades can help

NO BAD CHOICES

Hopefully, this chapter hasn't made you too nervous about picking the best feats and powers for your character. The game's power selection structure offers plenty of protection against making bad choices, so don't worry too much about accidentally making a suboptimal decision. Even a few subpar feats or powers can't reduce your character's effectiveness too much. When in doubt, pick the option that seems like it offers the most fun. After all, even if you decide later that you've made the wrong decision, you're only a level away from fixing it.

you do everything a little better, and Skill Training—or better yet, an appropriate multiclass feat—instantly boosts your competence in a specific area. The right utility power can also give you a trick useful outside the battlefield.

Before investing heavily in this type of versatility, talk to the other players. If you identify a noncombat talent that your character lacks, find out if someone else already has that covered, or if the group agrees that it's worth you adding it to your repertoire. No player likes being overshadowed, particularly at something he or she has decided is an important facet of his or her character.

Not Enough Damage

When you consider selecting or retraining attack powers, consider whether you're contributing your share to the party's damage output. If combat looks like a waltz that never ends, or if everyone locks enemies down with conditions but no one delivers the killing blow, choose a heavy-hitting power over one with fancy effects.

Not Enough Control

If you find your enemies are moving around the battlefield too easily—think about how often the wizard complains of taking damage and you'll know if this is true—pick up a power that slows, immobilizes, or even dazes the target.

Too Many or Too Few Targets

Sometimes you face the horde, and sometimes you square off against a lone monster. To handle either situation, your character should have a mix of single-target and multiple-target attacks. If you commonly have unspent encounter powers because you never see enough enemies within the blast or burst to make using an area power worthwhile, it's time to choose another single-target power. Similarly, if your DM really likes to throw an army of minions at you, even a low-damage multitarget power can be extremely effective.

Contingency Planning

Some powers deliver tremendous effects but function only in very specific situations. Choosing a couple of these powers—particularly as daily powers—gives you interesting tactical objectives to work toward. But if you have too many of these specialized contingency powers, you probably won't be able to set up the conditions to use all of them. If one of your impressive contingency powers hasn't been used since you last leveled up, it's time to trade it for something more versatile.

Another kind of contingency power is an immediate or free-action power triggered during your enemies' turns. If you can walk away from the table after your turn ends and not worry about missing the chance to do anything until your initiative count comes up again, consider taking a power that lets you strike in response to an enemy action. Being able to act throughout the round keeps your attention focused on the combat, which makes the time between your turns go by faster and makes the game more exciting. Just don't overdo it: If too many of your powers depend on a trigger from the Dungeon Master, you might find that your offensive output becomes unpredictable.

Class- and Race-Specific Options

Because these are available only to specific characters, the only one-size-fits-all recommendation here is always to consider these options when you level up. The best feats build upon your character's existing talents and party role, so those designed for your class and race are often tailor-made to fit your needs.

Who Are You?

Your character is defined by choices you make both during play and while away from the table. Your selections when you level up have a major effect on your character's image. You might be a barbarian, but will your comrades describe you as a ferocious savage who fights hardest after taking a beating, or as an imposing warrior who leads every charge into battle no matter the odds? The best guidance as you level up comes from understanding how you and your fellow players see your character, and how your choices enhance or lend contrast to that image. A feat or a power that you never use is like an elaborate ten-page background: It's written down, but because other players never see it, it has no effect on the experience at the table. As you level up, make selections that will have a vivid effect on the game, helping your friends see your character as you imagine him or her.

Retraining

No matter how careful you are in selecting character options, you inevitably end up with a power or a feat that doesn't pull its weight. Maybe it's too hard to use correctly, or it doesn't do quite what you thought it would, or a later choice makes it obsolete. Regardless of the reason, the answer is to retrain.

Each time you gain a new level, the retraining rules allow you to change one feat, power, or skill selection you made earlier in your character's adventuring career. The retraining rules aren't complicated.

Player's Handbook page 28 has the details, but as long as you remember to keep all your choices legal (both the new option gained through retraining and all your existing powers, feats, and skills), you're pretty much there.

By thinking about recent combats, you can recognize a power or a feat that isn't living up to what you want. Do you end up using one of your encounter powers only at the end of combat, or do you have a daily power that keeps going unspent? Similarly, has the situational attack or defense bonus from that

TELL US ABOUT YOUR CHARACTER

When Chris Tulach mentioned that he'd referenced my elf paladin Valenae in his sidebar for this book, I had to laugh . . . because in retrospect I had realized how very *un*optimized she was. Wrong ability score allocation, wrong powers, wrong feats, a mess of conflicting abilities that definitely kept her from being her paladin-y best. After the campaign ended, as an experiment I used the D&D Character Builder to recreate her using what I'd learned from playing the game. The revamped version turned out to be stronger, faster, and much, much more competent. The difference was astonishing.

And yet? While I played Valenae 1.0, this didn't make any difference to me. She felt plenty effective, holding her own against the ridiculously overpowered monsters Greg threw at us. That berbalang, for one, and most notably the angel of valor we were supposed to run from. Valenae held that thing off for round after round, soaking up massive amounts of damage and keeping its attention on her and away from her (capricious) fellow adventurers. Just like a capable defender should.

No question, it's a fun intellectual exercise to wring every last bit of possible efficiency out of your characters. But that should never get in the way of playing the character the way you want. As Valenae proved, D&D is robust enough that a character can survive with an inadvertently substandard build . . . and you might find that those hypothetical shortcomings matter far less than the drive for optimization suggests.

MICHELE CARTER joined TSR in 1992 as a roleplaying games editor and happily moved out to Seattle in 1997 to continue working with Wizards of the Coast. In that time, she has worked on nearly every game line produced for D&D (with some Star Wars and d20 Modern on the side). She maintains a special fondness for the PLANESCAPE campaign setting and was extremely pleased to see Sigil selected as the paragon-tier city for the 4th Edition Dungeon Master's Guide 2. You can recognize her desk by the army of comic book action figures, avatars of their owner's long-standing affection for the residents of Gotham City and the 30th century.

Offgood Martigan is a gnome sorcerer/dragon disciple. He's a ginger cherub dressed in plain robes, which at certain unfortunate angles can leave little to the imagination. He hails from a gnome town called Nittynan (which sounds particularly annoying when spoken in Offgood's nasal accent—and yes, I often speak in his voice at the game table). He visits Nittynan frequently to share stories and treasures with his wife and family.

He enjoys reminding his party mates (ad nauseum) that his great-, great-, great-, great-grandfather descended from a line of gold dragons. He one day hopes to unlock the secrets of his ancestry and tap into their draconic roots, but so far all he has to show for his efforts are a few deformed freckles that the local dermatologist has diagnosed as either pre-pubescent dragonscale or a searing case of dire acne.

While Offgood often serves as the comic relief of his adventuring party, he has an arsenal of powerful magic at his chubby fingertips and is loyal to the characters who treat him well. In short (no pun intended . . . well, maybe slightly intended), he has been a truly fun character to play. But even when I create characters with a bent for humor, I could not be more serious about my passion for playing them.

My player group is comprised mostly of men my age with Peter Pan syndrome (only without the tights, as far as I know) who welcome the chance to blow off steam once a week by engaging in interactive theatre and rolling some dice. Many of us grew up with some peripheral knowledge of D&D, but the majority of us discovered it for the first time as adults. We try to take the rule mechanics very seriously while keeping the experience loose and friendly. But sometimes even good friends can get into a debate about rules and the "right" way to play.

I once played a bard (Yorick) and put everything I had into his Charisma. This guy could charm a cyclops into wearing an eye patch. And although the party was happy when he negotiated with merchants to come down in price or intimidated prisoners for tasty morsels of intelligence, they did *not* enjoy his use of "diplomacy" to sway arguments about party leadership or loot.

The best thing about D&D is the human interaction.

But being human sometimes means having passions run high. We become deeply invested in our characters and can get prideful, defensive, and fearful about how we use (or lose) them.

I often hear about rules strategies, but rarely about social ones. How do you handle frustration with your role in the party, falling out of love with your character, or feeling like you're in competition with the other players or (worse yet) the DM? Ironically, the solutions to these problems often depend on your real-life Charisma and Diplomacy modifiers. When egos get bruised at your game table, it doesn't matter who's right: The fun gets spoiled for everyone.

Communication with the DM and your fellow players is just as important as communication between characters during a battle. I find it best never to disrupt gameplay at the table, even when I'm seething about something. Calm down, take a deep breath, and wait for the right moment to vent your frustration. Arguing during a play session only undermines the DM's authority and threatens to put egos on the defensive.

Instead, calm down and find a quiet place to settle disputes between game sessions. When we have grievances, my friends and I usually have a relaxed talk on the way home from a game, or type up an email the next day.

Remember that even the most serious and committed game is still just a game. You're all there to have fun with friends, roll dice, and tell stories. So when all else fails, ask yourself what's more fun: getting your way, or getting along. Because even though a good die roll might let my bard talk another character out of his loot, it's still a selfish, petty thing to do.

In the end, if the people at your table really just don't seem to prioritize each other's enjoyment of the game, then hit your friendly local game shop and check the forums . . .

. . . it's time to find a new crew to roll with.

DAN MILANO is a film and television writer. He co-created and starred in the shows Greg the Bunny and Warren the Ape, and he is a contributing writer/performer on Robot Chicken. His alignment is lawful awesome.

cool-sounding feat only come up once or twice since you chose it?

Do you find yourself using one of your at-will powers far more frequently than the other? It might be true that your best at-will is superior, but it could also be true that your other option just isn't the right choice for your character.

Does your new power outshine an existing power, doing the same thing only better? Many classes offer slight variations on iconic power themes as you level up. *Searing light*, for instance, does the nearly as much damage as the lower-level power *daunting light*, plus it blinds the target.

If you find that you are consistently passing over one of your powers, feats, or skills in favor of something that works better for your character, you should retrain the choice that isn't working for you. Here are a few details to remember when retraining:

ONE PER LEVEL

Unless your DM informs you otherwise, you can change only one choice each time you gain a level. This usually isn't a problem, but it means that major course corrections can take a few levels to pull off.

Plenty of DMs ignore this rule, preferring that their players enjoy their characters rather than follow strict retraining rules. Even if that's the case, don't abuse your DM's generosity by changing your whole character at every level. Unless your group really doesn't care about story continuity, this sort of activity can wreak havoc with the verisimilitude of the shared game environment.

KNOW YOUR LIMITS

You can't swap out Artful Dodger for Brutal Scoundrel, no matter how mean your rogue has gotten lately. Nor can you replace a power that's a class feature, which seems obvious until you remember that both of a warlock's at-will powers come from class features (which makes your pact choice all the more important). Perhaps it should go without saying, but you can't swap out your race, your class, your paragon path, your epic destiny, or any of the many other choices you make when building or advancing your character.

Again, some DMs allow slack on this restriction, so if you find one of your class features underwhelming, or if a new choice sounds more intriguing, see if you can work something out. Offer to make it part of the ongoing storyline, even if you have to wait a level or two.

WATCH YOUR TIER

During the paragon tier, you can use retraining to replace a heroic tier feat with one that has a prerequisite of 11th level. This means that, by the time you hit 16th level, all of your feats could be paragon tier feats.

The same rule applies when you hit 21st level. A 30th-level character who retrains a feat at every level could have sixteen epic tier feats.

REPLACING POWERS

In addition to the option of retraining at each level, during the paragon tier you can replace lower-level powers with newly chosen powers. This doesn't count as your once-per-level retraining. The replacement levels are easy to find on the Character Advancement table on page 29 of the *Player's Handbook*: They're the ones that start with "replace" rather than "gain." For example, at 13th level you might replace any of your lower-level encounter attack powers with a 13th-level encounter power.

You don't have to do a replacement, although the advantages of replacing a low-level encounter power (probably your 1st-level power) with a more potent encounter power should be pretty obvious.

You also don't have to replace your lowest-level power of that category. Maybe your battle cleric selected a Wisdom-based encounter power at 3rd level because the Strength-based powers didn't interest you. In that case, you might be better off replacing that less accurate 3rd-level power than your tried-and-true 1st-level favorite.

The power you replace also depends on the power you gain. If you like the way your character operates, you might want to avoid mixing things up too much, so look for a power at your new level that functions as a direct upgrade to one you already have. A warlock who reaches 13th level and replaces *diabolic grasp* with *harrowstorm* is still the same character, but with more kick. When your 17th-level warlord swaps *steel monsoon* for *warlord's rush*, you still have the same basic experience, with mechanical differences. And if that experience is what you want, then your character is the best that he or she can be.

When you reach 11th level, you hit a significant decision point in your character's career. Your class describes your character's job in the adventuring party; your paragon path defines the ideal your character strives toward. You've worked hard to get this far, and as a reward for reaching the new tier, you gain a nice suite of new talents, including paragon path features, a new encounter attack power, a feat, and a +1 bonus to all six ability scores.

Good thing, too, because your second reward will be deadlier monsters, life-threatening challenges, and even more world-spanning quests. Life is hard out there for the movers and shakers of the world, and guess what? That's you now.

You don't need to wait until 11th level to consider your paragon path choice. You can even pick out a likely option during character creation. Having a path in mind before choosing the rest of your character's options is perfectly reasonable. Most paragon paths require only a class or a race and perhaps one or two other prerequisites, but why wait until the last minute to qualify? An early choice can also help the DM weave your character's career arc into the campaign story.

On the other hand, waiting until 8th or 9th level to start seriously thinking about your paragon path choice allows you to adapt better to the events of the campaign. It can take many months of play to reach paragon tier, and who knows where the story (and your changing opinions of your character) might lead? Sure, you'd always expected that your eladrin would end up as a wizard of the Spiral Tower, but then your character got mixed up in Feywild politics, and now the shiere knight path in *Player's Handbook 2* seems to be the right choice. As mentioned above, most paragon paths have only minimal prerequisites. Even if you aren't on the right track when you first choose a paragon path, a level or two of retraining should get you where you want to be.

NARROWING THE LIST

You might be one of those fortunate players who knows your paragon path from the moment you see it. Maybe you see your character in the accompanying illustration. Maybe you hear your character's voice in the prose, or instantly recognize your character's style in the combinations offered by the powers and features. Congratulations! You're one of the lucky ones.

For the rest of us, choosing the right paragon path doesn't come easily. We pore over supplements, click every link in the D&D Compendium, and read the Wizards Community D&D forums to learn about other players' experiences. This is a significant decision—the biggest one since character creation—and we dread making the wrong call. You can't retrain away a poor paragon path choice the way you can a disliked feat or power. Who wants to be burdened with the disappointment of a bad call for the next 20 levels of play?

Worried yet? Don't fret; as with most choices in D&D, it's tough to make one that won't allow you to have fun at the table. Once you have an idea what you want to accomplish with your character, you can narrow down the options to a select few for deeper analysis.

To get started in your search, ask yourself which aspects of your character merit the most development during the next ten levels. Deciding that you want your paladin to focus more on healing and leader-style party support leads to a different set of paragon path choices than opting to become the ultimate, unkillable tank.

Although your paragon path doesn't define your character nearly as much as your class, it does have a significant effect both on story and on game play. You paragon path adds significance to your party role, your race, your faith, your preferred combat tactic, and your place in the campaign setting.

Each section below describes a category of options to consider when making your short list of potential paragon paths. At this point, don't worry too much about the details of each path—as long as you like the flavor, and as long as the powers and features seem interesting, add it to your short list for later evaluation.

CLASS PATHS: DESIGNED FOR YOU

A paragon path that lists your class as a prerequisite is designed with your class in mind, so it's likely to mesh reasonably well with your character. Refer to the original source of your character class for a selection of paragon paths aimed at you, and check the D&D Character Builder for more.

That said, not every rogue paragon path is equally good for your rogue character. If a path you find interesting lists a class feature in the prerequisite line that you don't have, even retraining won't make that paragon path right for your character. File that one away for your next character and move along.

If you like how your character works and you want more of the same flavor of powers and features, look for paragon paths that list your class as a prerequisite. Unless you're playing a very unorthodox character, at least half of your short list choices should come from this category.

SPECIALTY PATHS: SHOWCASING A SIDE OF YOU

Player's Handbook 2 includes a series of paragon paths based on the character's race. The EBERRON *Player's Guide* has paragon paths for heroes who have manifested dragonmarks. In the FORGOTTEN REALMS *Player's Guide,* your choice of deity or background allows you more options. These facets of your character might not affect game play as much as your class, but they still represent a significant part of your identity. Paragon paths built around these aspects allow you to highlight that part of your character, expanding your talents in interesting and meaningful ways that might go beyond the expectations of a class-based path. For example, do you want to be the ultimate dwarf in the campaign? The firstborn of Moradin paragon path allows you to forge a powerful connection with the earth and your revered ancestors.

Many of these specialty paths offer multiple choices for the ability score used for their attacks. This makes it easier for a variety of character types to choose these paragon paths and remain optimal—whether you're a Dexterity-based rogue or a Charisma-dependent bard, you don't give up any accuracy by taking the halfling scoundrel paragon path.

Even if only to provide a contrast to the various class-based paths, try to include one or two specialty paths on your short list.

MULTICLASS PATHS: BALANCING YOUR VARIETY

You can qualify for class-based paragon paths using multiclass feats or the hybrid character rules (see "Advanced Options," page 56). A burly half-orc fighter who has the Sneak of Shadows feat meets the rogue prerequisite of the death dealer paragon path just as easily as the sneaky halfling rogue.

Picking up a paragon path aimed at your secondary class offers a way to extend your multiclassing without expending more feats, since the features and powers you gain are designed for that secondary class. If you like the taste of your secondary class and want more, peruse the paragon paths offered to that class.

Even if you haven't multiclassed, it's not too late to consider it. A single feat—potentially gained through retraining at 11th level—opens up a wealth of paragon path options. If you've previously considered multiclassing but felt the pace of gaining secondary class options was too slow, you could change your mind at 11th level and take a multiclass feat and a paragon path tailored to your new class.

PARAGON MULTICLASSING: BUILD YOUR OWN PATH

Some players just can't find the paragon path that fits their vision of their character. Others get all the variety they want through multiclassing and don't care to add a third flavor. The paragon multiclassing option appearing on page 209 of the *Player's Handbook* provides another direction for such players. These rules allow you to gain additional powers from your secondary class instead of the normal benefit of a paragon path. Functionally, it's similar to selecting a paragon path designed for your secondary class, with a few significant differences.

Instead of gaining path features at 11th and 16th level, you can replace one of your at-will attack powers with an at-will attack power of the secondary class. This can dramatically change the variety of your always-available attack options, though it comes at the cost of the path features that come with each paragon path. This loss of path features dissuades many players from selecting this option. The feat cost—Novice Power, Acolyte Power, and Adept Power—is also significant.

If you choose paragon multiclassing for your character, you don't take gain the flavor or story provided by a paragon path. You might not notice this right away, but over time you might become jealous of your comrades playing the scion of Arkhosia, the keeper of the hidden flame, and the holy conqueror. If you choose the paragon multiclassing option, come up with your own story angle that describes how you've achieved these new powers. Did you train with a similarly talented master? Are you inventing your own unique path?

On the plus side, paragon multiclassing offers you a much wider range of powers to choose from than any paragon path offers. A careful choice of feats can make up for the paragon multiclass character's lack of path features. Search for "paragon multiclassing" in the D&D Compendium for examples. These feats give class features or other benefits from the second class.

For more details on multiclassing, see "Advanced Options," page 56.

PARAGON HYBRIDS

Perhaps the most complex option available for paragon tier characters, the paragon hybrid rules (appearing in *Player's Handbook 3*) offer yet another way your character can branch out into new areas. As the name suggests, this is only for characters using the hybrid rules from *Player's Handbook 3*. If that doesn't describe your hero, skip to the next section.

Like paragon multiclassing, this choice grants you more class powers in place of the powers normally offered by a paragon path. Unlike paragon multiclassing, the powers can come from either of your two hybrid classes, giving you twice the flexibility of the multiclass option. You also gain the Hybrid Talent feat, granting you another feature from one of your classes.

If your character uses the hybrid rules, you should include the paragon hybrid option on your short list.

For more details on hybrid characters, see "Advanced Options," page 56.

EVALUATING THE CHOICES

Hopefully, the preceding advice helped you to pare your list of options down to perhaps half a dozen potential paragon paths. This list might derive entirely from a single category—all fighter paths, for instance—but it's more likely that your list includes a few paths from your class, one multiclass path (even if you haven't multiclassed yet), and even a specialty path or two.

Thankfully, most paragon paths follow a very similar structure: three (or sometimes more) path features appearing at levels 11 and 16, an 11th-level encounter attack power, a 12th-level utility power, and a 20th-level daily attack power. This makes them pretty simple to compare side by side. You can easily line up the attack powers to see which deals more damage, applies a nastier condition, or fits your tactics best. Use the guidance on selecting powers earlier in this chapter to help you evaluate the choices.

But comparing the potency of powers can miss subtle but important distinctions that crop up in paragon path selection. Here are a few issues to consider during your evaluation.

Ability Score Mismatch: Look at the primary ability score used by the path's attack powers. Does it match yours? Even meeting the path's class prerequisite doesn't guarantee a match. Like many class powers, some paragon paths are designed for specific builds of a class, and some class builds use different primary ability scores. This commonly occurs when choosing a path matching your secondary class, or with specialty paths.

Matching secondary ability scores also helps you get maximum effect from your path. Even though your tiefling wizard can use his or her Intelligence score for the attack powers of the Turathi highborn paragon path, one of the path features benefits from a high Charisma score, and the 20th-level attack power uses Constitution to determine its damage.

Giving up a little accuracy or other secondary benefits to gain a useful variety of powers and features can be worthwhile. Your high-Dexterity half-orc fighter who pursues the death dealer paragon path probably misses only one or two attacks over the course of an entire session compared to a full-fledged rogue, and you might not even notice the difference. That said, avoid saddling yourself with powers that rely on an ability score lower than 19 at 11th level. Making an attack with an ability score 4 points lower than your primary ability score is like taking a -2 penalty to your attack roll.

Some multiclass path options allow you to sidestep this problem. The divine oracle path in the *Player's Handbook*, for example, has only a single power (and no features) that rely on an ability score. Any character who meets the cleric class prerequisite gets almost all of the benefits of the path, even if he or she has a low Wisdom score.

Action Point!: Each paragon path includes a feature that modifies the effect of your action points. (Paragon multiclassing and paragon hybrids don't offer this feature.) Some paths add effects to the action points you spend—a bonus to damage or to defenses is common—and others give you an entirely new way to spend action points. Since you spend action points in roughly half your encounters, and probably when you most need a boost, don't ignore the significance of this feature.

When comparing action point features between paths, think about how your character typically uses action points. Make sure the benefit won't go to waste. If you often use your extra action to take your second wind or to use a healing power on someone else, a path feature that grants you a bonus to attack rolls made as part of the extra action gained doesn't help much.

Feat or Feature: The features a paragon path grants at 11th and 16th levels are probably the hardest aspects to gauge when comparing paragon paths, because these features vary a great deal in their effects. It helps to compare them to your feats, since by now you have plenty of experience choosing good feats.

A paragon path feature should feel slightly weaker than the feats you already have. If you'd take both features together as a single feat, that's not bad. If you would strongly consider taking an individual path feature as a feat, that's great! You've found a near-perfect feature for your character. Most path features don't quite measure up to this standard, however, so don't expect that fit too often.

Feature Mismatch: Usually, a paragon path that relies on or bolsters a particular class feature includes that feature as a prerequisite . . . but not always. Check the path features and even the powers for any mention of a class feature you don't have. Even if you find one, you can still take the path, but you don't get as much benefit from it.

Even if you have a class feature that is the prerequisite for a paragon path, if you gained that class feature through multiclassing or the hybrid rules, you might not have a fully functional version of the feature. Increasing the output of Sneak Attack doesn't do much for a wizard who can only use that feature once per encounter thanks to the Sneak of Shadows feat.

Role Mismatch: Just as when you swap out powers by multiclassing, taking a paragon path that doesn't match your primary class means you risk losing some of your ability to fulfill your party role. Gaining more healing options for your paladin by picking up a cleric-focused paragon path seems like a great idea, but if everyone in the party looks to you as the lone tower of strength in melee, maybe you can't afford the trade-off. On the other hand, if you also have a fighter or a warden in the group, this sacrifice might not matter.

That said, you don't have to take a paragon path listing your primary class as a prerequisite to continue filling your role. A paladin who picks up a fighter-based path, or who picks up a specialty path that enhances survivability in melee, stays within his or her role but adds a unique flavor to his or her fighting style.

What's Your Story?: With all that talk about powers and features, you might think we've forgotten about all those words that come right after the paragon path's name. You know, the flowery sentences about great heroes and mysterious secrets known only to a chosen few. After reading too many entries, paragon path story text can run together. Don't try to keep every detail in your head. Instead, jot down a word or phrase next to each paragon path on your short list that captures its essence. Then, when evaluating your choices, see which phrases best describe your mental image of your character.

Just like when you chose your backgrounds, consider what story tweaks you might need to fit your character into the story of each paragon path on your list—and also what's required to bring the path into the campaign. Talk to your DM to gain his or her insights, and to allow opportunities to blend the addition to your character's identity with the game's ongoing storyline.

WALKING YOUR PATH

Because each paragon path comes as an entire unit, your short list almost certainly includes one path whose features appeal to you much more than its powers, or vice versa. Finding a path with six perfect entries (plus a compelling story) happens rarely. Don't dismiss a path just because one aspect doesn't exactly fit, and don't let yourself become enamored of a single power if the rest of the path doesn't help your character.

Before you make your final choice, think about the way that choice will affect the campaign. How will

your paragon path change the way your character acts in combat? How will it alter his or her outlook on the world, or his or her interactions with prominent nonplayer characters? Does the path magnify an aspect of your character that is already present, or does it represent a major overhaul? Throughout the paragon tier, your choice of paragon path will influence your actions, your party's success, and the overall story as you move toward level 21 and your next big decision—your character's epic destiny.

CHAPTER 1 | *Building Your Character*

Although implemented in similar ways, paragon paths and epic destinies are very different. Epic destinies are far broader in scope than paragon paths and represent your character in a totally new light. A paragon path represents your character striving toward an ideal. An epic destiny manifests that ideal in immortal legend, setting the scene for timeless myths of your greatness. That might sound overly poetic, but it is supposed to. As an epic-level character, you walk just beneath the gods, and that power comes with a responsibility to the ages yet to come.

Some players have an epic destiny in mind for their characters from level 1, but that kind of planning isn't necessary. Mechanically, the barrier to entry for a typical epic destiny is even lower than for most paragon paths. Some destinies list a class prerequisite, but even those rarely care about specific builds or features. Epic destinies don't grant attack powers, so primary ability scores don't matter much. As long as you meet the meager prerequisites (if you consider "21st level" as meager), you can likely make good use of everything offered by an epic destiny. So rather than worrying about eliminating mismatches, look for the destiny that best fits the immortal legend you want your character to leave behind.

Also, use what you've learned about the campaign so far. After 20 levels, you should have a good idea about the kinds of stories, foes, and encounters you can expect to see in later sessions. Choose a destiny that allows you to face those challenges and prove your mythic consequence.

BREAKING ALL THE RULES

The features and powers granted by your epic destiny are unlike any you've seen so far. For many players, the first look at an epic destiny results in a "You've got to be kidding me!" moment. Put simply, although epic-level powers often stretch the limits of reality, epic destinies shatter them. Here are just a few examples of the ways that epic destinies break the rules you've come to know and love over the previous 20 levels.

Every single-target martial encounter power used by your Martial Archetype becomes reliable. Given enough time, you're guaranteed to hit with every one of those powers.

Your Harbinger of Doom rerolls any natural 1 result on an attack roll. Say goodbye to the automatic miss.

The Avatar of War never grants combat advantage. Dazed, flanked, and prone . . . who cares?

Your Deadly Trickster gets to tell the DM that the roll the DM just made was actually a natural 1. I'm sorry, was that a crit?

If the epic destiny you're considering isn't going to give you an "I can't believe you just did that!" moment, think about finding one that will.

RECHARGING POWERS

Another significant group of epic destiny features allows you to recharge or otherwise reuse expended powers. For example, the Demigod and Chosen destinies each allow you to regain one encounter power of your choice after you've expended your last encounter power. In a long fight, this can either turn one of your encounter powers into an at-will power—quite a step up in potency—or it can let you cycle through encounter powers, selecting the right one for each new round of battle. The Deadly Trickster's 26th-level utility power allows you to recover all your expended encounter or daily powers (except itself), which quite earns its name of *epic trick*.

THE END IS NEAR

Before you salivate too much over that 30th-level destiny feature waiting on the horizon, remember that the game doesn't go to level 31 (at least not yet). You might get to use that shiny new toy for only a couple of sessions before putting your character up on the shelf and starting a new hero.

Give more weight to powers and features that you gain sooner. Sometimes, a weaker, lower-level ability can contribute even more to your overall enjoyment at the table than a "You did what?" feature.

On the other hand, if you prefer to go out with a bang—if a long, slow buildup is worth it for an unforgettable finish—forget everything you just read. Go read the Avatar of Hope, and save that automatic natural 20 for when you use your 29th-level daily power against Orcus in the depths of the Abyss. It'll be worth it.

MAKING YOUR MARK

As with every other choice you've made during your character's career, mechanics are only one factor in choosing your epic destiny. Not only does every destiny come with its own story, it also involves your character writing (or rewriting) that story for later generations to tell.

More than any other part of your character, your epic destiny comes with the opportunity, even the obligation, to influence the direction of the campaign. Over the next 10 levels, you will become an immortal part of history. Your character's legacy will alter aspects of culture, politics, religion, and perhaps even geography itself. How does this knowledge influence your decision of which epic destiny to pursue, and how does it affect your character's actions in upcoming sessions?

Players using a published campaign setting such as Eberron or the Forgotten Realms might be reluctant to upset existing, familiar structures to make room for their characters. Don't be! It's your world, not anyone else's, and no one can tell you that your demigod can't take the place of Torm or Dol Arrah.

But as always, with great power comes great responsibility. In this case, you're responsible for discussing your epic destiny choice—and your thoughts on how it might fit into the campaign—with your DM. Hopefully, after many similar conversations you're already on the same page regarding your character's place in the world. But know that the epic destiny discussion takes on a greater level of importance than almost any other chat since you first imagined your character. Your DM likely has an idea of where his or her plot lines are headed, and too much player input can overwhelm even the most accommodating Dungeon Master.

So start the discussion early. Although the benefit of deciding on an epic destiny during character creation is limited—who knows how many times you'll change your mind before you hit 21st level?—by the middle of paragon tier you should starting thinking hard about your destiny. A few casual talks with the DM—and the other players—can get the creative juices flowing. Story hooks can manifest earlier, key quests and plot lines can change to fit your epic plans, and the whole campaign can flow more naturally to accommodate your new identity.

Include the topic of Destiny Quests in your discussions. This concept appears on page 172 of the *Player's Handbook*; basically, it's about crafting an epic adventure tied specifically to the epic destinies of your group. Taking on the tarrasque might be a great final encounter, but wouldn't your Chosen of Bahamut rather storm the palace of Tiamat? The right Destiny Quest can provide a fantastic and fulfilling conclusion to your campaign, giving everyone at the table something to remember fondly for years to come.

Whether or not your group uses the Destiny Quest concept, the most important thing—as in all of D&D—is communicating and cooperating with your Dungeon Master. Learning enough about a setting to run a game requires a considerable amount of work, and creating a world from scratch takes even more. Your Dungeon Master has already put a great deal of time and preparation into the campaign, and embracing your character's epic destiny is your last chance to repay that hard work. Helping write this final chapter of your character's saga not only lightens the load on your Dungeon Master, it lets you determine how and why your character is remembered. Working together, you and your allies can establish the soaring temple, secret haven, or demiplane that will be your character's new home—and possibly a quest location for a new group of heroes just starting their rise to glory.

I AM UNKILLABLE! UUUNKILLAAABLE!

KALMAN ANDRASOFSZKY

Many players go through an entire campaign playing a traditional character, who has a normal race, a single class, and powers chosen entirely from that class's list.

But you need more options, don't you? Playing the best dragonborn fighter isn't enough when you could be playing a dragonborn revenant hybrid fighter/paladin specializing in the spiked chain. Yeah, we get it. We've been there, too.

The following sections describe some advanced character-creation options available in the game. Some, such as skill powers, are relatively simple. Others—hybrid character rules, we're looking at you—reward a mastery of rules and character optimization that can't be taught in a few pages . . . but that doesn't mean we can't give you some tips to evaluate these advanced options to determine if they're right for your character.

MULTICLASSING AND HYBRIDS

For some players, one class isn't enough. Perhaps you can't settle on a single character concept to play. Maybe your party needs a defender and a leader, and you want to fill both roles. Maybe the best way you can imagine to manifest your character's upbringing as a feral child taken in by mystics is by drawing on both the barbarian and the monk classes. Whatever the reason, you have two apparently similar yet very different options for blending elements from two classes into a single character: multiclassing and creating a hybrid character.

MULTICLASSING

A multiclass character uses one or more feats to get a taste of a second class. Each class offers one (or sometimes more than one) introductory multiclass feat. This feat typically offers training in a class skill and a lesser version of one of the class's features, which allows you to feel like a member of the class for a round or two in each encounter.

This entry feat also serves as a prerequisite for additional multiclass feats for that class, most notably the power-swap feats Novice Power, Acolyte Power, and Adept Power. Each of these feats allows you to replace a power from your primary class—encounter attack power, utility power, and daily attack power, respectively—with one of the same category chosen from your multiclass powers. If you take all four of these feats, you can even forego selecting a paragon path at 11th level in favor of more fully investing in your secondary class (see "Paragon Multiclassing," page 51).

Choosing to multiclass puts a burden on your feat selection. Fully embracing a secondary class in this manner can take up to four feats, which means you give up some of your ability to specialize your character's build or to enhance racial powers with feats.

That said, multiclassing doesn't significantly limit your ability to carry out the role of your primary class. A fighter with four rogue multiclass feats still feels more like a defender than a striker. If you prefer your primary class, but just want to borrow a couple of tricks from another class, multiclassing is a good option for you. The party that is always in need of one more healing power or that is missing a key trained skill appreciates a multiclass character.

HYBRID CHARACTERS

Unlike a multiclass character, a hybrid character doesn't have a primary class and a secondary class. Instead, a hybrid character acts more like two half-classes melded together into a unique whole.

When you create a hybrid character using the rules that first appear in *Player's Handbook 3*, you choose two different classes during character building. (Every hybrid character begins play as a hybrid; you can't later choose to become a hybrid character, unlike multiclassing.) Each choice grants you a subset (or lesser versions) of that class's features. When combined together, your two hybrid halves effectively form a brand-new class.

As a hybrid character, you choose powers from either of your two classes. This gives much greater flexibility than multiclassing, which at most grants three powers from your secondary class. You must always have at least one power in each category—at-will, encounter, daily, and utility—from each of your two classes to ensure a true blend.

Typically, a hybrid character can function as either of his or her two classes (and roles, if they are different) at any given time, but can't necessarily act as both classes simultaneously or for the entire encounter. For example, many role-defining class features come in hybrid forms that limit which powers they apply to. A hybrid fighter/rogue can't use Combat Challenge with rogue powers, nor can he or she apply Sneak Attack damage when using fighter powers. This limitation prevents hybrid characters from too easily overshadowing other characters at the table. If your hybrid fighter/rogue filled both the defender and striker roles simultaneously, the paladin and ranger in your party might rightfully feel irrelevant.

The hybrid option represents a more thorough blend of two classes than the multiclassing option. Hybrids are ideal when your character needs the flexibility to fulfill two roles, or when one or both of your hybrid classes' roles are already represented in your party. The undersized adventuring party welcomes a hybrid character, and in a large party it can help you stand apart from the other members.

CONSTRUCTING GOOD COMBOS

Choosing the right two classes to blend using the multiclass or hybrid rules can be challenging. The game wasn't built to cater to such characters, so even the most compelling concept can encounter problems when it hits the table. This section describes some of the issues arising from class combination and explains how to solve them.

Ability Scores: Selecting two classes that have the same primary ability score maximizes your effectiveness (that is to say, your accuracy) in battle. A fighter who picks up barbarian powers will be more successful than one who adds rogue or wizard powers.

However, this guideline excludes a lot of fun, compelling class combinations. If you can match your second class's primary ability score with your second-best ability score—particularly if your secondary ability score is near or equal to your primary ability score—you'll do fine. See the advice in "Setting Your Ability Scores," page 23, for more on this topic.

Bards: The bard is the unquestioned master of multiclassing, thanks to the Multiclass Versatility feature that allows him or her to select class-specific multiclass feats from more than one class. If your character concept involves more than two classes, consider starting play as a bard.

Complementary Stories: As mentioned earlier in this chapter, every class has a story. When building a character who has multiple classes, consider how those stories might blend together. Here are a few questions to get you started.

Does your character favor one class over the other?

Did you learn both classes from the same mentor?

Does one of your two classes represent a part of your training or background that you'd rather forget or a talent you don't like to talk about with others?

Does your character belong to a tradition of this class-blending, or are you a pioneer?

If your character combines two classes at the start of play, which class did he or she learn first?

When building a multiclass or a hybrid character, many players instinctively feel most comfortable with combinations that offer obvious explanations, such as cleric/paladin or fighter/warlord. Don't fear unorthodox combinations. Instead, see them as an opportunity to tell a unique story. Maybe the other players at the table can't imagine how you could combine the barbarian and paladin classes, but I'll bet you're already coming up with a compelling explanation.

Mixing and Matching Roles: Combining two classes with different roles can seem like a solution for the player in a party that doesn't cover all the roles, or for the player who wants to create a one-of-a-kind character. But blending different roles poses the risk of role dilution. Sometimes, a character who has two roles ends up fulfilling neither. This doesn't necessarily mean you don't contribute, but in a small party it can result in key talent gaps.

MULTICLASS AND HYBRID FAQ

The multiclassing and hybrid character rules are more complex than the rules for ordinary character creation. Understandably, users have questions about how these rules work. Here are a few of the more commonly asked questions.

Q: If a character already is trained in the skill granted by a multiclass feat, can the player choose one of the other skills from that class instead?
A: No.

Q: When my character takes a multiclass feat for a class of a different role than my primary class, do I qualify as a character of that secondary role for the purpose of meeting prerequisites?
A: Yes. A githzerai cleric who takes a swordmage multiclass feat could, for example, select the Marked With Iron feat (which requires the defender role).

Q: When a multiclass feat states "you can use (class name) implements," does that mean I can use those implements with powers of my primary class?
A: Yes. If you are proficient with an implement, you may use it with implement powers of any class, even if that class doesn't normally use that implement.

Q: Initiate of the Faith states that my character can use *healing word* once per day. Does that mean I can use it twice during a single encounter (since the power states it can be used twice per encounter)?
A: No. The feat only allows you one daily use of the power, regardless of what the power's Special line says. (The same is true of similar multiclass feats, such as Student of Battle, Bardic Dilettante, and Student of Artifice.)

Q: Can my character take the Hybrid Talent feat multiple times?
A: No. Like any other feat, you are limited to one Hybrid Talent feat unless some other rule provides a specific exception. (The Paragon Hybrid option, for example, allows you to take the feat a second time.)

Blending two classes of the same role can create a unique and compelling character: an entirely new, perhaps even more effective representative of the role. A rogue who has the Warrior of the Wild feat can double-up on striker damage output every now and then, and a hybrid cleric/warlord has an unparalleled range of healing and team-boosting effects to choose from.

Weapons Versus Implements: Picking two classes that both use complementary weapons or implements with their powers avoids the need to spend your hard-earned gold on an extra item. Some characters grapple with this issue even without multiclassing or playing a hybrid. Rangers have melee weapon powers and ranged weapon powers, and bards, clerics, and paladins each have both weapon and implement powers. The advice in this section applies equally well to such characters.

Many players of multiclass or hybrid characters get tripped up when they forget this advice. At a glance, your paladin who multiclasses as a warlock seems fine; both classes have plenty of Charisma-based powers. And for the first couple of levels, you probably won't notice a problem. However, most paladin powers work through weapons, and warlock powers use an implement. That means that the exciting new magic sword you find in the treasure chest doesn't contribute to the accuracy or damage output of your warlock powers. To keep up, you must find, craft, or purchase a second weapon or implement, which could represent a significant expense.

Thankfully, this only applies to a limited number of class combinations. Most class-specific multiclass feats grant you the ability to use the secondary class's implements with all your implement powers, and hybrid characters can use both classes' implements interchangeably, so your invoker/sorcerer shouldn't have a problem.

But even combining two weapon-using classes doesn't guarantee a match. The rogue's powers, for instance, rely on the use of a crossbow, a light blade, or a sling, which makes them suboptimal for a greataxe-wielding barbarian looking to multiclass. Look for a Requirement line in each class's powers to find such pitfalls before you stumble into them the hard way.

Thankfully, many workarounds exist that solve this problem. For instance, a number of magic weapons also function as holy symbols (including *crusader's weapon*, *disrupting weapon*, and *holy avenger*). The popular *pact blade* functions as a warlock implement, and the various *songbow* weapons function both as ranged weapons and as bard implements. Both the swordmage and the sorcerer wield weapons that simultaneously function as implements. Even if you don't belong to one of these classes, the Arcane Implement Proficiency feat grants you the ability to use one of these weapons as an implement.

If you avoid attack powers from your secondary class, you can ignore this drawback. For example, a fighter who multiclasses into cleric to get a *healing word* once per day and uses the Acolyte Power feat to swap in the *bastion of health* encounter utility power can get by without needing a holy symbol.

Secondary Class Options: By taking a second class, you open up a new range of options, such as feats and paragon paths, designed for that class (see the "Meeting Prerequisites" sidebar). Even so, you should be careful not to invest too heavily in options not designed for your primary class. Your primary ability scores might not match these options, or they might not fit your ideal tactics. Always think twice about grabbing an out-of-class option just because it has a cool name or makes your character feel more diverse; sometimes diversity has hidden costs.

That said, a number of hidden combinations arise only when you blend two classes in this way. For example, a sorcerer who has the Arcane Initiate feat gains great benefits from the Destructive Wizardry and Enlarge Spell feats, which are otherwise available only to wizards. Check out the Wizards Community D&D forums for more discussions and dissections of these odd combos.

ADDING DEFENDER

Multiclassing as a defender initially grants you a minor marking ability, available once per encounter. If you want to expand your ability as a defender, take powers that let you mark more frequently, such as the fighter's *close the gap* or the divine sanction powers of the paladin.

Hybrid defenders gain resilience through more hit points per level, and they gain the ability to mark when using defender-class powers. If you plan to serve as the primary defender of your party, consider taking the hybrid option that improves your AC, whether that's armor proficiency or something like the Warden's Armored Might hybrid option.

MEETING PREREQUISITES

One benefit shared by multiclass and hybrid characters is that they qualify for feats, paragon paths, and other options as if they were members of both of their classes. For example, a fighter with Sneak of Shadows can take a paragon path that lists rogue as a prerequisite just as if he or she were a rogue. Many hybrid character features count as the normal versions of the features for meeting prerequisites, which opens up even more options.

ADDING LEADER

The most popular reason to multiclass into a leader class is to gain more healing for your party. Having a second healer in the party is always nice, even if that second healer fills in only when the primary healer is down. Leaders also have great party-synergy powers, using partywide buffs or target designation powers to improve the performance of everyone around them.

Your first multiclass feat usually gives you a once-per-day healing power, but access to other such powers—a key benefit for leader multiclassing—requires more investment. Since many healing powers for leader classes are utility powers, multiclassing to gain one of these powers doesn't detract from your combat effectiveness.

ADDING STRIKER

Strikers focus on damage, so this option is for any character who wants to deal more damage. Even if you don't plan on further multiclassing, the entry striker multiclass feats provide a nice one- or two-round boost to damage. If you prefer dealing damage in occasional surges rather than reliably across multiple rounds, Sneak of Shadows (+2d6 damage once per encounter) is better than Weapon Focus (+1 damage per hit).

Hybrid strikers can use their striker-damage mechanic whenever they use powers from their striker class, following the hybrid model of letting them be a striker half the time. Use your nonstriker powers to help set up your striker feature. For example, warlock powers that daze or blind give your rogue combat advantage for Sneak Attack. An avenger benefits from using invoker powers that slide or push, which can properly isolate a target for *oath of enmity*.

ADDING CONTROLLER

More than other classes, the controller's role is defined by his or her powers. Controller powers lean toward multitarget powers and effects that limit enemy options, reduce enemy damage output, or force enemy movement.

As a multiclass controller, you can use an at-will power from that class as an encounter power. Choose a power that complements your normal class powers: Take a burst power if you have only single-target powers, or gain a power that targets a defense that your normal powers don't.

Hybrid controllers start out with fewer hit points than other characters but gain access to the controller power lists, where most of a controller's class identity comes from. Since a controller hybrid prefers combat from a distance, consider pairing your multiclass controller with a similar class to keep all your options equally useful . . . or combine your controller with a melee-oriented class to have the right answer in any situation.

UNUSUAL RACES

Two racial options offer the ability to add exotic details to your character. Coincidentally, both involve aspects of undeath, and both were first published in the online pages of *Dragon*™ magazine.

REVENANTS: SOULS RETURNED FOR A PURPOSE

The revenant is the soul of a dead person returned to the semblance of life by the Raven Queen. Revenants typically resemble gaunt, pale humans, with sunken facial features and eerie eyes. They walk the world for a reason, even if they don't fully understand it, and their dreams haunt them with fragmentary memories of a previous life.

Mechanically, the revenant is a race choice like any other. By choosing to play a revenant, you are choosing not to play a dwarf or a human or a tiefling . . . sort of. In fact, you also choose a second race that represents what you were before you died and the Raven Queen reincarnated your soul in this new form. You are treated as a member of that race for the purpose of meeting all prerequisites, so a dragonborn revenant could select dragonborn feats or choose a dragonborn paragon path or epic destiny. Certain feats even allow you to replicate your original race's racial power.

Choosing to play a revenant not only offers obvious story potential, but also allows you to blend two races together in unique ways.

DHAMPYRS: HALF-BLOOD VAMPIRES

From time to time, a mortal is born with vampiric powers. No matter the reason for this strange occurrence, the resulting individual acquires certain physical characteristics, including pronounced canine teeth, pale skin, a tendency toward immortality, and an unfortunate thirst for blood.

Unlike the revenant, the dhampyr isn't a race you can choose. Instead, you choose a race as normal, and your accursed bloodline manifests when you select the Vampiric Heritage feat. You retain all the traits of your base race and add abilities from the feat. This feat then serves as a prerequisite for many other options that expand your vampiric nature, including

NEW PARAGON TIER OPTIONS

Both the multiclass and the hybrid character have an extra option available when selecting their paragon paths at 11th level. Paragon multiclassing allows you to take additional powers from your secondary class, and the paragon hybrid option grants a class feature and powers from either class.

See "Paragon Paths," page 50, for more details and advice on these two options.

sprawl). However, they're different enough that they merit a separate discussion.

Most power-swap feats are designated as multiclass feats, even when they aren't linked to an actual class. However, instead of offering access to an entire class's list of powers, these power-swap feats swap in a single, specific, highly thematic power.

These feats offer a nice way to add some unorthodox flavor to your character, just like regular multiclassing. However, they don't provide the same depth of options, nor do they function as useful prerequisites for later feat or paragon path selection, so if that's what you want, don't bother with them. Since they're technically multiclass feats, you can't take more than one of them, nor can you take one of these feats and another multiclass feat (unless you're a bard).

Mini-Multiclassing

Bravo, Cutthroat, Poisoner . . . these could be D&D classes, but they aren't. Instead, they're special multiclass feats that exist without the need for a base class. The advantage they offer when compared to normal multiclass power-swap feats is that they don't care about your ability scores, weapons, or implements. Each attack power gained represents an effect that piggybacks on an existing power, using that power's information as a basis. For instance, the bravo power *death's messenger* adds extra damage and the rattling keyword to any at-will melee or ranged attack once per encounter.

Deity Focus

Still another subset of power-swap feats includes those that focus on the worship of a particular deity, such as Noble Indoctrination and Platinum Revelation. These feats offer any worshiper the option of swapping out powers for divine powers themed for his or her chosen deity. They provide a nice option for characters who want to play up their religious devotion, regardless of their base class's power source.

Weapon Training

Dragon magazine has published a number of power-swap feats for various unusual weapon choices, such as the blowgun and the whip. These feats represent extensive training with the weapons in question, weapons which otherwise pale in comparison to the reliable longsword or deadly battleaxe. If you want to build a concept around one of these odd weapons, the weapon training feats are a must.

feats and paragon paths. You can select as many or as few of these options as you choose, depending on how fully you want your character to embrace your half-breed identity.

Power-Swap Feats

Many feats allow you to give away a power you already have in exchange for a new power. These feats are commonly known as power-swap feats. Novice Power, Acolyte Power, and Adept Power are the most commonly known power-swap feats, but the game has expanded to include many more. Each power-swap feat uses terminology and rules similar to multiclass feats (and, in fact, they are called multiclass feats to simplify their use and limit character

Familiar Feats

Any character who has an arcane class can take the Arcane Familiar feat. Although Arcane Familiar is not a power-swap feat, it grants access to power-swap feats such as Shielding Familiar. Because your arcane familiar's defenses depend in part on the number of familiar feats you have, once you invest in the basic feat, you should consider selecting additional feats from the category.

Skill Powers

Player's Handbook 3 introduced this new category of utility powers that simultaneously belong to no class and every class. Unlike the various power-swap feats, which can only be accessed by selecting the appropriate feat, skill powers are automatically available to all characters who have training in the relevant skill. If you're trained in Endurance, you can select any Endurance power any time you'd normally choose a utility power from your class.

The low barrier to entry means that every player should become familiar with the skill power options available to his or her character. In most cases, the powers offer useful but not game-altering abilities (such as nimble movement, minor healing, and tricks of social interaction).

Typically, a skill power isn't as potent as a similar class utility power of the same level. The rogue's mobility powers, for example, might look a notch better than the Acrobatics powers, and the cleric probably wouldn't choose a Heal power. But every character should be able to find at least a few skill powers that offer options unlike those granted by his or her class.

Skill powers make your skill choices feel more meaningful, and they help you solidify your standing as a master of that skill. Plenty of characters have a high Arcana check modifier, but a true guru of such knowledge can use *arcane mutterings* to impress listeners.

TELL US ABOUT YOUR CHARACTER

Fareth Indoril is a 16th-level eladrin fighter who has the kensai paragon path.

A departure from the more traditional eladrin longsword-and-board swordsman fighter, the greatspear-wielding Fareth represents a little-known but incredibly vocal eladrin family of fighters and adventurers. Founded by Fareth's great-grandfather, the notorious Naidel "The Needle" Indoril, House Indoril's war college is known for training effective but unorthodox eladrin warriors: the Fey Lancers.

Naidel's wisdom is contained within a book only rarely spoken of within the eladrin noble houses. Called the *Tome of Infinite Battle*, the book is relatively new: only 700 years old. In every generation, one Fey Lancer is chosen to carry the book and update it with new discoveries, exploits, and philosophies of battle. In this generation, that person is Fareth.

Fareth's battle philosophies stem directly from his great-grandfather's teachings. The central theme of his fighting style revolves around two ideas:

1) Surprise is the key to victory.

2) The best way to win is to kill your enemies as soon as they show their faces.

Surprise comes not always through raw speed, but also from tactical and strategic action as well as battlefield control. For instance, if an enemy exhibits a strong offense but middling defenses, orthodox tactics prescribe a measured response: a strong defense to counter the enemy's offense, and a careful attack to gradually whittle the enemy down. A sword-and-board fighter would hold a chokepoint against strong offensive characters in the front line and allow the long-range strikers and controllers in the party to whittle down the opposition.

Fareth, on the other hand, immediately uses his *fey step* (possibly paired with the Fey Charge feat, against a lone ranged opponent) to blast past the front rank and strike at the heart of the damaging artillery and controller enemies with a powerful exploit.

Another of Fareth's favorite tactics is to use *fey step* to teleport into a knot of artillery enemies, then use *come and get it* to bring them within range of his powerful *bloodthirsty greatspear* attacks. Then, after finishing his initial attacks (usually boosted by Power Attack for maximum effect), he spends an action point to attack the knot of enemies with *thicket of blades*. This deadly combination deals a hefty amount of damage to a good number of opponents, all in the first round of combat. Not only that, every character within the knot is marked, fulfilling Fareth's duties as a defender.

Despite (or perhaps because of) his extensive use of teleportation in combat, Fareth also carries a *feyslaughter longbow* to prevent enemy controllers and such from escaping his reach through use of their own teleportation magic.

Ultimately, Fareth seeks to teach the other races the worth of the eladrin lancer, and to remind his own people that reliance on magic in battle is not always the solution, while also proving the value of his ancestor's fighting theories.

In game terms, he is very much a striker-flavored fighter and is best suited to a secondary defender role. He is designed to solo against artillery, controller, and lurker roles while the rest of the party deals with more immediate threats.

In addition to the powers noted above, Fareth's favorites include *shadowstep*, *advance lunge*, *rock steady*, *flanking assault*, and *bedeviling assault*.

DANIEL HELMICK *plays* Dungeons & Dragons *as much as possible. Once in a while, he shows up and works in Wizards of the Coast's Digital Studio, but mostly just to harass, intimidate, and cajole coworkers into letting him into their games.*

How to ...

The following pages describe various sample characters who specialize in a particular area of the game, such as healing or accuracy. This is not a list of optimization opportunities; it's a range of examples that demonstrate how far you can go beyond the obvious choices of class and build. If this kind of character concept appeals to you, you can apply the techniques described in this section to build your own specialized character.

... Make the Best Healer

"Nobody dies on my watch."

You know that being a leader requires more than using a couple of powers with *"word"* in the title. You take the role of healer extremely seriously. You have studied medicine, herbs, poultices, and first aid, and you know the tricks and techniques to keep your allies alive and kicking.

Being the best healer goes beyond just repairing damage in combat, although every healer must have that basic talent set. Your secondary focuses include granting and boosting saving throws and using rituals that eliminate negative conditions (such as Remove Affliction).

Follow these guidelines to maximize your healing potential. Your allies will thank you.

Class

Start by choosing your class, since this element contributes to the healing optimization build more than any other. Leaders are the only characters who have the potential to become top-notch healers. They have access to attack powers that feature secondary healing effects and to utility powers that have primary healing effects.

Of the leader classes, the cleric begins with the best healing, offers the most efficient healing powers, and gains the Ritual Caster feat for free. When building a healing master, choose the cleric and take *healer's mercy* in place of *turn undead*.

Bards, however, have an even greater potential as healers thanks to the Multiclass Versatility feature. Each time the bard selects a multiclass feat for a new leader class, he or she gains another daily healing power. The bard can also use multiclass feats to pick up the best healing powers from each class.

Race

Your character's race has minimal impact on your healing powers, but it can give you a small edge.

If you want to be a cleric healer, choose dwarf. The racial bonus to Wisdom improves your Healer's Lore class feature, and the bonus to Constitution and the Dwarven Resilience trait mean you don't have to spend as much effort healing yourself.

If you're building a bard healer, choose human or half-elf. The extra feat you get for being human lets you accelerate your acquisition of multiclass feats. As a half-elf bard, you could use your Dilettante trait to choose an at-will power that includes secondary healing, such as *invigorating assault* or *sacred flame*.

Ability Scores

Make sure your Wisdom score is high, so that you have a decent ability modifier for Heal checks. You need to be able to help others overcome disease and afflictions, and those restoration rituals require Heal checks. A high Charisma score helps you as a bard healer.

Feats

This section focuses on feats that fit the cleric or bard healers described above, but any class with healing powers can find feats that improve those powers.

The heroic tier is loaded with feats that enhance healing. Mark of Healing allows the target of your healing powers to roll a saving throw. Restful Healing maximizes the value of the healing powers you use outside combat. If you don't take Mark of Healing, the Mark of Hospitality feat offers a similar benefit to you and to your nearby allies. Bard healers should select multiclass feats as often as they can. By 8th level (or 6th level as a human), you could have five extra daily healing powers from multiclass feats.

In the paragon tier, look for ways to specialize your character's particular mix of healing options. By now, Healer's Implement—which adds the enhancement bonus of your holy symbol to cleric healing powers—becomes a worthwhile investment for cleric healers. Bard healers should take Improved Majestic Word to grant the target of that power temporary hit points. Majestic Rescue functions like Mark of Healing, but only augments *majestic word*. More leader multiclass feats can be useful, even if you aren't playing a bard.

The epic tier offers few very feats that boost healing. Supreme Healer and Supreme Majesty double the efficiency of *healing word* and *majestic word*, respectively, by allowing you to target two allies instead of one. Reactive Healing allows your epic-level healer to prevent an ally from dropping to 0 hit points.

MAGIC ITEMS

Look for magic items that improve your healing powers, allow the use of healing surges by allies, or increase you allies' healing surge values.

✦ *Gloves of the healer* and *healing brooch* add to every healing power you use. Grab both of these items early on.

✦ A *holy healer's weapon* improves your *healing word* and also lets an ally spend a healing surge once each day.

✦ *Armor of sacrifice* lets you spend a surge to heal another character, and a *healer's sash* allows you effectively to move a healing surge from one

ally to another. (The latter item received a substantial update in November 2009, so be sure to check www.wizards.com/dnd to confirm you're using the correct description.) The surge-trading power of a *belt of sacrifice* isn't as efficient as the other two items mentioned here, but it also adds to your allies' healing surge values.

✦ Use a *battle standard of healing* after each fight for a few extra points of healing.

✦ Avoid consumable items that provide healing; usually, your powers are more efficient than potions. The exception is *silver sand*, which increases the potency of your healing powers. By paragon or epic levels, you should use this reagent every time you use your basic class-granted healing power.

OTHER CHOICES

Take skill training in Heal. Even though you won't use this skill much at higher levels (because you have so many healing powers), it's a key skill for many of your preferred rituals.

Acquire any ritual that can help prolong or restore the life or health of your allies, such as Delay Affliction, Cure Disease, Raise Dead, Remove Affliction, Fantastic Recuperation, Soulguard, and Ease Spirit. These rituals won't keep your allies alive in the heat of battle, but they can revive allies later on and can cure afflictions and disease.

"Wanna race me?"

Speed thrills you more than anything else. You can run circles around everyone on the battlefield. Even at a walk, you leave enemies as if they were standing still. When you have room to move, stopping you is almost impossible.

You focus your options on increasing your speed, but gaining extra move actions and improving your ability to shift also demonstrates your talent for haste.

Since flight and teleportation are the cheater's way to win a race, this sample character intentionally ignores those options.

RACE

The race you choose for your character provides a head start on achieving the highest speed.

Elf is the only race that has a starting speed of 7 squares, giving it an edge over all other choices. An elf character also has the added benefit being able to ignore difficult terrain when shifting.

Razorclaw shifters also make good candidates for fastest character because of their *razorclaw shifting* racial power, which increases their speed by 2 when bloodied.

CLASS

A druid who selects Primal Predator as his or her aspect gains a +1 bonus to speed, and the class offers many other powers that increase speed.

The monk specializes in movement powers. You can easily increase your speed by 2 for most of the moves you make.

Most other melee-based striker classes have powers that temporarily improve their speed, grant extra movement, or include shifting as part of an attack. The avenger, barbarian, ranger, and rogue classes all provide good options for building a fast character.

ABILITY SCORES

Beyond the primary ability score required by your class, keep your Dexterity score high. Speedy heroes should have good Reflex. If for no other reason, think of it as a nod to realism—who's going to believe a fast but clumsy character?

POWERS

Look for powers that increase your speed for more than a single action or that can be used over and over. *Fleet pursuit* lasts for an entire encounter. The monk's *dancing cobra* movement technique is an at-will power that allows the character to move his or her speed +2.

Load up on attack powers that grant extra movement, such as *deft strike* or *evasive strike*. The square or two of free movement provided by a power works like a running start for your impressive cross-field sprint.

FEATS

Feats that directly increase your speed are rare, but some creativity and tactical thinking can allow the situational benefits from some feats to stack up nicely.

In the heroic tier, Bloodied Fleetness gives you a +1 bonus to speed while you're bloodied. Into the Fray increases your rogue's speed by 1 during the surprise round and the first round of an encounter. Fast Runner increases your speed by 2 when you run or charge.

A few feats do offer a direct bonus to speed. One heroic tier example is Vampiric Alacrity; if you're willing to spend the feat slot for the Vampiric Heritage prerequisite (and to become a dhampyr, described on page 59), you can pick up a +1 feat bonus to speed as early as 2nd level. Drow characters that have a primal class—such as druid—can take Spider's Swiftness to gain a +1 feat bonus to speed.

Paragon-level characters should take Fleet-Footed right away; for most heroes, it represents the earliest point at which they can gain a +1 feat bonus to speed. Fast druids could instead pick up Hunting Wolf Form for its +1 feat bonus to speed and its additional bonus to Perception checks.

At the epic tier, your speedy druid can replace Hunting Wolf Form with Swift Predator to keep the speed bonus and increase the distance of his or her shifts by 1 square.

Don't forget to look for feats that improve your ability to shift, such as Mark of Passage, Reckless Scramble, and Swift Slayer. The druid has many feats that allow him or her to shift when using particular powers, such as Pouncing Form.

Feats that grant extra move actions don't show up very often, so take them when you can. Avenging Opportunist gives your avenger another move action every encounter. Surprise Action lets your ranger take a full round's actions during a surprise round, effectively granting an extra move action whenever a surprise round occurs.

MAGIC ITEMS

Almost all speed-boosting items occupy the feet slot. Since you can only wear one set of boots or shoes at a time, you have some tough choices to make. Here are some of the best options to consider.

- *Wildrunners* (level 4) add 2 squares to the distance moved when you run.

- *Boots of rapid motion* (level 5) help prevent you from being slowed and can increase your speed by 1 for an encounter.

- *Boots of striding* (level 9) grant you a +1 item bonus to speed. Alternatively, you can pick up *boots of furious speed* at the same level, which give you a +2 item bonus to speed while bloodied.

- *Skalvani's anklets* (level 10) increase your speed by 2 for two turns every encounter.

- *Quickstride boots* (level 12) let you move your speed as a minor action.

- *Fleetrunner boots* (level 15) increase your run speed by 4 squares (and reduce the attack penalty for running by –2, making it a potentially viable option for every move action).

- *Sandals of the temporal step* (level 16) are like *boots of striding* that also give you a free move action once each day.

- *Boots of speed* (level 22) not only give you a +2 item bonus to speed, they let you spend a minor action to take a move action once per day.

- At the top of the list of speed-boosting magic items are *sandals of Avandra* (level 25), which grant you a +2 item bonus to speed, allow you to shift half your speed as a move action as often as you want, and once each encounter allow you to ignore opportunity attacks from movement for the next two turns.

- Outside the feet slot, look for *elven battle armor* (level 13 and up), which increases your speed by 2 for two turns, and *cloak of the cautious* (level 9 and up), which increases your speed by 5 for two turns but prevents you from attacking. Carry a few *elixirs of speed* for their +2 power bonus to speed, which lasts an hour.

OTHER CHOICES

All the speed in the world does no good if you can't move. A simple *ray of frost* spell can turn a speed of 20 into a speed of 2, creating a glaring weakness for your character. Make sure you have answers for when you become slowed, immobilized, or restrained.

Also, being fast doesn't actually defeat monsters. Although a fast character rarely gets killed—after all, you don't have to outrun the dragon, you just have to outrun everyone else in your party—this speed can't kill anything. Don't spend so many resources on speed that you forget about dealing damage.

"Look at that—I get to go first again!"

Getting the jump on your foe can provide a big tactical advantage. If you go first, you can outmaneuver your foes and get into position to pull off the perfect strategy.

Instigators love rolling a high initiative. Even if they don't optimize their characters to take advantage of it, they gain great pleasure from opening fire or charging enemies before anyone has a chance to tell them otherwise.

RACE

Any race that offers a bonus to Dexterity is a reasonable choice for this character concept, because Dexterity contributes directly to your initiative check.

Of all these races, the githzerai makes the best option, pairing a racial bonus to Dexterity with a +2 racial bonus to initiative checks.

CLASS

Your choice of class depends not so much on which option provides the best initiative-boosting options—because such options are rare—but rather on what benefits the class derives from rolling a high initiative. After all, if you just delay for something else to happen, what's the point of going first?

This question is covered in detail under "Winning Initiative," page 108, which points out the benefits for defenders, controllers, and ranged strikers. This section focuses on the ranger and the rogue. These two classes have the high Dexterity to boost their initiative, and (as long as they favor ranged attacks) they can use a high initiative score to pile damage onto an enemy before that foe can find cover.

The rogue's First Strike class feature gives that class an edge in this situation, allowing him or her to add Sneak Attack damage when hitting a target that hasn't yet acted. For a rogue, having the best initiative matters.

When considering paragon paths, the best choice is the githzerai rrathmal path, which allows you to roll initiative twice, keeping the better of the two results. If you multiclass as a cleric, you can receive a similar benefit from the divine oracle paragon path.

ABILITY SCORES

Dexterity is the only ability score that makes a difference here. Make it as high as possible.

FEATS

Several feats benefit your initiative, but make sure you don't accidentally take feats that have bonuses that don't stack with one another.

JOHN TYLER CHRISTOPHER

Start with Improved Initiative for a +4 feat bonus to initiative checks. If you can convince your allies to join your quest for a high initiative score, the Swift Jaguar feat's +2 feat bonus can easily become as high as +5.

Your first paragon tier feat should be Danger Sense, which allows you to roll twice and take the better result each time you make an initiative check. Unless you're a rogue, take Seize the Moment next; it effectively replicates the First Strike class feature.

If you're willing to invest in the Vistani Heritage feat as a prerequisite, the Vistani Foresight feat at 21st level offers an untyped +2 bonus to initiative checks.

Magic Items

Several lower-level items add to your initiative bonus, but this section focuses on those best for rangers or rogues.

Battle harness (level 4 and up) grants a power bonus to your initiative checks equal to the armor's enhancement bonus. *Feytouched armor* (level 12 and up) functions similarly, but provides an item bonus instead, which makes it combine less well with the items given below.

Helm of battle (level 9) grants you and nearby allies a +1 item bonus to initiative checks, but you might prefer to have either a *quicksilver blade* (level 2 and up) or a *timeless locket* (level 14 and up), either of which grants you an item bonus equal to its enhancement bonus. If you don't want to spend one of those slots on an initiative bonus, go for the *eye of awareness* (level 23) and its +5 item bonus to initiative checks.

Powers

Only a few powers improve your initiative or grant you a benefit for rolling a high initiative result. Here are some examples.

✦ *Hunter's privilege* (level 2) increases the damage dealt by the high-initiative ranger to his or her quarry by 3 for an entire encounter.

✦ *Avenger's readiness* (level 10) gives the avenger a +5 power bonus to an initiative check and a free 3-square shift when the first creature acts in that combat.

✦ *Seize the moment* provides a whopping +20 bonus to one initiative check each day, but as a 22nd-level rogue utility power it doesn't come up very often.

Other Choices

To take advantage of your high initiative score, choose powers that deal a lot of damage, injure or hinder many foes, or both. If going first gives you a particular benefit (such as from First Strike), find ways to maximize the number of attack rolls you can make on your first turn.

It doesn't hurt to try to talk someone in your group into playing a warlord so that you can benefit from the +2 power bonus to initiative granted by his or her Combat Leader feature.

TELL US ABOUT YOUR CHARACTER

Building a character with the express intention of beating the monsters and the rest of your party in initiative can be fun, but it has its risks. Consider my elf rogue, Adrin.

Adrin's initiative isn't even crazy-high: at 11th level, he's sporting a +12 initiative bonus (thanks to his *quicksilver blade*). But that's faster than just about everyone else in the party, and faster than most (but not all) of a random sampling of 11th-level monsters I found in the D&D Compendium. And that means it's just fast enough to get Adrin into trouble.

There was the fight where I used *handspring assault* in the surprise round to run up to a bunch of gnolls and stab one really hard, then won initiative and got in another good hit . . . and then got mobbed by gnolls. That didn't end well.

Considering that I'm a D&D professional, it has taken me a surprisingly long time to figure out that I should be using all these mobility powers I have to get *back behind the fighter*, not to put myself out in harm's way.

So this is my word of warning to those who pursue the highest possible initiative: Don't use your speed to get yourself into trouble you can't get out of.

JAMES WYATT is the D&D Design Manager for Wizards of the Coast Roleplaying R&D. He was one of the lead designers for 4th Edition D&D and the primary author of the 4th Edition Dungeon Master's Guide. He was one of the designers of the EBERRON campaign setting, and is the author of several EBERRON novels. He plays strikers and defenders, but things go badly when he gets them confused.

"Can we talk about this?"

A wily character can talk his or her way out of almost any problem, from a bar fight to a deadly dungeon encounter. You prefer to overcome challenges through wit and guile than by fire and steel. Others might call you "face man," "diplomancer," or just "the talky one," but you take it all as a compliment.

Not only does this approach appeal to actors and storytellers, it can also preserve valuable resources for more important battles. Talking your way past the guards saves healing surges, action points, and daily powers for later encounters.

This character works only if your Dungeon Master is amenable to the use of social skills. Some Dungeon Masters do not appreciate characters using Intimidate to force enemies to surrender. Other Dungeon Masters don't build encounters or adventures that encourage the use of social skills. Keep your Dungeon Master and his or her game style in mind before designing a character like this. These skills could shut a game down if the Dungeon Master is not prepared for them.

CLASS

The bard offers the best mix of primary ability score (Charisma), class skills, powers, and class features to build a good talker. Other classes—such as rogue or warlock—provide only some of these options, so

TELL US ABOUT YOUR CHARACTER

Oleander Fellswallow is a halfling who has a silver tongue. His philosophy is, "Why shed blood when words flow more easily and get more done?"

Since he has impressive bonuses in Bluff and Diplomacy, I've made a considerable effort to ensure that he can wield these bloodless weapons in as many situations as possible. The Linguist feat and the Mark of the Scribe feat (from the EBERRON *Player's Guide*) give him seven additional languages, and a *gem of colloquy* adds what he needs to speak every known language in the game. He can argue with and lie to any creature anywhere and listen in on conversations people think are private.

This pays off; the time when he convinced half of a Far Realm cult that he was the true prophet of the stars and got them to fight each other is a notable example.

PETER SCHAEFER *works in Wizards of the Coast R&D as a developer of such books as* Player's Handbook 3, Plane Below: Secrets of the Elemental Chaos, *and* Psionic Power. *This is a significant departure from his previous position as major-domo to an interdimensional emperor, and much less stressful.*

choose them only if you desperately need to fill a different role (and even then, the bard might do the trick).

RACE

You want a race that offers a bonus to Charisma to best pull off this character concept. Of all the choices, three races provide the best options.

The half-elf's racial bonuses to Diplomacy and Insight improve two key skills for a talker. The Group Diplomacy trait helps allies pitch in on important social interactions.

Changelings have a particular edge in this specialty because of their ability to change shape, which gives them an unparalleled ability to deceive others. With this ability, a changeling can expand his or her capability as the party's face.

The kalashtar offers an unusual but effective choice for this character archetype. Not only do the kalashtar"s ability score bonuses line up perfectly with the skills you need (skills you can also boost with the kalashtar's racial bonuses), but the race's telepathy allows a kalashtar character to plan with allies while carrying on a perfectly normal conversation with enemies.

ABILITY SCORES

As mentioned already, Charisma is vital for your social skills and bard powers, so max it out. A good Wisdom score boosts your Insight skill, which helps in skill challenges and negotiations.

SKILLS

Training in the following three skills is crucial: Bluff, Diplomacy, and Insight. Both Intimidate and Streetwise can be useful, but few characters can afford to train in all five skills without expending extra resources. If you're a bard, your Skill Versatility feature gives you a +1 bonus to untrained skill checks, so don't worry too much about missing one of these secondary skills.

FEATS

You can find useful feats in the D&D Compendium by searching for feats using your crucial skills as keywords.

✦ If you're serious about being the best talker, put your feat slots where your mouth is and boost your Bluff score and Diplomacy score with Skill Focus.

✦ You can't talk someone out of a fight if they can't understand you. Pick up the Linguist feat to broaden your language selection.

...AND I CAN TELL THAT DESPITE OUR CULTURAL DIFFERENCES WE HAVE **LOTS** IN COMMON! YOU KNOW, I EVEN OWN A BONE NECKLACE **JUST** LIKE YOURS!

- ✦ Fill in a missing skill with Skill Training (or better yet, a multiclass feat). Alternatively, Jack of All Trades stacks with Skill Versatility, and together they almost make up for a lack of skill training in all of your untrained skills.

- ✦ Friendly Deception allows a bard to apply the Words of Friendship feature to a Bluff check instead of to a Diplomacy check.

- ✦ Mark of Scribing, an EBERRON dragonmarked feat, grants a +2 untyped bonus to Diplomacy checks. The other benefits of this feat are also good.

- ✦ If you multiclass into a divine class and learn Supernal, Holy Speech can give you an extra success in any social skill challenge.

POWERS

Beyond *words of friendship*, the game doesn't include very many powers that enhance or benefit from your skill set. If you can afford to multiclass, though, the list of options grows.

- ✦ *Veil* (level 10) lets the bard disguise the entire party, making it easier to convince the guards that you all belong here. The same level offers *illuminating stars*, which grants the entire party a +5 power bonus to Insight checks and Perception checks for an encounter.

- ✦ The rogue has a few useful powers that require Bluff or Intimidate training, which you can pick up through multiclassing.

- ✦ *Beguiling tongue* (level 2) might be worth two warlock multiclass feats for a devoted talker.

- ✦ Look through the skill powers for Bluff, Diplomacy, Insight, Intimidate, and Streetwise for good alternatives to your class's existing utility

powers. Most of these powers allow you to use your prodigious social skills to gain advantages in combat, but *fast talk* (level 6) lets you replace a poor social skill check with a new Bluff check in every encounter, making it incredibly useful.

MAGIC ITEMS

Items that improve your social skills should form the backbone of your wish list.

- ✦ *Skald's armor* (level 3 and up) grants a +2 item bonus to Bluff checks and Diplomacy checks. At higher levels, though, a *choker of eloquence* (level 8 and up) provides a better bonus. If you're willing to take a smaller item bonus, choose a *gem of colloquy* (level 2 and up) for the extra languages. The top choice, though, is an *ioun stone of perfect language* (level 22), which grants a +5 bonus to Bluff checks, Diplomacy checks, Intimidate checks, and Streetwise checks and lets you communicate in any language.

- ✦ *Circlet of the urbane* (level 23) allows you to reroll Diplomacy checks, Insight checks, and Streetwise checks and keep the second result.

- ✦ *Fragrance of authority* (level 12) grants a +2 power bonus to Bluff, Diplomacy, or Intimidate for 1 hour each day.

OTHER CHOICES

The right background can give you another bonus to a crucial skill, or it can add to your list of languages.

A few rituals can come in handy for a talker, such as Speech Without Words, Call of Friendship, Anthem of Unity, and Tune of Merriment.

"Go ahead . . . just try to hit me."

You laugh in the face of danger, inviting enemies to give you their best shot. You're not worried: You are the bastion of defense.

Nothing keeps you alive better than a high AC. Brutes become nearly meaningless threats, and even the most accurate monsters rarely hit you. At the same time, nothing frustrates a DM more than not being able to hit a character. Expect your DM to find ways around your ultimate defense.

CLASS

Defender classes typically have the best AC. The paladin starts at the top, with proficiency with plate armor and heavy shields providing AC 20 at 1st level. However, fighters and battleminds can close this gap with a single feat, so don't count them out. Other heavy-armor wearing classes need at least two feats to catch up, so we'll rule them out for now, but if you have plenty of feats to spend, anyone wearing plate armor and carrying a heavy shield stacks up well.

You don't have to wear heavy armor to have a good AC. A 1st-level swordmage could also begin with AC 20 (+2 from leather armor, +5 from Intelligence 20, and +3 from the Swordmage Warding feature).

RACE

If you wear heavy armor, your choice of race doesn't matter very much (since you can't add an ability modifier to your AC). Instead, choose a race that fits well with the class you're playing. (See "Choosing Your Race," page 18, for suggestions.)

If you don't want heavy armor, racial bonuses to Dexterity or Intelligence, such as those of eladrin and humans, are critical for characters wearing light armor. A deva gains a +1 bonus to defenses against bloodied creatures, which gives a deva character an edge as a high-AC swordmage.

ABILITY SCORES

Many armor feats require good Strength and Constitution scores, so make sure you start with at least a 13 in each, and increase them to 15 by 11th level.

To get an equivalent AC wearing light armor, you must assign your highest ability score to Dexterity or Intelligence and improve it at every opportunity.

FEATS

Feats provide a great way of ramping up your AC.

+ Assuming you wear heavy armor, start by taking whatever Armor Proficiency feats you need to get up to plate armor. Take Shield Proficiency if you don't already have it.

+ Swordmages should take Improved Swordmage Warding, as well as Armor Proficiency (Hide).

+ At 11th level, heavy armor wearers should select Armor Specialization (Plate) unless they have the Dexterity 15 required for Shield Specialization (since this feat also improves Reflex).

+ Paragon tier swordmages can take Armor Specialization (Hide) or Greater Swordmage Warding.

+ A host of feats, such as Defensive Mobility and Shield Defense, improve AC in specific situations. To find them, search for "bonus to AC" in the D&D Compendium.

MAGIC ITEMS

Make sure you wear armor that has the highest enhancement bonus you can find. After filling that need, other magic items can boost your AC in particular circumstances. If you pick up enough of these items, you're almost always covered, but pay attention to bonus types so you don't waste anything.

+ If you wear plate armor, consider *salubrious armor* (level 4 and up), which adds +1 to AC for one round when you regain hit points; *agile armor* (level 5 and up), which adds the lower of your Dexterity modifier or the armor's enhancement bonus to AC while you aren't bloodied; or *bloodiron armor* (level 8 and up), which adds +2 to your AC against the attacks of an enemy you hit until the end of your next turn.

+ Wearers of light armor should look at *darkleaf armor* (level 4 and up). This armor adds +2 to AC against the first attack made against you in each encounter.

+ *Shield of the barrier sentinels* (level 9) adds to your AC and Reflex when you are flanked, but *force shield* (level 11) is even better, because its bonus lasts until you get hit (which shouldn't happen very often to your high-AC character). A *cloak of displacement* has a similar function, and its bonus stacks with that of a *force shield*.

- *Pavise charm* (level 8 and up) boosts your AC and Reflex as long as you stay in one place. Conversely, a *cloak of translocation* (level 9 and up) improves AC and Reflex when you teleport, which comes in handy for swordmages.
- The AC boost from *shielding girdle* it lasts until the end of your next turn.

POWERS

A search of the D&D Compendium turns up a number of defender powers that provide a bonus to AC.

- Fighters should pick up *defensive stance* or *shielded sides* at 2nd level, *iron bulwark* at 7th, and *defensive resurgence* at 10th (as long as your Dexterity is 12 or higher).
- Paladins should take *sacred circle* at 2nd level, but their next good option (*fortifying smite*) doesn't show up until 17th level.
- The swordmage can select *ward of brilliance* or *host of shields* at 2nd level, *silversteel veil* at 6th level, and *shield of besieged tower* at 16th level.
- Wardens have many AC-boosting powers, particularly in the category of guardian form powers.

OTHER CHOICES

A –1 penalty to an enemy's attack is as good as your receiving a +1 bonus to all defenses, so picking up some enemy debuffs can further enhance your unhittable nature.

If enemies can't hit you, find ways to share your unneeded healing surges with your allies, such as with a *belt of sacrifice* or a *healer's sash*. This comes in even more handy when the monsters start ignoring you altogether.

Don't forget that you have four defenses to support. Although AC covers about half the attacks you're likely to see, ignoring any of your other three defenses leaves a deadly gap for enemies to exploit.

No matter how high your defenses get, you can't kill monsters just by making them miss you. If you sacrifice offense for defense, make sure your allies can pick up the slack.

"How about I close my eyes, just to make it a challenge?"

You never miss. At least, that's your goal. You might not hit as hard as the raging barbarian who wields a greataxe, but you hit more frequently.

For the purpose of this section, we're assuming that making a weapon attack against AC is just as accurate as making an implement attack against Fortitude, Reflex, or Will. Obviously, this is not true of every monster. Expert optimizers can point out ways to take advantage of the four-defense system to increase accuracy even more.

CLASS

Some classes, such as the fighter and the rogue, offer accuracy through bonuses to attack rolls. Other classes, such as the ranger, provide multiattack powers that help ensure they hit at least once each round.

These are reasonable choices, but the avenger's *oath of enmity* power—which lets that character roll twice for every melee attack he or she makes against a chosen foe—leaves all these other classes behind.

Find a paragon path that further enhances your accuracy. Battlefield archer lets your ranger reroll a ranged attack roll by spending an action point, and beast stalker gives your ranger a +4 bonus to attack rolls against your quarry for a round. The shadow assassin paragon path provides a similar attack bonus for rogues. The avenger doesn't have many good options here, so if you decide on an avenger, multi-classing might be your best choice.

RACE

You must choose a race that has a bonus to your class's primary ability score, but that doesn't cut down the choices very much. Instead, look for racial powers and traits that increase accuracy. You won't find many traits that say "gain a +1 bonus to attack rolls," so think carefully when examining your options.

The elf's *elven accuracy* power lets you reroll one attack each encounter, which can turn a miss into a hit. The deva's *memory of a thousand lifetimes* racial power adds 1d6 to one attack roll each encounter; although this power is not as swingy as a reroll, its predictability of this power makes it more likely to have an effect when you use it. The changeling, the drow, the shardmind, and the wilden each have

a racial power that grants members of those races combat advantage (though the racial bonuses of first two don't match up with the avenger's primary ability score).

WEAPON

Select a weapon that has a +3 proficiency bonus, such as a greatsword or a longsword. The improved accuracy of these weapons compared to a greataxe or a battleaxe more than makes up for the small sacrifice in weapon damage die size.

POWERS

To find powers that maximize your accuracy, keep your eye out for options that include one or more of the following benefits.

+ *Inherent accuracy bonuses.* A few powers include a built-in bonus to the attack roll, such as the fighter's *sure strike*. Others grant you a temporary bonus to attack rolls, such as *dawn fire sigil* or *villain's menace*.

+ *Target non-AC defenses.* Any time you can use a weapon to attack Fortitude, Reflex, or Will, it's like getting a +2 bonus to the attack roll (since those defenses are typically about 2 points behind AC).

+ *Multitarget powers.* A power that lets you attack more than one target, such as *sweeping blow*, increases your chance of hitting somebody, although it doesn't improve your odds of hitting a particular enemy.

+ *Attacks that don't use standard actions.* Just like using multitarget powers, making more attacks means you hit more often. The rogue's *low slash* provides an example of such powers, which are admittedly rare.

+ *Effects that reduce enemy defenses.* A penalty to your target's defense is just as good as a bonus to your attack roll. *Menacing presence* is a great choice for an avenger.

+ *Avoid attack powers with Miss or Effect lines or that have the reliable keyword.* Although these might seem to fit well with your specialty, such powers are often balanced by delivering less punch on a hit. Since you expect to hit every time, why bother worrying about what happens when you miss?

ABILITY SCORES

Put your highest ability score in your class's primary ability. Everything else is less important.

FEATS

Few feats improve accuracy on all attacks, so take Weapon Expertise as your first choice. Once you have that, search the D&D Compendium for "bonus to attack" for options that best fit your character's class, powers, and preferred tactics.

ITEMS

Keep your weapon's enhancement bonus as high as possible. Once that's covered, search out items that provide conditional or situational bonuses to attack rolls, particularly if the bonus is untyped.

✦ *Master's blade* (level 4 and up) provides a +1 bonus to attack rolls with basic and at-will attacks while you're in a stance. A *berserker weapon* (level 10 and up) leaves you wide open to attacks, but its daily power bonus to attack rolls lasts the entire encounter. A *bloodthirsty weapon* (level 13 and up) adds +1 to your attack rolls against bloodied targets.

✦ *Barrage bracers* (level 10) give you a +1 bonus to attack rolls against a target when you hit it. Since the bonus lasts until the end of your next turn, multiple hits on the same target can build up a nice attack boost.

✦ *Hero's gauntlets* (level 17) add +1 to your attack rolls when you spend an action point.

✦ Planting a *battle standard of the vanguard* (level 20) provides a +1 power bonus to your attacks until the end of the encounter.

OTHER CHOICES

Don't forget to use your allies for additional accuracy bonuses. Flanking grants a +2 bonus to attack rolls, and most classes have powers that either grant bonuses to your attack rolls or penalties to enemy defenses.

This section only covers characters who improve their attack rolls to astronomical levels, but you could also build a "never miss" character by selecting powers with guaranteed effects on a miss and by taking other options to improve those powers.

"Don't worry—I'll be fine."

You feel better knowing that no matter what an enemy throws at you, you can shake it off. Even if you fall unconscious, you won't bleed to death. You just don't share the same worries as other mortals. And why should you? You've maxed out your saving throws.

This character concept appeals to risk-averse players, as well as to those players who just can't succeed on a saving throw to save their lives (sometimes literally). Saving throws are a great mechanic to max out because when all else fails, at least you'll make your death saving throws.

TELL US ABOUT YOUR CHARACTER

My name is Devon Avery, and I tell people that I am a paladin of Moradin. Many find it odd that a human would worship a dwarven god, but that is not what I am here to confess today. I came to the depths of the dwarven cities to hide from something so evil I have trouble speaking of it. This journey has proven to be in vain, however, because whatever this evil is, I have brought it with me.

When my wife lay dying from childbirth and my gods ignored my pleas to spare her life, I made a dark pact. At first it was only words, and I thought nothing more of the things I said that night. After all, my son and wife survived and I had nothing to worry about. But I am haunted now, and I have left my home in search of a way to rid myself of this thing that grows inside of me.

I went to the dwarven kingdom, where no one would recognize my face, and I studied their religious ways in hopes on concealing the demon in me . . . and the demons around me. One of them I see frequently. I call him Gorahk, and he is no bigger than a pint of ale. The creature seems invisible to all others, so my babbling appears madness-induced. I try to keep my talking to a minimum. Even as we speak now, Gorahk sits upon my shoulder whispering things to me, unpleasant things and always whispering.

Now I must find another way out; I must venture forth and be rid of this once and for all. I want to return to my family, but not like this. Moradin shall grant me the courage I need and shall lead me to the right path.

I hope.

CRAIG KROHN works as a lead software test engineer for DUNGEONS & DRAGONS Digital Tools. When he is not at the office or playing D&D, he spends most of his time at his dojo teaching karate and aikido.

CLASS

Increasing the number of chances you get to succeed on a saving throw is the best way to shake off lasting effects. Most defender classes offer a variety of powers that do this, but no class does it better than the warden, whose Font of Life class feature grants one extra saving throw every round.

RACE

Many races grant bonuses to particular subsets of saving throws. For example, eladrin and dwarves have large bonuses against charm effects and poison effects, respectively, and other races have bonuses against different effects. If you fear death saving throws more than any other, the Warforged Resilience trait means your warforged character will never die from failed death saving throws.

However, none of these races hold a candle to the saving-throw potential of humans, who have access to key saving-throw boosting feats. If you really want to max out your saving throw success rate, play a human.

FEATS

You want feats that grant you a bonus to saving throws or that provide extra saving throws. This section focuses on feats appealing primarily to human characters or to wardens, since those options offer the best opportunity for optimization.

Your human character should start with Human Perseverance, which grants a +1 bonus to all saving throws. Stubborn Survivor grants an additional +2 bonus to saving throws when you have no action points, so go ahead and spend those action points as soon as you get them. Action Recovery lets your paragon tier human make extra saving throws each time you spend an action point. If you play a paladin, Divine Approval grants your human an extra saving throw each time he or she uses a Channel Divinity power.

As a warden, take Revitalizing Font of Life at 1st level; it grants a +2 bonus to the saving throws you make following a successful saving throw from Font of Life. At 11th level, pick up Enhanced Font of Life for the +1 bonus it gives to the saving throws granted by that class feature. When you hit the epic tier, grab Enduring Font to get another extra saving throw every round.

Timely Respite gives any character an extra saving throw when he or she uses second wind or total defense, giving you the opportunity to roll an extra saving throw every turn if you want to.

MAGIC ITEMS

The armor slot contains many choices for enhancing your saving throws.

- ✦ *Delver's armor* (level 2 and up) retroactively adds 2 to a saving throw you just rolled.
- ✦ *Armor of cleansing* (level 3 and up) grants a +2 item bonus to saving throws against ongoing damage, which is one of the most common effects that a save can end.
- ✦ *Verve armor* (level 4 and up) adds 2 to your death saving throws, and turns one saving throw each day into a natural 20.
- ✦ Wardens should pick up *lifefont armor* (level 4 and up) for the +1 item bonus to the saving throws granted by Font of Life.

Another common slot for save-boosting items is the neck slot.

- ✦ *Amulet of resolution* (level 2 and up) lets you reroll one saving throw each day.
- ✦ *Resilience amulet* (level 8 and up) lets you react to an attack that deals ongoing damage by rolling a saving throw to negate that damage before it occurs. A *steadfast amulet* (level 8 and up) works similarly against the dazed or stunned conditions.
- ✦ *Amulet of bodily sanctity* (level 14 and up) grants a +2 bonus to saving throws against ongoing damage and lets you (and your nearby allies) roll an extra saving throw against ongoing damage once each day.

Many other items enhance particular types of saving throw, such as a *survivor's belt* (level 11), which lets you roll twice when making death saving throws.

Finally, consumable items offer many effects that boost saving throws, such as *antivenom's* bonus to saving throws against poison and the extra saving throw offered by a *potion of vitality*. These options can prove cheap alternatives to permanent magic items.

POWERS

Your power choices don't help your saving throws as much as your feat and magic item choices, but that doesn't mean you should ignore them.

- ✦ The paladin gains extra saving throws from *trial of strength*, *fear not*, *comeback smite*, *guiding verse*, *cleansing spirit*, and other powers.
- ✦ The swordmage gets extra saving throws from *mythal recovery*, *unicorn's touch*, *borrowed confidence*, and *bravado strike*.
- ✦ The warden doesn't need many save-improvement powers, but *cleansing earth*, *vine poultice*, and *panacea* all come in handy.

OTHER CHOICES

Consider options that grant you extra benefits when you succeed on a saving throw (since you'll be doing that frequently). For example, *erupting font* lets your warden mark multiple enemies when you succeed on a saving throw granted by Font of Life. *Torc of fortune* (level 24) lets you shift 2 squares whenever you succeed on a saving throw during your turn.

Don't forget to figure out how you defeat the enemy. Many of your feat and item choices don't directly contribute to winning a fight, and if you can't deal damage, your successful saving throws just prolong an inevitable defeat.

EMPTY ROOM STUDIO · PETER LAZARSKI

"I'm not sure I can be killed."

Let the rogue or sorcerer brag about how much damage they deal. You know that the true mark of success is how much damage you can take before falling down.

At the end of each session, show the other players the piece of paper (or the entire note pad) that holds your chicken-scratched hit point updates. Then blow them away by totaling up the damage you survived.

CLASS

Defenders offer the most hit points, both at 1st level and beyond. The barbarian keeps up well, particularly for a striker. Of all the classes, though, the warden has an edge of about 1 hit point each level.

Take the dreadnought paragon path, even if you have to multiclass to do so. It gains 10 extra hit points at 11th level and has plenty of other features and powers that make your fighter's hit points last longer.

RACE

Choose a race that has a bonus to Constitution to pick up a couple of extra hit points.

Goliath is a good choice because of the racial power that negates incoming damage (which is a lot like having more hit points), and because a goliath's

TELL US ABOUT YOUR CHARACTER

You know what I hate? When my character dies . . . or, to be more precise, when my character is close to death. Do I risk triggering that opportunity attack? Oh, crap! That dragon's gonna breathe on me again. I'd better get away from that aura or it'll kill me.

The threat of death led to way too much tension in-session, and it caused too many post-session questions of "Why didn't I have more fun?" After years of living with my mortality issues by playing characters who didn't want to be anywhere close to the front line, it was time for me to confront this problem. It was time to warforge up.

Hammoth Stoutarm, Dreadnought of Brindol, is there to negate the best shots the bad guys can offer. In basketball terms, he's the defensive stopper. Put Hammoth on that brute one-on-one and he will shut it down. That ogre's no longer wreaking havoc on the squishy rogue Adrin, or threatening our cleric and lifeline Boldrik. Hammoth's got its attention, and like the tide, he will wear it down from boulder to pebble if given the time.

A high AC and a font of hit points make all this possible. The quality of Hammoth's armor will always be a higher priority than his weapon. Along with a ton of hit points, he has a few easy ways to stock up on temporary hit points. By taking warlord multiclass feats, Hammoth can pass around a few healing surges in each fight, but he always saves at least one healing power for himself. After all, if he falls in battle, he has failed his comrades.

Hammoth's ideal turn? After absorbing a wave of punishment that would have floored anyone else in the party, a bloodied Hammoth looks like he's on his last legs. The foes start circling, ready to put him down for good. And then the comeback starts . . . *warforged resolve* gives him a little healing and some temporary hit points. An action point spent for a *comeback strike* gets him farther away from death's embrace, marks the biggest, baddest foe out there ("Hey buddy, I'm not done with you yet!"), and gives Hammoth resist 10 for a turn thanks to his paragon path. Bloodiron plate armor boosts his AC against that target for a turn. A *rousing word* or second wind has Hammoth back up to nearly full hit points. If it looks like the fight's going to last a while, he throws in *boundless endurance* for the safety net of near-constant regeneration.

You thought you had me whipped? Think again, chump. I'm better at this than you, and it's gonna be a loooooooong fight.

GREG COLLINS is a web producer for magicthegathering. com at Wizards of the Coast. A D&D player for almost 30 years, he's recently taken up the mantle of DM and finds the experience of screwing with his players' heads highly enjoyable. What's in the box?

racial bonuses to ability scores match up well with the warden.

Similarly, the mix of ability bonuses and the racial power possessed by the warforged marks that race as another excellent option.

Revenants cheat at this contest, because they can stay conscious after dropping to 0 hit points. Since that kind of survivability isn't due to a spectacular number of hit points, we won't include revenants in this discussion.

ABILITY SCORES

Put your highest score in Constitution to maximize your hit points.

FEATS

If you want to be a hit point machine, start with Toughness.

✦ Consider multiclassing into fighter to gain access to powers and feats that grant temporary hit points (such as Grit, a solid paragon tier feat choice).

✦ Warforged characters should pick up Improved Warforged Resolve to gain an extra 5 temporary hit points from *warforged resolve*.

✦ Similarly, goliaths should take Unyielding Stone to gain temporary hit points when they use *stone's endurance*.

POWERS

Powers don't generally grant extra hit points, but many provide temporary hit points.

✦ Many fighter powers, such as *boundless endurance*, *bolstering stride*, and the various powers that have the invigorating keyword, grant temporary hit points. (If you select invigorating powers, be sure to train in the Endurance skill.)

✦ The warden has only a few powers that grant temporary hit points, but those include the at-will attack power *strength of stone*, which gives you the option of gaining temporary hit points every round.

MAGIC ITEMS

As with feats, most of the hit points you get from magic items are temporary. Don't get too many of these items, since temporary hit points from multiple sources don't stack.

✦ Most armors that grant temporary hit points are heavy, making them suboptimal for wardens. *Heartening armor* (level 3 and up) grants a few temporary hit points when you use second wind. *Stoneborn armor* (level 3 and up) gives you a decent chunk of temporary hit points once each day. *Champion's armor* (level 9 and up) gives you temporary hit points equal to the damage you just took from an attack.

✦ When you reduce an enemy to 0 hit points with a *lifedrinker weapon* (level 5 and up), you gain 5 temporary hit points.

✦ *Amulet of false life* (level 9 and up) grants you temporary hit points equal to half your surge value once each day.

✦ *Hero's gauntlets* (level 17) give you temporary hit points when you deal damage with an attack made by spending an action point.

✦ A *cord of foresight* (level 18) lets you start the day with temporary hit points equal to your healing surge value. Even better is an *eager hero's tattoo* (level 10), which gives you temporary hit points every time you take a short rest.

OTHER CHOICES

Increasing your healing surge value doesn't feel like increasing your hit point total, but it makes your hit point supply last longer.

Similarly, relying on leaders for your healing can nearly double the efficiency of your hit points by making each surge worth much more than normal.

"Still hurts, doesn't it?"

After your allies perform an attack, the story is over, but your powers are gifts that keep on giving. Enemies that face you suffer prolonged agony from poison in their veins, fire burning their bodies, and acid searing their flesh—occasionally, all at the same time. When you strike an enemy, a clock starts ticking slowly down to the enemy's inevitable death.

Attack powers that deal ongoing damage might not seem as powerful as more traditional options, but when used properly, they can be much more devastating. These attacks represent a type of gamble, betting that failed saving throws by the target will result in much more damage than a typical power would have dealt.

Building a character who focuses on dealing ongoing damage can be a long, difficult road. For the first few levels, you are limited to a single power that grants the effect. Your patience, however, will be rewarded.

TELL US ABOUT YOUR CHARACTER

Mar'lik is a 2nd-level shadar-kai hybrid rogue/swordmage. I envision this character as one part Huron-haired, pierced-and-tattooed goth, one part musketeer with a flair for stylish attire and weaponry. He wears fencer's attire, a short, dark cape, and a rapier hanging from his broad leather belt. He also sports a short, neatly trimmed, pointy beard below his roached hair.

At only 2nd level, Mar'lik already displays tremendous talent at Stealth (with sylvan leather armor and a Luskan background, his Stealth skill modifier is +14). With his trusted *farbond spellblade* rapier stowed elsewhere for quick retrieval, he can confidently bluff his way into fancy receptions completely unarmed, all the better to disappear and investigate mysteries using Acrobatics and Thievery.

His powers include *piercing strike, dazing strike, lightning lure,* and *frost backlash.* He spent his first feat to gain proficiency with the rapier, and the second to take Hybrid Swordmage Warding to help his AC. He relies on his *shadow jaunt* racial power to escape when he is surrounded.

DIDIER MONIN started playing AD&D in 1980 at the History Games Club of St. Sever in Rouen, France. At the University of Jussieu, Didier helped start both an RPG gaming club at the university and an RPG fanzine. He worked for Wizards of the Coast for nearly 14 years, first in the French office then in the U.S. office, where he managed the data system for Organized Play and later produced the D&D Insider client applications.

CLASS

Almost every class has a few powers that deal ongoing damage, but only a few classes use them extensively. Invoker and wizard offer a decent range of options, but the two best choices are sorcerer and warlock.

The primordial channeler is a great paragon path choice for sorcerers, since it can add ongoing fire damage to all your attacks. The life-stealer paragon path for infernal warlocks adds ongoing fire damage to any attack made with an action point.

RACE

Since you need accuracy to deal ongoing damage, start by narrowing your race choices down to those that offer a bonus to your class's primary ability score. Of those options, focus on races that increase your accuracy. (See "Never Miss," page 72, for tips on finding these races.)

ABILITY SCORES

If you plan to create a warlock or a sorcerer, Charisma is by far your most important ability score. Most powers that deal ongoing damage rely on Charisma, and many of them gain a damage bonus equal to the character's Charisma modifier.

POWERS

Finding appropriate powers is easy: Just search the D&D Compendium for powers that have the word "ongoing" in their descriptions. (Searching for "ongoing damage" misses all the powers that include a damage type between those two words.)

Most of your options will be daily attack powers, since that's where ongoing damage generally resides. Try to vary the ongoing damage type so that you can stack their effects onto an individual enemy.

A few encounter attack powers deal ongoing damage, including *fire shroud* (wizard 3), *word of fiery condemnation* (invoker 7), *unholy glee* (warlock 17), and *hideous tether* (spellscarred 23). Pick one of these up if you have the chance, since you'll use it much more often than any of your daily attack powers.

At 10th level, you should select *storm of energy,* even if you must use multiclass feats to do so. The 10-point increase in each target's ongoing damage value makes this power essential for this character specialty.

Look for powers that give a target vulnerability to one of your ongoing damage types (*ruinous resistance* is a great choice for warlocks). This combination can drastically increase your damage output.

ADAM PHILLIPS

FEATS

Until you have a good selection of ongoing-damage powers, don't invest too heavily in feats that enhance them. You can always retrain to take such feats later on in your career.

As with powers, feats that give a target vulnerability to damage (such as Arcane Fire) can help increase the efficiency of your ongoing damage.

Sorcerers should pick up Arcane Spellfury. The attack bonuses it provides can help you hit with your crucial daily ongoing-damage powers.

If your campaign includes dragonmark feats, the Aberrant Mark of Contagion applies a penalty to saving throws against ongoing damage.

If you plan to use alchemical items to augment your collection of ongoing-damage effects (see "Magic Items," below), snag the Alchemist and Alchemical Opportunist feats.

MAGIC ITEMS

Magic items can significantly increase the variety of ongoing damage that you deal.

✦ A *robe of quills* (level 3 and up) gives you another source of ongoing damage, although it's probably not worthwhile to get one until you reach paragon tier. A simpler choice is *counterstrike armor* (level 10 and up), which deals ongoing 5 damage to the first enemy that hits you in each encounter.

✦ *Skin of agonies* (level 13 and up) lets you turn an enemy's ongoing-damage attack away from you and onto another foe.

✦ Look for items that add ongoing damage to other attacks, such as *burning gauntlets* (level 6), *orb of fiery condemnation* (level 15 and up), *rod of the churning inferno* (level 12 and up), and *rod of silver rain* (level 15 and up).

✦ A *lifesapper rod* (level 9 and up) lets you deal ongoing damage to a target just by subjecting the target to your Warlock's Curse.

Plenty of alchemical consumables create ongoing damage, such as *alchemist's acid*, *dragonfire tar*, *bloodstinger poison*, and *acidic fire*. Just make sure you buy new consumables periodically to keep their attack bonuses relevant.

OTHER CHOICES

All classes are limited in the number of ongoing damage powers they can use in one combat. Typically, only daily powers deal ongoing damage, so be prepared to round your character out with more standard attack abilities, as well.

Search for options that reduce your enemies' saving throws to make your ongoing damage effects last longer.

"There you go, using your feet to move around again. What a waste of energy!"

Why exert yourself—not to mention risk all those opportunity attacks—by walking around, when you could just teleport wherever you need to go?

As a master of teleportation, you can escape the nastiest deathtrap and close the distance to engage the foe of your choice. Although you might face jealousy from the other players at your carefree method of movement, try to be humble: Remember what it was like to be a slave to traditional measurements of time and space.

CLASS

Several classes offer a range of teleportation powers. Most of them are strikers, but you can have teleportation fun in many roles.

The avenger uses teleportation to pursue his or her chosen enemy. Despite a vast selection of teleportation powers, many of the avenger's powers are limited in their flexibility.

The assassin can choose from many teleportation options, including an at-will class feature. Again, however, several of these powers restrict the assassin's options of where to teleport.

The swordmage and warlock have the most versatile groups of teleportation powers; however, the fey pact warlock is clearly ahead of all other classes.

RACE

Three races have a racial teleportation power. The eladrin's *fey step* has the longest distance (5 squares), and the shadar-kai and wilden gain extra benefits when they teleport.

TELL US ABOUT YOUR CHARACTER

How do I know if I've created a character I'll enjoy playing? It has nothing to do with statistics, race, or class. It's all in the behavior and mannerisms. When other players in my D&D group start quoting my character and speculating on what he will do, then I know I've created a character worth keeping.

Take the wizard I created for Rodney Thompson's FORGOTTEN REALMS campaign, for example. Harold Glimmerswick was an 70-year-old spellcaster who had spent most of his life cloistered in Blackstaff Tower studying magic. What's more, he was obsessed with reviving Mystra.

Most of Harold's personality came out of this single character concept: If a person spent his entire adult life in a tower with little social contact and only books to inform him about the outside world, then he would have a very distorted view of reality. With a strong background and a powerful motivation (reviving Mystra), Harold had the makings of a fun, comedic character.

The best hijinks were the ongoing jokes poking fun at Harold's naivete and headstrong nature. For example, even in the Frozen North, Harold wore nothing underneath his robes, believing this to be a perfectly natural thing, since he never bothered back in the warm quarters of Blackstaff Tower. Whenever meeting people, he brazenly announced himself: "I am Harold Glimmerswick, wizard of Blackstaff Tower, and I am going to revive Mystra." The other characters inevitably groaned at Har-

old's missteps, but I made sure not to get so wrapped up in my character that I derailed the game.

Harold adventured with several morally questionable characters, such as an escaped convict and a drow with a penchant for torture. Creating a character who is something of a fish out of water, who has a background and an outlook that are much different from those of the rest of the party, can lead to great roleplaying opportunities. For instance, as the drow threatened grievous injury to one of our wererat foes, Harold quizzically wondered why his books about adventurers never recounted such things.

So, coming back to my point: I know I've made a character I'll enjoy when the other players can vividly imagine my character and describe what that character might do. If the DM tells us there's a big red button and before I can do or say anything, the other characters turn to me and say, "Harold, NO!" then I feel like I've achieved the infamy I want. If my wizard flies overhead and the other characters all announce, "Don't look up!" then I count it as a success. For me, having a character I enjoy is more than filling out a character sheet, it's about making someone who feels distinct and alive.

GREG BILSLAND is an editor and a designer at Wizards of the Coast. His recent credits include Monster Manual 2, the EBERRON Player's Guide, Martial Power 2, and Monster Manual 3. You can learn more about Greg's characters and campaigns at twitter.com/gregbilsland.

ALL GLORY FOR MORADIN!

UM, MORADIN?

MORADIN! YAH!

POWERS

Searching the D&D Compendium for "teleportation" brings up a list of appropriate powers. You can choose the powers that fit your style.

Pick up some teleportation powers that are activated with a move action or a minor action, such as *ethereal stride* (warlock 2) or *dimensional warp* (swordmage 2), so you can teleport without having to make an attack first.

Ethereal sidestep (warlock 10) is the ultimate "lazy" teleportation power, allowing you to teleport 1 square instead of shifting. Your allies will stop teasing you about it, though, once they watch you teleport out of a grab, or atop a low wall, or through a hole too tight for squeezing.

FEATS

Shorten your search term to "teleport" when looking for appropriate feats.

✦ Mark of Passage increases your the distance you can teleport with all powers by 1 square. Other similar feats include Devious Jaunt (for shadar-kai), Improved Misty Step (for fey pact warlocks), and Feyborn Pursuer (for eladrin avengers).

✦ Eladrin swordmages should grab Eladrin Swordmage Advance to get a free melee basic attack every encounter.

MAGIC ITEMS

With the right magic item selections, you can drastically increase your teleportation options.

✦ A *robe of contingency* (level 4 and up) is a favorite of many lightly armored characters because of its immediate-reaction teleportation power.

✦ *Translocating armor* (level 14 and up) lets you teleport after being missed.

✦ *Bracers of escape* (level 7 and up) allow you to teleport when attacked, effectively negating the attack.

✦ *Feystep lacings* (level 12) provide great teleportation flexibility, giving you 5 squares of teleportation each day that you can divide as you choose.

OTHER CHOICES

Even though rituals don't offer much help in combat, if you want to be known as a master teleporter, you'd better pick up Linked Portal and similar rituals.

Of these races, the eladrin has the most other teleportation-affecting options available, but any of these races makes a good choice.

ABILITY SCORES

Your ability scores have little effect on your ability to teleport, except in specific circumstances. Instead, the powers and feats you choose determine which ability scores benefit you most.

CHAPTER 2

BUILDING YOUR PARTY

YOU'VE FOLLOWED the advice in Chapter 1, and now you have a well-designed character who has a fascinating personality and an intriguing background. All you need is for the other players at the table to have the same, and then fun and success inevitably follow, right?

Unfortunately, even with an entire party of compelling, optimized characters, your game might still end up a miserable failure. If every player makes a bad-boy, long-ranged striker who doesn't work well with others, you might find that you can't get much done, and you won't survive many encounters. Failure to collaborate with the other players to make a party that works well together can ruin your gaming experience before you even roll initiative in your first encounter.

D&D is a social game. Most players feel the game is most rewarding when it provides the same feeling of camaraderie that we get from working well with others in any other environment. By spending a little time early on discussing the details of your adventuring party, you can avoid hours of dull roleplaying, aimless wandering, failed encounters, and stalled adventuring later on.

Before anyone starts building a character, you should talk with the other players about character roles, party optimization, group and individual strategy, and teamwork. This chapter explains how to plan your party for both efficiency and enjoyment. It includes the following sections.

✦ **Character Roles:** How the four roles work together to build a successful party, and how to deal with a nonstandard party size or role array.

✦ **Group Characterization:** How to optimize the social side of your party, including advice on creating complementary personalities and crafting interlocking backgrounds.

✦ **Party Optimization:** A discussion of advanced tactics for party-building, including group character design and power choice.

✦ **Sample Parties:** Each sample party shows a different way of thinking about building a unified group and includes explanations of how and why it was created.

The ideal party of D&D characters includes one character from each of the four roles described in the *Player's Handbook*: a defender to soak up damage, a controller to manipulate the battlefield and quell the mobs, a striker to take down key monsters, and a leader to keep the party on their feet while they do their jobs. If you have at least four characters in your party, aim for at least one player to assume each of these four roles. (See page 14 for more details on character roles.)

Of course, most parties don't have exactly four characters, and even those that do might find themselves down a character occasionally (or even welcome a guest). So how do you decide which roles to double up in a large party, or which ones to live without in a smaller group?

BUILDING A LARGE PARTY

In our experience, tables of five players are quite common. In fact, the game's advice for the DM on building encounters and assigning treasure assumes a party of five characters. But we also know that some of you out there routinely play with six, seven, or even more players all vying for the Dungeon Master's attention. So let's talk about how to choose the best roles for a big group.

DOUBLING A ROLE

Many players have strong opinions about the right role for a fifth (or sixth, or seventh) character, and they back up their opinions with all kinds of claims about critical redundancies or the like. In truth, the right extra character for your group depends on many factors, including the style of game the DM plans to run, the enemies you expect to face, and your group's tactical skills and preferences.

Controller: No character can affect a greater area of the battlefield than the controller. Wielding a variety of long-range, multitarget powers, the controller devastates mobs and reshapes the battle with a wave of his or her hand. If one controller is good, two must be better, right? Not always. Unless you commonly face particularly big mobs or wide battlefields, one controller is usually sufficient to get the job done.

That said, if your DM loves throwing endless waves of minions at your party, or if you spend more time fighting in the great outdoors than in narrow dungeon corridors, multiple controllers make a huge difference. Two controllers working together can easily block off entire swaths of the battlefield with deadly zones or can coordinate their efforts to eradicate swarms of enemies.

Controllers are at their most effective when facing large groups of enemies. If your DM prefers solo monsters or small groups of monsters, doubling up on controller can leave both characters feeling like low-damage strikers.

Also, since few controllers can survive extended contact with the enemy, make sure your controllers have good defensive or escape powers. The defender probably can't guard more than one controller simultaneously, so each controller needs to be self-sufficient enough to get out of trouble on his or her own.

Add a second controller if you anticipate many large-scale combats, and if both controllers can reliably survive occasional melee encounters.

Defender: Adding a second defender gives your party a lot of control over who gets attacked. If the two defenders divide their attention among different enemies, the party has locked down twice as many foes as before. Two defenders near each other can set up a virtual wall to protect their squishy allies. In a typical dungeon crawl, this tactic can easily render the monsters incapable of posing a serious threat.

A second defender also comes in handy when your party is facing a two-front battle. If your DM likes bringing enemies at you from all directions, strongly consider adding a second defender to the party.

In a battle with few enemies, a second defender can feel redundant. Multiple defenders facing a solo monster occasionally squabble over who should mark the foe; this can result in one character feeling left out. (See "Defenders: Tank-Teaming," page 90, for tips on managing multiple defender marks.)

Add a second defender to your group to gain durability and reliability. You might not kill the enemies quickly, but it takes a catastrophe to lose the fight.

Leader: Adding a second leader allows your party to bounce back quickly from any development. No matter what the DM throws at you, your group has the healing and party buffs to survive and thrive.

In some groups, the leader serves as the character who gets others out of trouble, whether with healing, extra saving throws, or other benefits. Having two leaders makes it tough to screw up badly enough to ruin your chances for victory. Even when the cleric goes down to the ogre's crit, the warlord's there to save the day.

The same goes for groups with unpredictable attendance. If you can't reliably forecast which players (and thus which characters) will show up for any given session, adding that extra leader ensures you have the problem-solving skills you need even if one player is missing.

A second leader can result in slow and undramatic encounters. With twice the healing of a normal party, monsters have difficulty piling damage on quickly enough to endanger any character. But since leaders lack the damage-dealing capability of strikers and controllers, the characters also win slowly.

Two leaders can also overlap, resulting in wasted effects and bored healers. Two daily powers that both

grant power bonuses to AC, for instance, have little benefit when used in the same encounter. And unless the monsters get lucky with attack rolls, your second leader might find his or her healing unused in many encounters.

Add a second leader to your party to cover for tactical mistakes or absent players.

Striker: It's tough to have too many strikers in a party. After all, dealing damage tends to win fights, so dealing more damage wins more fights, right? Unlike defenders, multiple strikers rarely have overlap problems (with the exception of two warlocks, since you can't place your Warlock's Curse on a creature already cursed by another warlock unless you have the Accursed Coordination feat). Your rogue can use Sneak Attack against an enemy already chosen as the ranger's quarry; in fact, that's often the best tactic to end fights quickly and efficiently.

If you have multiple strikers in your party, make sure at least one of them is melee-friendly. Otherwise, you risk having too many characters who want to stand at the back of the party and not enough on your

TOO MANY STRIKERS

Even with a normally sized group, you might end up with an unbalanced party. The most common manifestation is the striker-heavy team. Striker classes are the sexiest in the game, not just for power gamers and slayers but also for many actors because of the strong flavor associated with some of these classes.

With a party full of strikers, you desperately need a leader or at least a defender to keep an eye out for problems. While the warlock, rogue, ranger, and avenger run around the battlefield, poking holes in the enemies and cracking jokes about the decor, your "fixer" patiently cleans up the problems these strikers inevitably create.

front line. Barbarians and two-blade rangers work well as melee combatants, and rogues and Constitution-based warlocks don't mind getting into the thick of battle now and again. Avengers prefer melee, but they also prefer fighting a lone opponent.

A striker-heavy party performs best against small groups of enemies. Most strikers can't deal well with large groups, and their damage-dealing talents are wasted against mobs of minions.

When in doubt about which character to add to your large party, go for a striker. Even if it's not always the best choice, it's rarely a bad choice.

COVERING A TACTICAL GAP

Even if you have all the roles filled, your party might still be unbalanced. Sketch out where each character in your party prefers to stand during battle. Now, imagine a half-dozen monsters charging across the room. Where do they go, and what's the result? If you're the lone defender protecting three or four ranged attack specialists, how can you guard everyone, and who steps up when you inevitably fall?

The ideal adventuring party should have two characters devoted to melee combat, two focusing on ranged and area attacks, and one character who can switch between melee and ranged attacks as needed. Use the following descriptions to help plan your tactical group.

Melee Focused: ardent, avenger, barbarian, battlemind, fighter, monk, paladin, runepriest, swordmage, warden, warlord. These characters need to get up close to do their best work.

The warlord is a special case. *Martial Power 2* introduced the skirmishing warlord build, which focuses on making and enhancing ranged attacks. This character can easily fit into the highly versatile category.

Ranged Focused: invoker, psion, sorcerer, wizard. These classes rarely bring any melee prowess to the table. They need other characters to stand in the way of the monsters.

Highly Versatile: artificer, assassin, druid, rogue, skirmishing warlord. These classes can switch between melee and ranged attacks without giving up power or accuracy.

Potentially Versatile: cleric, ranger, seeker, warlock. These classes can be built to include both melee and ranged attacks. However, such builds typically need multiple primary ability scores or have other drawbacks, making achieving versatility with these classes more challenging. When bringing such a character to the group, make sure everyone knows whether you've built a focused or a versatile member of the party.

BUILDING A SMALL PARTY

If you drool at the thought of having too many characters at the table, you're probably one of those poor souls who can't assemble a full adventuring party. We empathize: Everyone's been there, whether as a new arrival in town or just cursed to live in a game-scarce region. So how do you deal with the party of three or fewer players?

Well, get rid of the idea of having a well-balanced party. No matter the workaround, you're bound to come up against situations that expose your team's gaps. But with a little discipline in class selection— and some cooperation from your DM—you can still have plenty of fun and success with a small group.

FOREGOING A ROLE

Many of the arguments about which roles to double up on also apply to small-group situations, but in reverse. If having two leaders means it's tough to lose a fight, having no leaders makes every battle tougher to win. Since you know you're missing a role, which one do you choose to forego and how can you compensate?

These descriptions are ordered from most expendable to least expendable.

Striker: The striker is the most expendable, because this role specializes in dealing damage. Sure, the other roles can't deal damage as quickly as a striker, but that just means the fight lasts longer. The striker lacks the leader's ability to heal, has only a limited ability to affect multiple enemies like a controller, and has no marking ability and weaker defenses than the defender. So if necessary, your party can manage without a striker.

Compensate for your lack of a striker by choosing classes with higher damage output or with plenty of accuracy and damage boosts. The right wizard or invoker can make up some of the damage gap. A warlord can pass out extra attacks and offensive buffs. A bard can easily load up on powers that increase his or her party's offensive output. A predator druid in beast form makes a decent striker replacement.

Controller: A controller is slightly more important to a party than a striker because of the multitarget aspect of the controller's abilities. With no controller in your party, you can't quickly destroy large groups of minions and you can't easily manipulate the battle

PLAYING IN A LARGE GROUP

If by choice or by chance you find yourself in a group with six or more players, you might think the extra players ensure success in combat and a fun game for everyone. It's true, pitting more characters against the same group of monsters likely results in an easier win. But in reality, the situation presents a number of challenges.

Big groups are slower than small groups. You might find that a seven-player team takes longer to finish a combat than the five-player group, even against the same group of monsters. The more players you have, the harder it is to know what you're going to do before your turn. And let's face it, some players just make decisions more slowly than a dwarf wades through a gelatinous cube. Encourage players to focus on simple, straightforward character options: powers without secondary attacks, feats without complicated situational benefits, and so forth. Even if each player sacrifices only a little of the complexity that slows the game down, it adds up to a big time savings.

Big groups mean less roleplaying time for each player at the table. Dividing the same number of playing hours between more people means less face time for each player. Don't hog the spotlight. Respect the other players' turns. Know when to sit back and let other people talk.

Big groups can lead to spotty attendance. Ironically, having more characters in the party can sometimes result in fewer players showing up. If you don't feel that your attendance is crucial for the group's success, you might find it easier to skip a game. Unpredictable attendance introduces all kinds of problems, both for the group's success and the DM's sanity in crafting encounters and intricate storylines. Let the DM rely on your presence; work hard to attend at least 75 percent of the sessions. If you can be one of these reliable players, offer to take charge of tracking treasure or quests, or offer to keep the party's journal. (see "The Campaign Journal," page 148.) Have a backup for this task; if you're going to miss a session, send that player any notes he or she needs to step in for you.

Talk with the DM and the other players to agree on a standing rule for how many players will have to attend to keep a gaming session on the calendar. As much as it hurts to tell a player that the group isn't rescheduling a game to account for his or her absence, putting your game at the mercy of seven or eight competing schedules is a recipe for madness. Pick a night and stick with it—the player who misses a session can always catch up with the story next time.

through conditions, zones, and walls. Although you can get by without a controller, having one definitely makes your party stronger.

Compensate for your missing controller by having each player pick up multitarget powers, if possible. Every dragonborn can take out a couple of minions in each fight with *dragon breath*. Most classes have at least a couple of close burst or close blast attack powers; the fighter's *come and get it* is a good example.

Also, look for powers that restrict enemy options or reduce an enemy's effectiveness in combat. Both the sorcerer and the warlock can stand in for a controller in a pinch, with the variety of controlling or debuffing powers available to these characters.

Defender: Without a defender, strikers and controllers have difficulty doing their jobs. Strikers start taking more hits, forcing them to flee melee. Controllers lose their safety buffer, making them vulnerable to enemy brutes and soldiers. Even if the monsters cooperate by attacking your melee-focused leader, he or she doesn't have the defenses or hit points to stand up for long. And when your leader falls, the party's in big trouble.

Compensate for the lack of a defender by ensuring that everyone has either the durability to survive melee or the mobility to escape it. For strikers, use barbarians or two-blade rangers rather than sorcerers or warlocks.

Pick up some powers that mark foes—the bard has a few—to pull the monster off your bloodied wizard before it's too late.

Leader: It's tough to survive without a leader for very long; second wind only goes so far. Without a leader, every combat becomes a nail-biting race to

defeat the monsters before you run out of hit points. The margin for error becomes razor-thin, mandating smarter play and stronger tactics from everyone at the table.

Compensate for your missing leader by picking up as many healing powers as you can. The paladin is your best choice, but several classes (such as the fighter and the warden) have the ability to restore their own health. Check out the Heal skill powers for options for any class. Although multiclassing is a good solution for any missing role, it's almost mandatory when your group goes without a leader.

POWER TRIOS

If you need help assembling that three-character adventuring party, here are some combinations that might work for you.

No Striker: fighter, invoker, warlord. The fighter-warlord team-up can deal massive damage in a hurry while the invoker keeps the rest of the battlefield locked down.

No Controller: bard, swordmage, warlock. This all-arcane team brings plenty of battlefield control to the table. With the right powers, any of them can stand up against a mob for a round or two until help arrives.

No Defender: barbarian, druid, shaman. The first two characters can handle themselves in melee combat, and the shaman can lock down foes with his or her spirit companion.

No Leader: druid, paladin, warlock. The druid and the paladin can provide much-needed healing and defensive buffs. The warlock can easily get out of trouble before getting too injured.

Just as when lacking a defender, make sure you have the melee chops to handle the incoming monsters. Alternatively, you could try making everyone slippery; if the monsters can't keep up with you, maybe they can't hurt you.

One subtle effect of playing in a leaderless party is that it costs more healing surges to bounce back from a battle (since you don't have all those extra dice of healing normally gained from leader powers). Expect to play only half to two-thirds of the number of encounters between extended rests that you would play if you had a leader.

GENERAL-PURPOSE CHARACTERS

The best solution for a small party comes from abandoning the game's preference for specialization in favor of more generalized characters. The multiclassing and hybrid character rules provide two methods for building a team member who can potentially cover two of your four bases.

A multiclass character spends feats to pick up some features and powers from another class. However, a single multiclass character doesn't fully compensate for a missing role. Multiclassing in leader or controller provides a bit of support for a party lacking that role, since so much of those roles lie in their power selection. On the other hand, multiclassing as a defender or a striker supplies only minimal role support and probably won't accomplish what you need.

Adding a hybrid character is another story. Built properly, with a good mix of two roles and the appropriate ability scores to support both classes, a hybrid

character is a godsend to the small party. Although your hybrid fighter/cleric can't necessarily act as both a defender and a leader every round—or as either role for the full encounter—he or she certainly brings more of each role to the table than a multiclass character.

If everyone at the table can handle the complexity, consider encouraging each player in a small party to build a hybrid or at least a multiclass character.

WORK WITH THE DM

Make sure your Dungeon Master knows about your party's role gaps. If you're worried about not being able to handle a particular type of challenge, ask your DM for advice on how to deal with it. Maybe he or she will agree to avoid placing your party in those situations very often, or maybe your plight earns you a "get-out-of-TPK-free" card.

The companion character system presented in *Dungeon Master's Guide 2* provides a potential solution for exactly this problem. Rather than crafting an entire extra character, the system allows you to build a simple character to fill in on either a temporary or a long-term basis. Running the character doesn't require much brainpower, due to its limited options, but the extra body can make the difference between success and failure.

A good DM knows that his or her job is to make the game fun for everyone. Any DM can build an encounter that kills off the entire party; the challenge comes in building encounters that come close without quite getting there.

TELL US ABOUT YOUR CHARACTER

Kael, the Hand of Io, is a 16th-level dragonborn deva cleric/invoker who has the angelic aspect paragon path in Chris Perkins's Wednesday night Iomandra campaign. (See the Iomandra page on the Wizards Community D&D forums for more details on this island-based campaign inspired by the D&D core world.)

Jumping into a Chris Perkins campaign is no easy feat. I polled the crew to see what the group needed, and a leader/controller topped the list. As I pondered jumping directly into a paragon-level campaign rich in detail and story, with a solid cast of characters who have already had crazy adventures together, I wanted to make something a bit unique. Using the deva's racial description, the angelic aspect paragon path, and the write-up for Bahamut-worshiping invokers in *Divine Power*, I created a twist on the deva story. Kael is an angel who descended to be the Hand of Io in the world, acknowledging both Tiamat and Bahamut in his code of action. This allowed me to retain a direct tie to the powerful draconic influences in Chris's game, yet still leave the "dragonborn spotlight" on the unique storyline of the paladin of Bahamut already in the party. I was a draconic deva. Go figure.

So I had a cool, unique race and character, and an easy-to-integrate background. Starting as a cleric, I swapped out some powers using the multiclass feats to give him some invoker/controller flavor while retaining the core healing this group of bleeders needed.

Also, reading the blog posts of the campaign, these guys fall all the time, so sprouting angel wings in a clutch seemed like a really, really good idea. Especially when diving out the window is the typical "Hail Mary" maneuver intended to save the party members from something deadlier inside the room. Seriously, they get sucked into vortexes, blown out windows, and dropped from heights on a regular basis. Read the blogs to find out how things turn out.

We should be okay, right?

CHRIS CHAMPAGNE is the studio director of the team that makes great D&D applications like the Character Builder, Monster Builder, and D&D Compendium. An avid D&D player and DM since the summer of 1978, Chris uses the phrase "Just livin' the dream" when asked what it's like working for Wizards of the Coast.

Crafting a mechanically balanced group represents only half the task of building a strong party. In addition to functioning well together on the battlefield, your characters must get along well enough to stand adventuring as a team. Work together to create complementary personalities and interlocking background stories for your characters, and you'll be rewarded with a much more entertaining game.

LINKING STORIES

Share your character concept and background elements with your fellow players and encourage them to do the same. Look for places where your stories might link together, and take advantage of those opportunities to build connections before the campaign even begins.

Your links might have been forged in the past. Perhaps two characters hail from the same village, or studied under the same mentor, or were orphaned by the same war.

If such coincidences seem too strained, find another way to connect yourself to a person, a place, or an event significant to another character. Maybe your character knows another character's home town because you used to make delivery runs there as part of a merchant caravan. The paladin in the party knows your mentor because the paladin's father served with him in the war . . . the same war that orphaned the wizard.

On the other hand, the connections you build might involve plans for the future. You know that one of the characters likes to play practical jokes, so you decide that your dwarf will become the unwitting straight man for your friend's tricks. Two dragonborn characters in the same party might share a desire to see the glory of Arkhosia reborn in the world.

These links don't just provide common points of reference for small talk between your characters, they begin to build a framework upon which the DM can later place adventure hooks, significant nonplayer characters, and storylines. A person known to two or three characters provides a more compelling contact than one who's a stranger to everyone but you. A goal shared by two characters is twice as likely to become significant in the campaign setting.

You don't have to decide that every character knows everyone else before the first adventure starts. Instead, craft an interesting link between your character and two others in the party. Each of those characters, in turn, builds a link between two others, and so on, until you have a web of connections that bring you all together.

COMPATIBILITY TEST

Make sure that your various character personalities don't clash too badly. Friendly rivalries and occasional differences of opinion can make for exciting roleplaying, but heated arguments and obstinate refusals to work together lead to broken groups and ruined friendships.

In some cases, you might have to tone down an aspect of your character concept to fit in. D&D isn't just about showing off your creativity or theatrical talents—it's about everyone at the table having fun. If your fun comes at the expense of the fun of other players, throttle back a bit and let others share the enjoyment.

Include the DM in these conversations, as well. Some Dungeon Masters can roll with any character personalities, but most have at least one behavioral quirk that rubs them the wrong way. Maybe your DM doesn't want a punster in his or her spooky game about undead. Be reasonable, and find a way that both of you can play the game you want.

WHY ARE WE HERE?

Some gaming groups are satisfied just playing a team of treasure hunters without a greater purpose. Often, however, groups create a story that gives the party a reason for their adventures. Do your characters all work for the same mysterious benefactor? Have you come together for vengeance against the dragon who laid waste to your home region? Are you all escaped slaves, bored children of nobles, or graduates of the same military academy? Agreeing on the central purpose of your gathering can suggest adventures and quests to the DM while simultaneously reminding everyone why your characters risk life and limb to go on these crazy escapades.

Some groups go one step further, building their characters around a shared mechanical theme. It's never been easier to craft an entire party that shares a power source, but you could also share a race, use tribal feats, or find some other element of the rules to brand your group as a unified team.

Without exploiting the rules, a party can benefit from choosing classes, powers, and other options that work well together. This section aims to ensure that your party becomes a well-oiled machine.

DEFENDERS: TANK-TEAMING

When you have two or more defenders in a party, it takes discipline and planning to avoid unnecessary canceling of each other's marks. Sometimes, trading marks is a great strategy, but many multiple defender groups unintentionally spend half the battle with only one marked enemy. Before you get to the table, figure out how to pair the right two defender classes to avoid this problem.

Place extra value on defenders who can easily select the target of their mark. The battlemind and the swordmage have the greatest flexibility in this regard, since they can mark a specific target other than the creature they're fighting right now. The fighter must mark the target he or she attacks, and the warden marks all adjacent enemies without any ability to pick and choose. The paladin falls in the middle of the continuum—he or she can select a particular enemy within 5 squares, but the paladin must then engage the marked foe.

Don't overrate multiple marking powers. With two or more defenders, you already have multiple marks on the battlefield, and multiple marking powers increase the chance that you'll override (and thus waste) an ally's mark.

Remember the value of durability. Although all defenders rely on high defenses and hit points, having two defenders means each one must be patient when it comes to getting healing. Also, it's unlikely that your two defenders can evenly split the incoming attacks; one or the other probably ends up taking the brunt of the assault. Paladins, fighters, and wardens are the toughest and most self-reliant defenders. Choose one of these characters as your primary defender, relying on him or her to take point in your defensive wall.

The swordmage makes the strongest secondary defender. Since your swordmage character can trigger your mark's punishing effect from range, you can effectively keep your attention on two places at once: the enemy in front of you, and the marked enemy across the room. Even if your aegis doesn't include teleportation, your own class powers offer many options for blinking across the battlefield at a moment's notice. Also, *arcane deflection* allows your swordmage to protect any adjacent ally, even another defender, from attacks.

The battlemind is another solid choice for a secondary defender; the class's precise yet flexible marking powers provide great options on the battlefield.

STRIKERS: FOCUSING FIREPOWER

When you divide damage between multiple foes, you draw out the battle and allow the enemy more opportunities to hurt you. Having a striker or two on your team avoids this problem by piling lots of damage on individual targets. Usually, having multiple strikers doesn't cause problems, since dealing more damage is almost always a good call. However, some parties that have multiple strikers encounter difficulty with competing striker priorities.

The most common problem with multiple striker parties comes from an overreliance on ranged attacks. The sorcerer, the warlock, and the archer ranger are popular striker choices, but none of these characters necessarily wants to face monsters in melee. Assuming that they don't stand together in the fight, all those fragile strikers are going to need multiple defenders to protect them. Pair a ranged-focused striker with a melee-friendly striker, such as the barbarian or the monk, to avoid this problem. Alternatively, make sure your strikers all have strong mobility, self-healing, or escape options so they can get themselves out of trouble.

Two striker classes, the ranger and the warlock, each have the Prime Shot class feature. If these two characters try to maximize accuracy against the same target, it's tough for both characters to gain the Prime Shot bonus. Either avoid pairing these two classes in the same party, or accept the inefficiency that comes with splitting attacks or foregoing Prime Shot.

Sometimes, two strikers' preferred tactics don't work well together. For example, the avenger prefers to fight a lone opponent. That usually means the character doesn't want any allies nearby—multiple characters usually draw multiple monsters. On the other hand, most rogues require a teammate fighting the same enemy to perform at full effectiveness. Having both an avenger and a rogue in the same party makes it tough for the strikers to focus their damage on a single foe.

Coincidentally, many strikers have similar skill lists. Keep in mind the party's desired distribution of trained skills (see "Skill Training," page 92) when choosing which strikers best fit your group's needs. The class skills lists of barbarians and rangers, for instance, overlap more heavily than the lists of sorcerers and rangers.

CHOOSING THE RIGHT LEADER

The *Player's Handbook* suggests that leaders are essentially interchangeable, but don't mistake this to mean that all leaders are identical. Although any leader fills the party's basic needs for healing and buffs, each leader class brings a different flavor of party assistance to the table. Matching the right leader to your party can make a significant contribution to your success.

Ardents have many powers that boost allies' accuracy and damage. Characters specializing in multitarget attacks (such as controllers, sorcerers, and rangers) can easily double the effectiveness of their attacks because of these boosts.

The artificer's conjuration powers often function as minicontrol effects, helping to keep a battle from getting out of hand. Like the ardent, the artificer also has many offensive buffs.

Bards are masters of minor repositioning, both of allies and enemies. Your bard should view the combatants as his or her toys to move around at will. The bard also provides great benefits outside combat, and has a long skill list, access to rituals, and *words of friendship*. Rogues and avengers appreciate the help in getting enemies into unpleasant positions, controllers love being slid out of melee, and the bard helps fighters lock down the battle as well. The Multiclass Versatility feature means your bard can easily slide into other roles when needed; small parties love having a bard.

No class brings more efficient healing to the party than the cleric. You could easily choose nothing but powers that heal damage or provide temporary hit points. Clerics also have a plethora of both melee and ranged attacks, which means that you can add the class either to a melee-focused group (to stand in the back rank) or to a ranged-focused team (to hold the front line). A group with plenty of other forms of healing might not need those powers as much.

The shaman can spread healing out to great effect but can't heal individual allies quite as quickly as other leaders. The shaman's spirit companion functions as a minidefender (if near allies) or as a zone of battlefield control (if elsewhere). You can safely bring low-defense characters to a party including a shaman, thanks to the many defensive buffs the class provides.

Warlords function best in a melee-focused party. Many warlord powers grant extra melee attacks to nearby allies or provide bonuses to melee attacks. Surround your warlord with fighters, barbarians, and rogues to maximize your party's damage output. The skirmishing warlord build in *Martial Power 2*

favors ranged allies, so make sure you have an archer ranger, a seeker, or a warlock at hand.

Of the leaders, only shamans lack at least one social interaction skill; ardents and bards have all three. Most leaders have Diplomacy as a class skill, so if you have two or more leaders, take care to avoid unintentional skill overlap.

CHARACTER REDUNDANCY

The basic advice on building parties earlier in this chapter handled balancing melee and ranged attackers (see "Covering a Tactical Gap," page 85). Try to have at least two of each kind of attacker in your party, to avoid putting too many of your eggs into either basket. The members of a melee-heavy group might find themselves tripping over each other to get into combat, and an all-ranged party lacks the ability to effectively deal with brutes and soldiers.

Sometimes, though, you just can't avoid this imbalance. If you need to fill out a group that leans in one direction or the other, try these suggestions.

All-Ranged Group: This party needs a defender or a leader who can provide melee support for the rest of the team. For a defender, you can't beat the swordmage, who can keep one enemy marked while engaging a second enemy on the other side of the room. This class also has great mobility, allowing the swordmage to move between different threats with ease. For a leader, try a skirmishing warlord to enhance your party's ranged attacks. Make sure the warlord has a few melee powers, as well. The druid is a good choice for controller, since he or she can step into melee without difficulty.

All-Melee Group: An excess of melee characters offers fewer problems than an all-ranged group, but these characters still encounter difficulty handling flying enemies or cramped battlefields. Choose a leader who has ranged attack powers, such as an artificer, a devoted cleric, or a cunning bard. Make sure your strikers, even if they are melee-focused, have ranged attack options. The rogue and the hunter ranger are good choices for strikers with ranged attack abilities.

Equipment: Diversify your characters' choices of weapons, implements, and armor. Even if your DM is diligent about using character wish lists, when multiple characters want the same type of items, treasure distribution can get a bit testy.

Rituals: Every party should include a character capable of learning and using rituals. Several classes gain ritual use as a class feature; if you don't have one of these characters in your party, have someone select the Ritual Caster feat no later than 8th level. (That's when the really important rituals start appearing.)

MATCHING CLASSES TO SKILLS

Skill	Best Choices	Other Choices
Acrobatics (Dex)	assassin, avenger, monk, ranger, rogue, seeker	bard, barbarian
Arcana (Int)	*artificer*, *bard*, invoker, psion, shaman, *swordmage*, warlock, *wizard*	assassin, ardent, battlemind, cleric, druid, runepriest, *sorcerer*
Athletics (Str)	barbarian, fighter, monk, ranger, runepriest, seeker, sorcerer, swordmage, warden, warlord	ardent, assassin, avenger, bard, battlemind, druid, rogue, shaman
Bluff (Cha)	ardent, assassin, bard, psion, rogue, sorcerer, warlock	—
Diplomacy (Cha)	ardent, bard, battlemind, cleric, paladin, psion, sorcerer, warlord	artificer, druid, invoker, monk, swordmage, wizard
Dungeoneering (Wis)	artificer, psion, *ranger**, warden	bard, rogue, sorcerer, wizard
Endurance (Con)	ardent, barbarian, battlemind, druid, fighter, invoker, runepriest, seeker, shaman, swordmage, warden	assassin, avenger, monk, paladin, ranger, sorcerer, warlord
Heal (Wis)	ardent, artificer, avenger, battlemind, cleric, druid, monk, paladin, ranger, runepriest, seeker, shaman, warden	barbarian, bard, fighter, warlord
History (Int)	artificer, bard, invoker, psion, shaman, swordmage, warlock, warlord, wizard	cleric, druid, paladin, runepriest, sorcerer
Insight (Wis)	ardent, battlemind, cleric, druid, invoker, monk, paladin, psion, runepriest, seeker, shaman	assassin, bard, rogue, sorcerer, swordmage, warlock, wizard
Intimidate (Cha)	ardent, barbarian, bard, battlemind, paladin, psion, rogue, sorcerer, warlock, warlord	avenger, fighter, invoker, seeker, swordmage, warden
Nature (Wis)	*druid*, *ranger**, *seeker*, *shaman*, *warden*	barbarian, bard, sorcerer, wizard
Perception (Wis)	artificer, avenger, druid, monk, psion, ranger, seeker, shaman, warden	assassin, barbarian, bard, rogue
Religion (Int)	*avenger*, bard, *invoker*, shaman, warlock, wizard	*cleric*, monk, *paladin*, *runepriest*
Stealth (Dex)	*assassin*, avenger, monk, ranger, *rogue*, seeker	—
Streetwise (Cha)	ardent, assassin, bard, rogue, warlock	avenger, fighter
Thievery (Dex)	assassin, monk, *rogue*	artificer, runepriest, warlock

*The ranger automatically receives training in either Dungeoneering or Nature at 1st level.

A party can benefit from having more than one character who has the ability to use rituals, but only if each of those characters focuses on different kinds of rituals. Having multiple characters learn the same rituals serves little purpose, and the characters end up feeling less interesting and special. The party also wastes money, because learning rituals costs gold. So have your leader learn healing and restoration rituals while your controller learns scrying, exploration, or deception rituals.

Languages: Speaking a wide variety of languages is nice, but if the characters share a second language, they can speak to each other without others outside the party understanding. You might have difficulty convincing your Dungeon Master that all the characters speak Supernal, so learning a more common language, such as Elven or Goblin, might be better.

SKILL TRAINING

An optimized party is ready for any skill challenge the DM might craft. Aim to have at least one character trained in each skill, saving redundant skill training for only the most important skills. A five-character party can easily cover all seventeen skills as long as you take a little care.

Smaller parties have more difficulty covering all skills and might have to rely on characters who combine high ability modifiers with bonuses from race or background. Having a human or an eladrin character in your party can help cover all the bases, since those races gain extra trained skills.

Use the Matching Classes to Skills table to figure out which character will train in each skill. If possible, assign every skill to a character who has a score of 16 or higher in the skill's key ability. Classes appearing in the "Best Choices" column offer the skill's key ability score as either a primary or a secondary ability option; characters from these classes are likely your best options for that skill assignment. Other classes that include the skill in their class lists, but which are unlikely to have a high score in the skill's ability, appear in "Other Choices."

After you have chosen your classes, assign automatic skill training. Class names that are italicized in the table automatically receive training in the skill. In some cases, these classes might not be in the "Best Choices" column.

Assign the rarest skills first. Dungeoneering, Nature, Streetwise, and Thievery have the fewest "best matches" among the skills, so make sure you handle those before moving on to the more common skills.

Next, cover the skills most likely to prove mission-critical. The other knowledge skills—Arcana, History, and Religion—and the observation skills (Insight and Perception) should never go untrained in a party. You should also have at least one character trained in each of the social skills: Bluff, Diplomacy, and Intimidate. It's good to have a character trained in Stealth, but it's often more important to have no character who has a negative skill modifier in Stealth (since the group that sneaks together stays together).

The last few skills—Acrobatics, Athletics, Endurance, and Heal—aren't as likely to require a high level of expertise, so you can fill them out last.

After covering the list, your party should still have a few more skills left to train. Use these to gain a second expert in the most commonly used skills (Arcana, Diplomacy, and Perception) or to help cover weak points in skills that often require the whole group to succeed (Acrobatics, Athletics, and Stealth).

TACTICAL COMBINATIONS

Talk with the other players about your character's preferred tactics to ensure the party isn't working at cross-purposes. Few game experiences prove more frustrating than the realization that your character's careful build is negated by another character's power selections.

Here are a few examples: Although many leader powers boost adjacent allies, these powers rarely help the avenger, since that character prefers to fight alone. And if you chose powers that allow you to slide enemies around the battlefield, remember that the fighter needs to stay adjacent to foes to maximize his or her ability to lock them down. The battlerager fighter rarely needs more temporary hit points, so the cleric's *sacred flame* becomes less useful to the fighter.

Look for ways your powers can benefit your allies, even if you aren't playing a leader, and tell them about it. Any character who can daze, restrain, or knock enemies prone makes it easy for the rogue to gain much-needed combat advantage. Your warlock's *dread star* helps your allies hit the enemy's Will just as much as it helps you. Remind the bard that your rogue appreciates being slid into a flanking position before your turn starts.

HAVE PATIENCE

Not everyone has the skill, experience, time, resources, and motivation to ensure that a character is optimized with the latest updates from *Dragon* magazine, the newest supplement, and the most recent campaign setting. Not everyone wants to crunch the numbers, read the optimization boards, plan out interparty dynamics, or create nifty spreadsheets displaying damage output per level. Understand each player's talents and preferences and respect them.

Avoid building characters that marginalize the efforts of other players at the table. As you carefully optimize your fighter, make sure to leave some room for your friend playing the paladin to shine. Let the paladin have higher defenses than you, or more hit points, or a couple of trained skills that you don't have. When building your perfect rogue, try not to eclipse the defender's AC—it makes that player feel like he or she doesn't need to be there.

Even though being awesome certainly is awesome, D&D is not about being the best—it's about everyone at the table having fun. If you are better in every way than another party member (particularly one playing the same role), the other player probably isn't having much fun. If you are the only defender, then go right ahead and be mega-amazing at defending your allies, but if your party has another defender, consider making other choices. Otherwise, you risk diminishing your friend's enjoyment of the game. And what's the point of that?

We come from different races, different lands, different backgrounds. And yet our knowledge and appreciation of the arcane mysteries bring us together in a shared quest for the secrets held by the many worlds.

The Spellblades bonded over a common interest in arcane magic. Some characters dabble in magic, using it to enhance their martial attacks. Others are full-fledged magic users who revel in the thrill of spell and ritual.

Even with this shared power source, subtle differences and rivalries exist within the Spellblades. The feyborn eladrin, Taellaen, sometimes wonders if the shadowy Delaia keeps secrets from the rest of the group. The characters compete for the highest Arcana check result, seeing it as a point of pride.

RUEL, SHIELDING SWORDMAGE

Role: Defender
The heart of the party, Ruel blends magic and martial art into a seamless fusion. The human's calming presence provides a balm to the passionate energy that can spark in such a magical group. As the party's defender, Ruel stands in the front line, soaking up attacks and damage. Ruel focuses more on defense than on offense; he uses a longsword to maximize the AC boost of his Swordmage Warding class feature. Ruel uses his high Constitution score to deflect away from his allies the damage dealt by marked enemies.

Powers: Ruel prefers a variety of powers that can strike both adjacent and distant enemies—such as *frostwind blade*, *lightning lure*, *lightning clash*, and *whirling blade*—so that he can keep pace with the party when ranged combat is a better option.

Feats: Ruel starts with Toughness and Improved Swordmage Warding, knowing that staying alive and active keeps his party safe. He expects to continue to focus on defensive feat options, looking forward to Human Perseverance at 2nd level.

Skills: Arcana, Endurance, History, Insight.

TAELLAEN, TACTICAL WARLORD

Role: Leader
Taellaen, the party's primary leader, focuses on getting his allies to optimal positions on the battlefield.

Powers: Taellaen leads off with *inevitable wave*, encouraging Ruel to follow him into battle. *Opening shove* helps get enemies into the right position, and *warlord's favor* makes his allies' attacks more potent. *Lead by example* combines both aspects of this eladrin's leader role.

Feats: Because of his high Intelligence score, Taellaen has become a multiclass wizard with Arcane Initiate, taking *scorching burst* to add an attack useful against distant foes or groups of minions.

Skills: Arcana, Athletics, Heal, History, Intimidate, Perception.

ZULOT, DRAGON SORCERER

Role: Striker
Zulot, a dragonborn, is the party's firepower, both literally and figuratively. She is the striker of the party, and she can deal a great deal of damage.

Powers: *Acid orb* is a solid long-range attack (and functions as a ranged basic attack, for times when Taellaen uses powers that grant free basic attacks). *Dragon breath* and *burning spray* allow Zulot to routinely damage multiple enemies, making her almost as much a controller as a striker. *Tearing claws* helps her defend herself when enemies slip past the front line.

Feats: Zulot wants to deal as much damage as she can, so she likes the accuracy boost of Implement Focus. Later, she looks forward to Arcane Spellfury.

Skills: Arcana, Athletics, Diplomacy, Intimidate.

DELAIA, CONTROL WIZARD

Role: Controller
The least impulsive Spellblade, Delaia prefers to know what she faces before acting. If the shadar-kai can't figure it out, she keeps it away from her.

Powers: As a control wizard, Delaia specializes in powers that affect enemy movement, such as forced-movement powers (*thunderwave* and *spectral ram*), powers that immobilize (*web*), and powers that create barriers and difficult terrain (*icy terrain* and *wall of ice*). Dealing damage is a secondary concern to her; she leaves that to Zulot.

Feats: Enlarge Spell increases the size of three of Delaia's starting powers, dramatically widening her area of effect on the battlefield.

Skills: Arcana, Dungeoneering, Nature, Religion.

RASKEL, VALOROUS BARD

Role: Leader
Raskel is an archetypal half-elf wandering minstrel. He picks up a bit of knowledge, story, and song everywhere he goes and from everyone he meets.

Powers: *Vicious mockery* and *war song strike* offer Raskel a nice variety of at-will power choices. *Fast friends* can help an ally in need, and *slayer's song* helps speed the battle to a victorious conclusion. *Eyebite*, which Raskel gained by multiclassing, comes in handy when he needs to maneuver past enemies to aid a friend.

Feats: Raskel starts by multiclassing into warlock with Pact Initiate (selecting Thievery and the fey pact). He intends to continue selecting various multiclass feats; he has his eye on sorcerer and paladin.

Skills: Arcana, Bluff, Diplomacy, Perception, Streetwise, Thievery.

PARTY OPTIMIZATION

Working the Front Line: Two of the party's five members, Ruel and Taellaen, are pure frontline fighters. Ruel tends to absorb blows for Taellaen so that the warlord can heal him and keep the other party members alive. Raskel is a decent third melee fighter. The three of them make sure that their striker and controller can avoid melee.

Long-Range Combat: All five members of the party have some ranged combat ability, although Zulot, the sorcerer, and Delaia, the wizard, are the primary ranged combatants. But even the warlord and the swordmage—classes that don't traditionally favor ranged combat—have a few ranged attack options. Because of the party's versatility, it can handle both melee and ranged combat with ease.

Arcane Link: Because they share a power source, these characters have developed an uncommon unity. The Spellblades' shared interests lead to adventure hooks that speak to the entire party rather than to a single member. Such unity might not seem like a form of optimization, but in a sense it is, because it leads to enhanced cooperation.

Skill Challenges: Raskel and Zulot take the lead on social skill challenges. Ruel and Delaia handle most of the knowledge skills, but anyone in the party can ace an Arcana check. The party lacks a Dexterity- or Wisdom-focused character, so it's weak on those skills.

PARTY TACTICS

Synergistic Front Line: Ruel and Taellaen bring an important synergy to the front line. Ruel uses his mark to deflect blows away from Taellaen or reduce damage to the warlord when attacks do land. Taellaen keeps Ruel alive with healing and buffs. These two maintain a wall in the front to give the others room to maneuver.

Keep 'em Guessing: With their mix of attacks, the members of the Spellblades make guessing what they might do difficult for enemies and the Dungeon Master. The defender is capable of speed and of both ranged and area attacks. The dragonborn sorcerer uses more area attacks than most strikers. The warlord leader specializes in combat leadership, which keeps the party alive and kicking hard. And the bard keeps the enemy guessing with his never-ending array of tricks, finding something with which to baffle enemies at every turn. He thinks of unique ways to avoid combat when possible and rolls with the punches when the situation gets dirty.

ADJUSTING THE PARTY

Of the five characters, either Raskel or Delaia is the most expendable if there are only four players at the table. True, keeping Raskel means having two leaders, but he has enough other talents that losing him would be hard on the group.

If we expanded this party, we'd consider adding either a second defender or a second striker. Assuming we wanted to keep the arcane theme, we might choose an assault swordmage, a warlock, or even a paladin/warlock hybrid.

We could also trade out the warlord for an artificer. This strengthens the arcane flavor of the team while keeping a mix of melee and ranged powers in each character.

Originally hired by a militia captain to take care of bandits, the Guardians of Eastfall quickly proved their worth. After eliminating the bandit problem, the heroes remained to protect the area. The next mission will be something even greater, and it's just around the corner.

Instead of using a fixed tactical plan, synergy between various characters enables the party to operate equally well either as a group or in small teams. The Guardians focus on adaptation to solve whatever challenges they encounter.

KRIZZ, BATTLE CLERIC

Role: Leader

By any measure, Krizz is a frontline leader. Although he is the party's only healer, Krizz still likes to fight a little recklessly to get the benefit of his Dragonborn Fury racial trait as often as possible.

Powers: Krizz focuses on Strength-based powers that make the most of his racial ability bonus. He uses *righteous brand* to set up enemies for powerful attacks by Brugar. Rather than choose powers that grant redundant attack bonuses, Krizz prefers options that grant healing, such as *healing strike*, or that apply harmful conditions to enemies, such as *rune of peace*.

Feats: To compensate for his rash fighting style, Krizz has the Toughness feat, and he plans to take Battle Healer next.

Skills: Diplomacy, Heal, History, Religion.

KALIRIA, ENSNARING SWORDMAGE

Role: Defender

Kaliria, a tiefling, anchors the party's frontline defense, keeping monsters from getting too close to Sherran or Hobor, the ranged attackers in the party.

Powers: *Aegis of ensnarement* and *lightning lure* enable Kaliria to pull a stray enemy to the front line, and *booming blade* keeps those enemies close. When choosing her other attack powers, Kaliria opted for those that had interrupts, such as *frost backlash* and *dimensional vortex*.

Feats: Kaliria's regular use of at-will attacks triggers her White Lotus Enervation feat, which in turn softens up enemies for Brugar or Sherran. Kaliria already wants to multiclass into bard, believing it her destiny to tell the tales of the Guardians for many years.

Skills: Arcana, Athletics, Diplomacy, History.

BRUGAR, THANEBORN BARBARIAN

Role: Striker

Brugar is a quintessential half-orc barbarian: big mouth, big weapon. Bonuses from Krizz help Brugar bring his powerful attacks to bear. When he drops a foe, the barbarian uses *roar of triumph* and his Thaneborn Triumph class feature as lead-ins for Krizz or Hobor to drop an area attack on enemies.

Powers: *Whirling rend* lets Brugar deal damage to two foes at once. Even though Constitution is only his third-best ability score, Brugar took *recuperating strike* for the constant stream of temporary hit points. *Escalating violence* boosts the damage his allies deal, and *rage drake's frenzy* maximizes the value of his weapon.

Feats: Brugar likes big weapons, so he took Weapon Proficiency and selected the mordenkrad. He also likes hit points, so Toughness might be next.

Skills: Athletics, Endurance, Intimidate, Perception.

SHERRAN, ARCHER RANGER

Role: Striker

Sherran stands at a distance, peppering foes with arrows and insults in equal measure. The elf prefers to target the victim of Kaliria's aegis (the one enemy that definitely can't get to Sherran).

Powers: Sherran uses *twin strike* to thin enemies out after Hobor softens them up. *Rapid volley* and *hunter's bear trap* backs up her allies in the front, filling a minor crowd-control role. *Nimble strike* allows Sherran to escape when she is pinned down.

Feats: Elven Accuracy helps Sherran land key attacks. She's considering Hunter's Aim to ensure that she always has a clear shot, even when enemies stand between her and her quarry.

Skills: Acrobatics, Dungeoneering, Nature, Perception, Stealth.

HOBOR, WRATHFUL INVOKER

Role: Controller

Hobor is a typically gruff dwarf who has a penchant for area attacks. Although he prefers to stand in back, Hobor occasionally welcomes bold enemies who think they can drop him.

Powers: Hobor opens with *grasping shards* or *thunder of judgment* to keep distant foes at bay. *Armor of wrath* and *angelic echelon* take care of nearby enemies. Krizz's tendency to fight while bloodied brings the extra damage from *avenging light* into play frequently.

Feats: Scouring Wrath turns the target of *armor of wrath* into a pincushion for ally attacks.

Skills: Arcana, Endurance, Insight, Religion.

PARTY OPTIMIZATION

Working the Front Line: The party uses a two-line battle formation that puts the three melee-ready characters–Krizz, Kaliria, and Brugar–between the monsters and the ranged combatants. These front-line fighters focus on blocking positions to frustrate enemies trying to get behind them.

Long-Range Combat: If enemies with ranged attacks get bothersome, Brugar can chase them down, and Sherran and Hobor are more than capable of beating them at their own game. Kaliria also has a few ranged powers to use after other enemies are under control, but if an enemy is protected by terrain, she prefers to approach close enough to use *aegis of ensnarement* to bring the enemy out where everyone else can get at it.

Skill Challenges: The party has decent skill coverage. Sherran's advice comes in handy when an ally needs to succeed on a Stealth check or a Perception check. The Guardians have a notable lack of talent in Bluff or Thievery; Sherran might consider multiclassing into rogue with her next feat to address this gap.

PARTY TACTICS

Line 'em up, Take 'em Down: Hobor is in charge of clearing out minions, and Krizz uses *dragon breath* to help out when necessary. The two strikers take injured enemies down quickly, but tougher foes require more time and usually get a few hits in before finally taking their turn in the meat grinder. Krizz's healing keeps the front line intact; Kaliria acts as a failsafe if Krizz starts acting a little too recklessly.

Big Enemies, Big Penalties: The Guardians of Eastfall particularly excel against elite and solo monsters. The swordmage marks the foe, and Krizz's *righteous brand* and Kaliria's White Lotus Enervation feat help everyone pour on the damage. Although

these big enemies have loads of hit points, the two strikers don't allow them to stick around too long, and the party avoids having to deal with monster powers recharging time after time.

Have a Backup Plan: The Guardians pride themselves on adaptability. If an encounter involves two fronts, Krizz and Brugar keep together, as do Sherran and Kaliria. Hobor joins either pair as fits the situation. With his defensive powers and minor-action second wind, Hobor can take care of himself for a round or two. Splitting into two teams gives the Guardians a solid fallback plan for encounters that don't go as hoped.

ADJUSTING THE PARTY

A smaller group could drop either Brugar or Sherran. The loss of Sherran costs the team valuable skills that might require more precise background choices or even multiclassing for the other characters to cover. Brugar's departure leaves the team with only two melee characters, making the "pair-off" tactic more difficult. Without the barbarian, Krizz would have less use for *righteous brand*, so he might switch to a different at-will attack power.

A larger group should add another leader. With three hard-fighting characters and a current leader who doesn't exactly play it safe, more healing and protection would be welcome. A shaman would be a fine choice, especially since a spirit companion could act as another barrier along the front line.

Trading Sherran for a warlock would retain the group's ranged prowess and give the party the Bluff and Thievery skills it lacks, but at the cost of its Nature skill and its best scout. A bravura warlord might better fit Krizz's style while still providing strong leadership in battle.

The Moonlit Watchers originally met at an inn, although nobody believes them when they tell the story. The members caught the eye of the local baron, and the party's star rose quickly in the region. Before long, the Watchers found themselves hunting an ancient conspiracy. The leaders were successfully brought to justice, but the organization concealed secrets deeper than anyone suspected.

These four characters were created to gain maximum benefit from positioning during battle. Their mobility and their powers granting slides make sure they can always flank.

SHADE, TRICKSTER ROGUE

Role: Striker
Shade deals damage quickly and in large batches. The revenant stays mobile and keeps her enemies from standing where they want.

Powers: For her at-will attack powers, Shade took two options useful either as melee or as ranged attacks. *Disheartening strike* debuffs enemies, and *deft strike* maximizes her mobility (Artful Dodger keeps her from worrying about opportunity attacks). *Positioning strike* slides a foe into a flank. *Trick strike* keeps an enemy off balance until the end of the encounter.

Feats: Eladrin Soul grants Shade *fey step*, just as she had in life. She looks forward to Distant Advantage to allow her to deal Sneak Attack damage with her thrown daggers.

Skills: Acrobatics, Intimidate, Perception, Stealth, Thievery.

HURIN, PROTECTING PALADIN

Role: Defender
Hurin focuses on keeping enemies marked with *divine challenge* and most of his starting powers. However, on a marked enemy's turn, Hurin is usually nowhere around, thanks either to Gan-turil helping him shift away or Shade sliding the creature. So the enemy must choose between attacking another foe or chasing down the paladin.

Powers: *Ardent strike*, *valorous smite*, and *majestic halo* all deliver divine sanction to Hurin's enemies. *Enfeebling strike* hinders those marked enemies, and *bolstering strike* (the extra at-will power Hurin gains from being human) keeps him alive in tough situations.

Feats: Durable gives Hurin the extra healing surges he needs to fuel *lay on hands*. He's waiting until 2nd level to see whether he needs Toughness or can go with Weapon Expertise to boost accuracy.

Skills: Diplomacy, Insight, Religion, Streetwise (through Poor background).

DUSK, PREDATOR DRUID

Role: Controller
Dusk's build and power selection moves the razor-claw shifter toward a secondary role as a striker.

Powers: Dusk's *savage rend* and *cull the herd* fit the group's penchant for moving foes around. *Swarming locusts* encourages enemies to move to avoid granting combat advantage. *Chill wind* also provides useful battlefield control. *Summon giant toad* adds a valuable ally to the combat.

Feats: Dusk uses Ferocious Tiger Form to maximize the benefit of any combat advantage granted by the team's positioning. At 2nd level, Agile Form will increase her mobility.

Skills: Dungeoneering (through the Mountains background), Heal, Nature, Perception.

GAN-TURIL, TACTICAL WARLORD

Role: Leader
Gan-turil, a genasi, serves as the party's leader, both by class and by the player's nature. A diehard thinker, Gan-turil's player knows how everyone else's character can move people around the battlefield and stays aware of any potential flanking situations that arise.

Powers: *Earthshock*, *wolf pack tactics*, *opening shove*, and *lead by example* keep everyone positioned exactly as Gan-turil wants them. *Diabolic stratagem* provides a useful marking option.

Feats: To aid the party's lone defender, Gan-turil took Student of the Sword.

Skills: Arcana (through the Chaos Born background), Athletics, Endurance (through Student of the Sword), History.

PARTY OPTIMIZATION

Working the Front Line: All four Watchers are built for melee combat. The characters' numerous movement and forced-movement powers ensure that they can rearrange the line easily to hold enemies at bay.

Long-Range Combat: Against ranged attacks, Dusk and Shade can respond in kind with their

own powers. Hurin and Gan-turil each carry a few javelins, but they prefer to close the gap with attackers.

Skill Challenges: For a small group, the Moonlit Watchers exhibit excellent diversity, with each party member using a different primary ability score. They lack only Bluff, but make up for it with strong Diplomacy and Intimidate skill modifiers.

Party Tactics

Positional Advantage: The party members use their powers to slide enemies into flanks or to move themselves into advantageous positions. Either way, the damage dealt by Shade and Dusk climbs. These powers also enable the group to control choke points, high ground, and any other terrain features.

A Deadly Double Team: If the battlefield is wide open with no real features to exploit, Gan-turil and Shade can instead work together to set up Sneak Attacks. This pairing has great synergy that lets them quickly mow through weaker enemies.

Beat the New Boss, Same as the Old Boss: Against an elite or a solo monster, Shade stacks *disheartening strike* with Hurin's *enfeebling strike* and marking penalty to suppress an enemy's ability to deal damage until it is finally brought down. Against an enemy that has burst or push attacks, Shade and Dusk move back to use ranged attacks from a safe distance. Otherwise, the party members move into a four-corners formation so that even if the enemy shifts, it remains flanked by two characters. If the enemy moves farther, it takes opportunity attacks.

Stay on Your Toes: Monsters bring their own abilities to the table. When something nasty mucks up the plan, the Moonlit Watchers' flexibility enables them to adapt to whatever the bad guys throw at them. Shade and Dusk can transition between ranged and melee attacks if necessary. Hurin has some healing and Gan-turil has some defending abilities, so they can also trade off or step in for each other if required. When handled well, these overlaps don't make anyone feel obsolete or overshadowed, but they do ensure that whoever's turn it is, the necessary job gets done.

Adjusting the Party

The Moonlit Watchers are built as a tightly knit four-character party; reducing the group size would require serious reconcepting.

If a fifth character is added, a wizard would be a good choice to bring more battlefield control and ranged attacks to the group. Alternatively, a cunning bard would be an excellent fit, using powers such as *majestic word* for added healing and *blunder* to move enemies into position for the others to hit. Another bard would free up Dusk to use powers such as *flame seed* to create dangerous zones for the rest of the party to play off.

They tell us our destiny is already written, and that these runes we bear mark us for future legends. We say our only destiny is the one we make in battle!

The adventurers who would later become known as the Marked Ones met for the first time in the port city-state of Bahar, at the edge of a tropical jungle. Each one came to the city with his or her own secret past, but together they have vanquished many enemies . . . while making still more. Recently, strange, twisting runes have manifested on each character, marking them as the bearers of mythic destinies. But whether these destiny marks portend the heroes' weal or woe remains to be seen.

Unlike the other sample parties, this entry shows the characters at 11th level. Each character has developed in response to the DM's campaign (which features a mix of city intrigue and jungle adventure). When one player had to bow out halfway through the heroic tier, his warlord became a simplified DM-controlled NPC version of the character, and the group added a paladin to have another player character at the table.

BAHAMUS, BATTLERAGER FIGHTER

Role: Defender
Bahamus fearlessly wades into battle against any number of foes, relying on his comrades and his own abilities to see him through. He's still learning how best to coordinate marks with the new defender on the team, since many of his powers mark multiple enemies.

Powers: Bahamus is a one-dragonborn brute squad who can handle crowds of enemies with ease thanks to *dragon breath*, *come and get it*, *rain of steel*, *sweeping blow*, and *passing attack*.

Feats: Armor Specialization (Scale) helps Bahamus feel more comfortable when surrounded by deadly foes. Draconic Arrogance significantly increases the effect of *tide of iron*.

Skills: Athletics, Endurance, Intimidate.

MIDGARD, AVENGING PALADIN

Role: Defender
This dragonborn paladin of the Raven Queen spends most of his time on the front line, standing near Bahamus, Tyrellius, or both. However, as the party's second defender, Midgard can afford to follow trouble wherever it leads.

Powers: *Holy strike* and *valiant strike* offer Midgard a high-damage and a high-accuracy option in melee. *Knightly intercession* allows him to guard an ally from a distance, and *dragon's wrath*—just gained from the scion of Arkhosia paragon path—gives him a useful area burst power.

Feats: Healing Hands and Devoted Paladin boost the potency of Midgard's *lay on hands*, allowing him occasionally to stand in as the party's main leader.

Skills: Athletics, Diplomacy, Endurance, Heal, Religion.

INDULGENCE, DECEPTIVE WARLOCK

Role: Striker
Indulgence carries herself with confidence and mystery. Equally at home with royal company and in cursed tombs, the tiefling never shows any sign of anxiety or discomfort. Tyrellius might see himself as the party's leader, but everyone knows that Indulgence is the true brains behind the operation.

Powers: Indulgence relies on *eldritch blast* as her primary ranged attack. She once used *eyebite* to help her move safely around the battlefield, but now teleportation effects such as *ethereal stride*, *otherwind stride*, and her Misty Step pact boon provide all the movement she needs. Slashing Wake (from her feytouched paragon path) turns every teleportation power into a damaging effect, drastically increasing her destructive output.

Feats: Jack of All Trades helps Indulgence cover the party's skill needs, or to back up the resident expert. Bardic Dilettante has opened up a new suite of power options for Indulgence as she explores her evolution into the party's secondary leader.

Skills: Arcana, Bluff, Diplomacy, Intimidate, Streetwise (from bard multiclassing).

CYRIK, WAR WIZARD

Role: Controller
This headstrong eladrin loves to rain down fire and ice upon the battlefield, destroying as many foes as possible (even at the risk of his own teammates).

Powers: Cyrik brings a variety of attack types to any combat, to ensure that he always has the right answer. *Ray of frost* and *scorching burst* provide a versatile pair of at-will options, with *icy terrain*, *fireball*, *flaming sphere*, and *winter's wrath* contributing to his battlefield control talent. He also packs plenty of defensive powers, including *fey step*, *shield*, and *wizard's escape*, to help stay out of danger when a defender isn't nearby.

Feats: Arcane Fire allows the wizard to mix his fire and cold powers to great effectiveness. Improved Initiative helps Cyrik use control effects before enemies have time to react and spread out.

Skills: Arcana, History, Insight, Religion, Perception (from Eladrin Education). Cyrik provides most of the group's knowledge expertise.

Vahara, Archer Ranger

Role: Striker
Vahara stays well out of melee, sending arrow after deadly arrow into enemies. With her slayer motivation, Vahara's player is perfectly satisfied dealing piles of damage and not worrying too much about the other characters.

Powers: *Twin strike* remains this elf's favorite power, since it all but ensures that she deals her extra Hunter's Quarry damage. Her other ranged attack powers provide control (*hunter's bear trap*) or situational options (*evasive strike*).

Feats: Lethal Hunter boosts Vahara's damage output, and Elven Precision helps make up for the occasional low roll.

Skills: Acrobatics, Athletics, Nature, Perception, Stealth.

Tyrellius Vex, Inspiring Warlord

Role: Leader
Tyrellius leads with his chin, daring enemies to take shots at him (and thereby provoke the wrath of one of his defender allies). He heals comrades before looking to his own needs, due to his belief in his own immortality. (It's a long story.)

Powers: Tyrellius is strong, but not as strong as either defender, so he often lets them do the heavy lifting with powers such as *brash assault*, *furious smash*, and *hammer and anvil*. He saves *war of attrition* for late in the battle, when his encounter powers are exhausted.

Feats: This warlord focuses on simple feats to ease the DM's burden of running an extra character. Improved Inspiring Word help the group's survivability, and Toughness and two Armor Proficiency feats keep Tyrellius alive despite his bold tactics.

Skills: Athletics, Diplomacy, Intimidate, Streetwise (from background).

Party Optimization

Defense and Healing: To avoid having all its healing eggs in a single basket, the party has wisely spread its healing and defensive resources among many characters—Midgard and Indulgence each have healing powers, Bahamus can pick up temporary hit points whenever needed, and Cyrik can escape from danger easily.

Balanced Attack: The group's mix of melee and ranged specialists allows it to handle any threat. Even the specialists have access to nontraditional attacks, from Bahamus's throwing shield to Indulgence's *all the sand, all the stars*.

Skill Challenges: Due to frequent social skill challenges that call upon multiple characters' efforts (such as the gala party held by House Nacato last month), the Marked Ones find it valuable to overlap with skills useful in those situations.

Party Tactics

The Wall of Steel: The two defenders set up the front line, with Tyrellius moving between them as needed. Vahara and Cyrik stand safely behind the armored warriors, launching ranged and area attacks without fear of harm.

Teleportation Tease: Indulgence relies on her teleportation powers to go wherever she wants, leaving damage behind with Slashing Wake. Cyrik also uses teleportation to get out of danger. This mobility helps the characters reorient the battlefield at a moment's notice.

Adjusting the Party

Even when one player doesn't show up, the party's balance means it can get along fine without one character. If you were building a similar but smaller party, you could drop one of the defenders or one of the strikers without losing that balance.

The players in this group expect that one day their DM will decide that running the party's leader is too much work. When that time comes, they will need to expand their healing options, either with heavier multiclassing or skill powers, or by working with the DM to turn one character into a hybrid.

CHAPTER 3

STRATEGY AND TACTICS

SOMETIMES, a single +1 bonus to AC or to an attack roll for a character can mean the difference between living or dying. This makes it vital for characters to work together to keep each other alive.

Not every character needs to be a tank. It's more important for each player to know his or her character's role in battle and to understand how to keep the other characters alive and move combat forward.

To achieve this goal, players must possess a combination of combat strategy, rules knowledge, table organization, resource management, and tactical positioning.

This chapter includes the following sections.

✦ **Tactics 101:** Your primer for playing effectively in combat, including understanding your role, focusing fire, and the importance of positioning and timing.

✦ **Healing:** How to manage healing surges as a resource.

✦ **Know Your Enemies:** How to learn the strengths and weaknesses of your enemies without wasting time or resources.

✦ **Using Your Powers:** How to manage your power selection efficiently.

✦ **Tracking Effects:** How to keep track of conditions, battlefield alterations, and other crucial in-game effects.

✦ **Troubleshooting:** What to do when nothing else is working.

✦ **Tactics in Action–Irontooth:** How to approach an encounter that seems impossible to win.

✦ **Tactics in Action–Storm Tower:** How to beat the denizens of the Storm Tower.

ADAM PHILLIPS

This section provides tactical advice to help you and your party succeed in combat encounters. In some cases, the text also suggests places to deviate from these basic tactics.

Unless things go horribly wrong, you rarely fight on your own. Each of your allies brings his or her own sets of skills and powers to the fight, and many of those powers might influence you directly. To understand how your character should behave in combat, always consider how your actions can assist your allies, and how your allies can help you. When in doubt about what you should do, ask the other players.

ROLE-BASED TACTICS

Each character class is associated with a primary role. This role defines your basic tactics in combat. If you've built a balanced party, you can be reasonably confident that as long as each character plays his or her role appropriately, you'll cover the key tactics you need to win the battle.

Defender: Your primary job is to get the monsters to attack you. By marking a target, the defender not only gives a -2 penalty to attacks, but also threatens

MORE LIKE GUIDELINES

These tactics aren't a strict set of rules that you must follow to play correctly. Being aware of the tactical ramifications of your actions helps you make successful decisions, but you should also consider how your character thinks and acts.

Is your character a brilliant strategist, a commanding battlefield presence, or just lucky enough to end up in the right position at the right time? Alternatively, what common tactical errors does your character make? Your character might choose these tactics—whether positive or negative—deliberately, or because of some sort of code or behavior that he or she follows. It's up to you to decide, but you can make tactical thinking a part of your character, in as subtle or overt a way as you want.

One way to internalize your character's preferred tactics is to adopt a particular stratagem and use it as often as possible. For example, you might decide that your character prefers not to fight fair and goes to great lengths to attack with combat advantage. This, in turn, means that you often need to move around or ready actions to set up your attacks, perhaps even provoking opportunity attacks. Alternatively, your bloodthirsty character might attack only monsters that have already been hit, which helps focus fire but also might lead to pursuing a foe that no longer poses a threat.

the marked enemy with a negative effect—such as the radiant damage dealt by the paladin's *divine challenge*—that triggers when the enemy ignores the defender to attack someone else.

Defenders usually have more hit points and healing surges than other party members, and they often have slightly higher defense scores. More hit points also means a higher healing surge value, which makes healing a defender more efficient.

As a defender, you should stand on the front line of combat, adjacent to as many enemies as possible. Use your marking ability to mark as many targets as you can, and make sure those marked foes stay within the range of the negative effect you impart. For fighters, this means staying adjacent to the marked target, but each defender class can affect marked enemies at a different range.

Striker: You deal damage without taking hits. If you must meet special criteria to deal extra damage—such as having combat advantage, for a rogue—work hard to meet that requirement every round.

But moving to the right place to deal damage isn't the only way that positioning helps you. Since you probably don't have the durability of your defender comrade, avoid placing yourself in harm's way too often. Use your powers and your allies' positions to dissuade monsters from attacking you. Engaging a target marked by your defender is a great way of keeping the enemy focused on someone other than you.

Controller: You spread damage over multiple foes while preventing enemies from bringing the full weight of their offensive firepower to bear. If that explanation sounds a bit complicated, look at it this way: Your defender influences the actions of the foes he or she has marked, which usually means one or two enemies standing near the defender. You get to influence the rest of the monsters on the battlefield.

Use your multitarget powers to wipe out minions. They might not deal much damage individually, but three or four can exceed the output of a single monster of their level.

Use your control effects to prevent enemies from attacking, or at least to reduce their options or potency. A slowed brute standing 5 or more squares away from your party can't hurt you. A dazed artillery monster standing next to your fighter can't shift back and use a ranged attack in the same turn. The fewer attacks your enemies make, the less damage your allies take.

Due to your relative fragility, keep away from melee combat. Standing close to your defender can help, but sometimes he or she draws more enemies than he or she can handle, and then those monsters turn to you, so find a place that limits enemy approaches altogether. Avoid placing your blasts and bursts where they will hurt your allies. Remember, they're keeping you safe.

Leader: You provide your allies the healing they need to stay alive in battle, as well as crucial bonuses and benefits that speed victory in combat.

More than the other roles, you must think about the rest of your group when you start each turn. Recognize who needs healing or a defensive boost. Determine which character can benefit most from a bonus to attack rolls or damage rolls, or which enemy should become the next target of your allies' attacks. Don't think you need to figure all this out on your own—the other players will happily tell you what you need to know if you ask them.

Once you identify the current needs of the group, communicate your intentions and the benefits you grant. Until the other players get used to your powers, you might have to remind each player on his or her turn of the bonuses in effect.

Most leaders can (and should) safely join the defender on the front line. These leaders wear heavy armor and boast good melee attacks. Other leaders, however, favor ranged attacks and should stand a few squares away from the main battle.

No matter where you stand, make sure you can heal the characters who need it. Many healing powers require you to stand adjacent to the target, or at least within 5 squares. Thankfully, most of these powers require only a minor action to use, so that you can move into range before using them and still retain your standard action to make an attack.

Focusing Fire

In simple terms, your characters defeat the monsters by dealing damage. When the damage you deal equals or exceeds your enemies' hit points, you win. But this simplistic approach overlooks a number of key facts about the attrition-based combat of D&D.

Damage can be wasted. When your 1st-level rogue blows a daily power to deal 23 damage, you feel pretty good. But when the DM tells you that monster only had 4 hit points left—or worse yet, that it was a minion—you realize that all that extra damage doesn't make the monster any more dead. In a perfect world, you'd reduce every enemy to exactly 0 hit points. Since that's impossible, settle instead for identifying the right foes for your high-damage and low-damage attacks.

Not every point of damage is created equal. Because most monsters fight at full potency until they reach 0 hit points, only the last point of damage you deal—the one that reduces a monster to 0 hit

FOCUSING FIRE

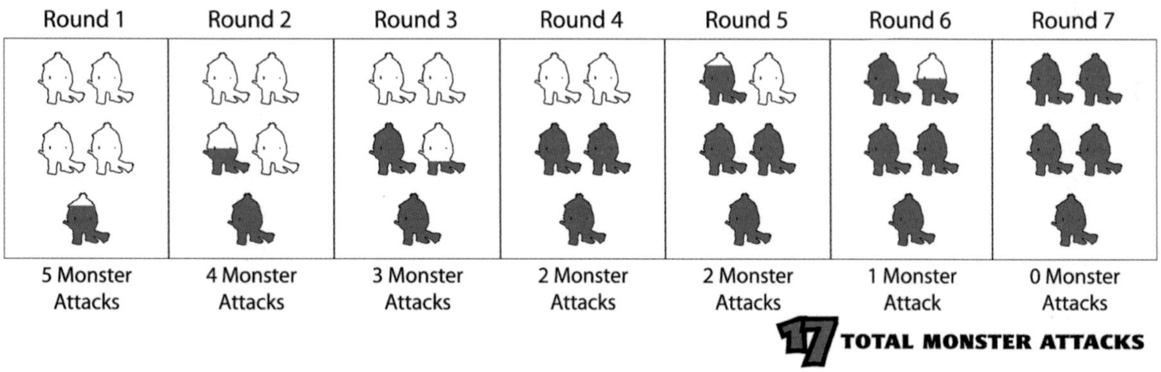

Round 1	Round 2	Round 3	Round 4	Round 5	Round 6	Round 7
5 Monster Attacks	4 Monster Attacks	3 Monster Attacks	2 Monster Attacks	2 Monster Attacks	1 Monster Attack	0 Monster Attacks

17 TOTAL MONSTER ATTACKS

SPREADING OUT ATTACKS

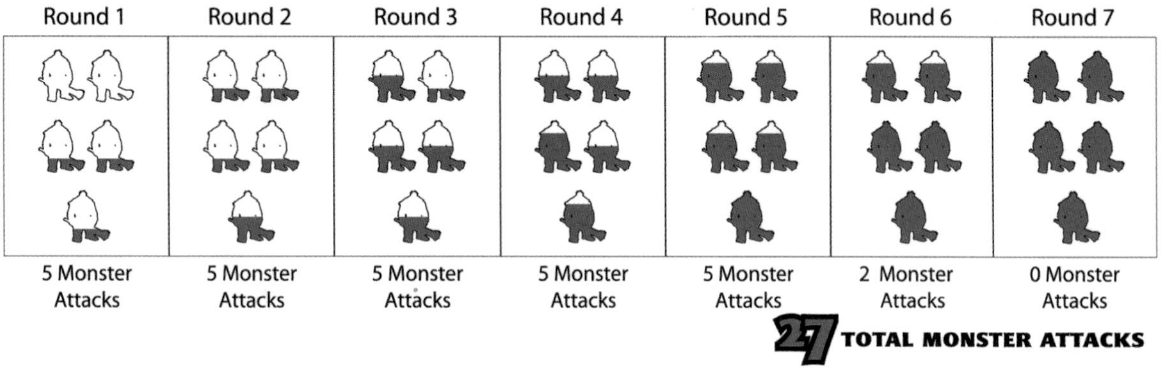

Round 1	Round 2	Round 3	Round 4	Round 5	Round 6	Round 7
5 Monster Attacks	5 Monster Attacks	5 Monster Attacks	5 Monster Attacks	5 Monster Attacks	2 Monster Attacks	0 Monster Attacks

27 TOTAL MONSTER ATTACKS

points—makes any significant contribution to winning the fight. Avoid spreading your damage out too much. Dealing 9 damage to five different targets isn't the same as dealing 45 damage to a single enemy (unless those targets are minions).

Some characters—particularly controllers—can't help but spread their damage out. That's okay—usually, their powers also include useful control effects, and the more enemies you control, the better.

Eliminate enemies. Each round that an enemy remains standing, it attacks one or more characters. When an enemy falls, the number of attacks the characters must endure on subsequent rounds drops. The fewer enemies remaining, the less dangerous the combat becomes for the characters.

By focusing your attacks on as few enemies as possible, you accelerate the point at which those enemies leave combat. It can be hard for some players to leave an annoying enemy alone to attack someone else, but barring some compelling reason to split your attacks, you'll win more battles with focused fire than not.

Assume that your heroes can kill a typical monster with four successful attacks. That means you need twenty hits to win an encounter against five monsters. If each character attacks on his or her turn, your party is likely to score three hits each round (because the average character hits about 60 percent of the time). That means you need about seven rounds to score the twenty hits needed defeat those five monsters.

Imagine the worst-case scenario, in which each character fights individually against a different monster. If each character scores a hit on 60 percent of his

or her attacks, assuming one attack each round, each monster will last for nearly seven rounds. This means that each character gets attacked six or seven times in this encounter, for a total of thirty to thirty-five monster attacks against the party.

On the other hand, what if the characters work together? After one round, four of the monsters remain undamaged, but the fifth has only 25 percent of its hit points remaining. By the end of the next round, that monster is down and another one is bloodied. Now the characters are taking only four attacks each round from the monsters, rather than five—they're already ahead of the worst-case scenario. In round three, another monster drops and damage starts accruing on a third. Now the monsters have only three attacks left. By the end of round six, only one monster remains (compared to the five still standing in the worst-case scenario). Overall, the characters face significantly fewer incoming attacks in the focused-fire combat than in the worst-case scenario.

Of course, D&D combat doesn't always match this abstract example: critical hits, control effects, and other battlefield conditions change the course of individual fights. But the basic principle is sound: If the party focuses fire on one target at a time, it can significantly reduce the number of attacks the monsters make during the fight. This tactic leads to less damage taken and fewer healing surges used by the party, which means that the characters are more capable of continuing through more encounters.

MOVEMENT AND POSITIONING

Once the battle starts, many players ignore their move actions, leaving their characters in the same place for round after round. But being in the right square can significantly increase your chances of success in battle. Positioning is about placing your character where he or she can hit the enemy. But good tactical positioning is also about providing advantages to your allies through your character's position. It can also involve controlling or limiting your enemies' movement.

Try to use your character's move action every turn. Even if walking or running isn't the right option, you can often shift 1 square into a more tactically optimal position. (And if you truly can't or don't want to move, consider whether a second minor action might prove useful.)

FLANKING

Most players quickly learn the value of flanking. Combat advantage is a great way of gaining a big edge on your attacks, and moving to a square where you flank the enemy is the easiest way to get it.

Even if you can't flank a foe on your turn, try to move into position for another ally to gain a flank on his or her turn. If you do this, be sure to tell the other player about it.

Use your forced-movement powers to maneuver enemies into positions where your allies can flank them. Drawing an enemy away from its allies is a great way of breaking up their defensive line and rendering the foe more vulnerable to your assault.

Normally, flanking helps only two characters (the ones standing opposite one another). But if you use timely shifts, three characters can all use flanking against the same enemy. Here's how: Imagine two characters flanking an orc. After the second character attacks, he shifts clockwise around the orc into a different square, still adjacent to the same orc. This allows a third character to move to the square just vacated, thus flanking with the first character. On the first character's next turn, he or she shifts clockwise before attacking, which means she's now flanking the orc with the second character again. Repeat until the orc drops, adjusting your positions to respond to enemy movement as needed.

Flanking can also keep an enemy from easily escaping combat. Imagine that you want to prevent an evil mage from safely using his ranged attacks (or worse yet, from fleeing the battle to warn his masters). By taking up the right flanking positions, you can set it up so that even by shifting, the mage can't avoid being adjacent either to you or your ally.

Imagine overlaying a phone keypad on the battlefield, with the 5 hovering over the enemy. By flanking orthogonally—that is, occupying the 2 and 8 squares, or the 4 and 6 squares—you cut off any opportunity for the mage to shift into a safe square. Every square adjacent to 5 is also adjacent to one of you.

Don't forget that monsters can also flank your character. When you are adjacent to an enemy, look at the square that would provide flanking against you. What's keeping another monster from moving into that square? If the answer is "nothing," consider shifting to a different position.

Similarly, if you can use a power to get an ally out of a flanked position before the enemy can take advantage of it, that's like giving your ally a +2 bonus to defenses.

PINNING THE ENEMY

Use your allies and the terrain to restrict enemy movement options. If an enemy moves adjacent to a wall, moving to a square that places the enemy between your character and the wall prevents the enemy from escaping, because even a shift leaves the enemy adjacent to you. (Think of this as flanking with the wall, as described under Flanking, above.)

Use your immobilizing powers wisely to negate attacks. Immobilize an artillery monster while it stands next to your fighter to make its ranged attacks provoke opportunity attacks. Immobilize a brute or a soldier that stands across the room and watch it fume as its turn goes by and it is unable to attack.

Used in the right situation or combination, other conditions can replicate immobilization. Knocking a ranged-focused monster prone while it is adjacent to you or an ally means it can't shift away before attacking. Knocking a melee-focused monster prone when it isn't standing adjacent to one of your allies likely means its only attack option is a charge (which usually means it can't use its best powers). And if that prone enemy lies exactly 2 squares away from an ally, it can't even charge. Knocking a dazed enemy prone (or dazing a prone foe) is almost as good as stunning it, since it likely uses its lone action to stand up.

MAKE ROOM, MAKE ROOM!

Give your controller room to put down the blasts and bursts that maximize his or her damage output. Learn the sizes of the area attacks commonly used by your allies and keep them in mind when moving around the battlefield. Sometimes a single shift can clear enough space to allow a safe burst.

Bunching around a monster to gain bonuses from flanking helps, but it can also make it tough for your controller to use an area power without harming an ally. Flanking along a diagonal, however, allows your wizard to catch the enemy in the corner of his or her *scorching burst* without risking either flanker.

Also, use those forced-movement powers to herd enemies together into the burst or blast zones. Your controller will thank you.

COVER AND CONCEALMENT

Just as standing in the right square can grant you a +2 bonus to your attack roll from combat advantage, standing in the right place can also grant enemies a –2 penalty to attack rolls if it gives you cover or concealment. Particularly if you're a ranged attacker, taking up a defensive position like this can increase your survivability.

Look for corners, pillars, or furniture to stand behind. In most cases this provides the equivalent of a +2 bonus to your defenses against area, close, and ranged attacks without hindering your powers at all.

Your allies also provide cover against the ranged attacks of enemies. Keep the fighter or cleric between you and the enemy artillery whenever possible.

Most battlefields don't offer many opportunities to gain concealment, but that doesn't mean you can't look for them. If you can find a shadowy corner, a thick fog, or underbrush, you can make it harder for enemies to hit you.

Savvy monsters use these same tactics. When going after a monster that has cover, figure out where you'd have to stand to negate that cover. Assuming it's not too dangerous to do so, move around until you occupy that spot.

Fiddling around with cover and concealment can slow the game down dramatically. Review the appropriate rules (see "Cover and Concealment" in Chapter 9 of the *Player's Handbook*) to help you make quick judgments in battle.

USING TERRAIN

Cover and concealment aren't the only benefits you can derive from smart use of battlefield terrain. When combat begins, figure out where the advantageous and disadvantageous positions are. Where would you most like to stand, whether to gain offensive or defensive bonuses, to limit enemy options, or both? Where would the enemy prefer to stand? And what squares do you (or your enemies) want to avoid?

Difficult Terrain: Standing in an area of difficult terrain makes combat positioning harder, since most characters and monsters can't shift through difficult terrain. If you're an elf, use your Wild Step racial trait to frustrate less nimble opponents. Or use the difficult terrain as a buffer to slow the approach of oncoming monsters. A single square of difficult terrain can sometimes mean the difference between a monster reaching you in one turn or two.

Choke Points: The narrower the front line, the easier it is for one or two characters to hold it. When possible, take up battle positions that prevent monsters from easily bypassing your wall of defense. Look for halls, doorways, corners, pillars, and difficult terrain—anything that obstructs or limits movement can work.

Beneficial Terrain: Keep your eyes open for terrain elements that might provide bonuses or offer extra options in combat. Use your character's skills and your own creativity to assess the situation. Ask the DM if a skill check might allow you to recognize a potential advantage, or if your character could manipulate an object to gain a benefit. Even if the encounter designer didn't take your creativity into account, your DM should be amenable to interesting, creative solutions. *Dungeon Master's Guide 2* includes a discussion on creating ad hoc attack powers from the landscape, such pulling down a tapestry or pushing over an unstable wall. Don't abuse this option; if you win every fight by hitting the monsters with furniture, your DM might wonder why you bothered to choose all those powers.

TIMING

Adventurers have a saying: "He who strikes first strikes last." Winning initiative is a lot like getting an extra turn in the battle. In addition to the benefits of going first, managing the order of your party's actions during combat can also drastically improve your chances of success.

WINNING INITIATIVE

Nobody likes to roll a low initiative result. Waiting around for everyone else to act is boring. But before you spend your precious resources on increasing your initiative check modifier, take a moment to figure out whether that's worthwhile.

As a general rule, it's more valuable for defenders and controllers to go first. Defenders use a high initiative result to move to the position they want to defend. Letting enemies go first allows them to define the battlefield instead. The controller's high initiative result lets him or her make an area attack before the monsters have a chance to scatter (and before allies have a chance to get in the way). In both cases, a high initiative score allows these control-focused characters to preempt the enemy.

The strikers out there are already hollering. "We have to go first," they're saying, "because if we get lucky we can drop the enemy before it even acts!" This claim has some truth, particularly if your striker is highly optimized for first-round damage output (sometimes called an "alpha strike"). But in most cases, a striker acting first doesn't reduce the number of enemies, nor does it substantially alter the tenor of the battlefield. And if you're a melee-focused striker, going first can leave you exposed to enemy attacks before your defender comes to your aid.

One important exception to this rule is the rogue, whose First Strike feature grants him or her combat advantage during the first round against enemies that haven't acted yet. Every rogue should have a ranged option that he or she can use during the first round. Even a ranged basic attack (with Sneak Attack added in) beats getting mobbed by monsters.

Leaders gain the least benefit from going first in combat. Many of their powers are reactive, and they have little reason to charge out in front of their allies, so a leader who rolls a high initiative often ends up delaying anyway.

At the higher tiers of play, most characters need help to keep up with the ever-increasing initiative modifiers of the enemies. Unless Dexterity is your primary ability score, consider picking up Improved Initiative (or a similar feat) to help you stay competitive.

DELAYING AND READYING

Once you establish the initiative order, combat often plays out in a "players' turn, then monsters' turn" fashion, sometimes staggered if multiple monster types are in the fight at wildly varying initiative scores. But just because it's your turn in the initiative order doesn't mean that you have to act immediately. Instead, time your attacks to gain the maximum benefit of the conditions or effects they apply.

For example, if you have a power that dazes a monster until it succeeds on a saving throw, delay your turn until after that monster acts, then daze it. Now your entire party can benefit from the monster's dazed condition before it gets any opportunity to shake it off.

If you want another ally to move into a flanking position before you attack, ready your attack for when the ally takes up a flanking position. That way you both get the benefit of flanking.

Don't outsmart yourself. Unless your DM keeps the initiative order public (or you have a flawless memory), it's easy to forget the exact order of combat. If you try to get too tricky, you risk wasting turns on fancy readied actions or badly timed delays.

MANAGING YOUR RESOURCES

Many gamers have a tendency to hoard their resources, reluctant to use them for fear of needing them more on a later occasion. In fact, for people who routinely engage our minds in exciting power

fantasies, we're a remarkably risk-averse bunch. We'd often rather win a long, drawn-out battle with powers left unused than mount an all-out blitz that might leave our characters gasping for air by the end.

Other players—particularly some newbies—use the shiniest options first. These players forget that sometimes you need to save a big gun for when the battle gets unexpectedly tougher.

Learning how to identify the right time to expend a key resource—such as a power, an action point, or a potion—is perhaps the most demanding skill required at the table. That said, don't feel that the game requires mastery in this area. Unlike a chess match, D&D has too many variables and uncertainties to ever know absolutely that one choice is superior to another. Instead, focus on making tactically sound decisions that carry an appropriate payoff. Making a good decision quickly is much better than spending a lot of time trying to make the perfect decision. Learn a few basic tenets of good resource management, and keep the game moving along; fun and success will be your rewards.

Due to the prominent role occupied by healing, managing the resources related to character hit points and healing surges merits its own section (see "Healing," page 113).

ENCOUNTER RESOURCES

Once you've gained a few levels, your encounter powers form the core of your resources. Many of your tactics revolve around these powers, and your successful use of these powers influences ensuing tactics.

Some players blow through their encounter powers in the opening few rounds of combat, regardless of the threat. These players see these powers only as carriers of damage: An encounter power that deals 2d10 + 9 damage is better than an at-will power that deals 1d10 + 9 damage, so why not use the good one first?

Most encounter powers, however, reward smart tactical use. Even if that encounter attack power deals more damage than your at-will attack powers, does it also apply a condition to the enemy or grant a boon to an ally? If so, ask yourself if now is the right time for that effect. Immobilizing a brute standing next to your fighter has little impact on the battle, since that monster was likely to keep standing there anyway. Saving that power to use against the enemy archer standing in the same place, however, might prevent it from attacking.

Several encounter powers grant temporary hit points, an area in which players display wasteful behavior. Since two sources of temporary hit points don't stack, don't waste the effect of a power that grants temporary hit points on a character who already has some. Instead, use a different power, or wait until your preferred recipient has exhausted his or her current pool of temporary hit points.

You never know when a battle might get tougher than it looks. Maybe that monster turns out to be elite, or perhaps reinforcements arrive. Worse yet, the monster could score a lucky hit and drop your bloodied ally, changing the odds considerably. However it happens, if you waste an encounter power to deal only a few extra points of damage, you might regret not having it when a fight heats up.

All that said, you don't want to end the fight with multiple encounter powers left unused. If you find this happening routinely, examine your tactics and your power choices. Are you being too conservative, letting battles run longer than necessary for fear of spending encounter powers too quickly? Or have you selected encounter powers that rely too heavily on situations that don't occur?

If you've chosen your at-will and encounter powers carefully (see "Choosing Powers," page 31), you should rarely find yourself in a situation in which using an encounter power represents a "same effect but more of it" situation. This makes saving those powers a simpler decision, since you can more easily identify the situation that calls for your specialized encounter power.

ACTION POINTS

Using action points can be an even tougher decision than using encounter powers, since they renew only every other encounter. It seems reasonable to save your milestone resources for a fight against a really difficult enemy, but they can easily pile up. It doesn't help to have two action points when the climactic battle starts, since you only get to spend one in each encounter.

Opinions vary, but many experienced players advise spending your action point the first time you think it can have a significant effect on combat. If you think you can drop an enemy by taking an extra action—particularly if that enemy's turn is coming up soon—it's probably worth it. If you can keep a bloodied ally from falling, or revive a dying comrade, by all means spend the resource.

This advice doesn't mean "use your action point as soon as possible." Dealing another 10 damage to an enemy that isn't even bloodied is a waste of an action point. Using your action point to move up to an enemy without having an action left to attack it opens you up to unnecessary damage.

Use your action point to double up on bonuses that would otherwise benefit only one of your attacks. When the warlord uses *war of attrition*, which gives allies a one-round bonus to attack rolls and damage

rolls, consider using your action point to make a second at-will attack on your turn.

If you accrue additional benefits from spending an action point, then using your action point becomes more like using an encounter power. If your inspiring warlord lets you heal 9 damage whenever you spend an action point, wait until you've taken a hit before you spend it. If your paragon path lets you deal damage to each enemy affected by your Warlock's Curse when you spend an action point, make sure you have a couple of cursed foes when you spend it. Consider keeping an action point power card in your hand that lists the various benefits you gain from its use, particularly if some of these benefits come from other characters.

You can use your action point at any time during your turn. Spending an action point to take an extra minor or move action doesn't sound exciting, but if it helps set up a devastating standard-action attack a round earlier, it might be the perfect way to use it.

Many paragon path features, such as Battle Mage Action, grant you a bonus to attack rolls or damage rolls when you spend an action point. If this bonus lasts for more than a single attack, spending the action point during that turn means you can apply the bonus twice: during the extra action and again during your normal standard action.

DAILY RESOURCES

No decision causes some players more anxiety than the choice of when to use their daily powers. Some of these players labor under the misconception that a) there exists such a thing as the perfect moment for using every power, and b) they'll be able to recognize and take advantage of that moment when it arrives. Other procrastinators falsely imagine that such resources must be saved for the last encounter of the day, since that fight will inevitably prove more difficult than any other battle.

Don't fall victim to either of these two worries. Combat is unpredictable. If you wait for the moment when five enemies gather closely enough for your *fireball*, or for the mists of uncertainty to part and present you with the unmistakably correct time to cast that *wall of ice*, you might end the day with your most spectacular powers unused. Or worse, you might lose a battle because you didn't unleash havoc when things started to get hairy.

Instead of obsessing about perfect situations, think about the circumstances that make each of your daily powers a good choice. The number of squares covered by *blast of cold* means that you want to include many enemies in it. But the power also automatically damages and slows targets (or immobilizes them on a hit). Slowing even a single enemy might be more valuable than damaging two or three, and maybe that guaranteed damage is enough to drop the target. Sure, you'd love to save *evade the blow* for when a brute crits you with a big attack, but if you use it early in the day, you probably go into the last fight with one more healing surge than you otherwise would.

Some players hoard daily powers, fearing that once they're out, their characters will have to drag the rest of the party back to camp for an extended rest. Don't assume that a character without daily powers can't keep up with his or her allies. Unless you suspect a truly grand combat lies ahead, only a lack of hit points and healing surges should keep you from going on.

Daily powers provide your character with a chance to turn the dial up to 11. Sometimes, you need this option because a fight's gotten tough. Other times, though, using a daily power lets you step into the spotlight for a few moments and say, "Look what I can do." Take advantage of those opportunities to shine.

Magic Items

Like action points, magic item daily power uses come at each milestone. Unlike action points, you can safely accrue them over the course of a day, using them all in the final encounter.

That said, think of magic item daily powers much like your other daily powers: Use them when a good opportunity comes up, rather than waiting for the perfect opportunity. If your item grants a reroll on an attack or a saving throw, use it as soon as a successful roll would be meaningful rather than waiting for the most important daily attack power or the dreaded third failed death saving throw.

Make sure that your choice of magic items with daily powers matches up well with the number of uses you expect to accrue. Carrying ten different items with daily powers gives you flexibility, but even at the epic tier you're unlikely to get the chance to use more than half of these items. Conversely, don't carry so few items that your daily uses go to waste. On average, a heroic character should carry one or two items with daily uses, a paragon character two to four, and an epic character three to five.

Consumable Resources

This last category includes resources that don't renew each encounter, each milestone, or even each day. Consumable resources, such as potions and whetstones, function only once and then they're gone forever (or until you buy another one). For the risk-averse player, deciding when to use these resources can prove paralyzing. When can you be certain it's the right time to add ongoing acid damage to your weapon's attacks with a *caustic whetstone*, or which encounter merits drinking that *fire beetle potion*? From reading this section, you know that such certainty rarely if ever presents itself.

Just like a daily power, figure out ahead of time what circumstances would lead you to use a consumable item. As soon as you know that you face a high-AC opponent, chug that *elixir of accuracy*. When minions appear on the board, pull out the *elixir of dragon breath*.

Many consumables use up other resources, such as healing surges or magic item daily power uses. Don't accidentally create a drain on those resources by carrying around too many of the same kind of consumable.

Be wary of spending too much gold on consumable resources. Using the ones the DM places in treasure parcels is fine—in fact, you should usually consume these within a few levels, or you risk them becoming obsolete. But if you routinely spend money on potions, reagents, or the like, you undermine your ability to buy permanent magic items later on. Spending 100 gp per session on *elixirs of dragon breath* might not seem like much, but the gold for ten of those potions could have bought you a 5th-level magic item that lasts the rest of your career.

DEFINING SUCCESS

Standard combat encounters set the players up to win the fights. In fact, the game's math places a significant edge on the side of the characters. Unless your DM runs a particularly difficult campaign, even a single character death in combat—much less the complete defeat of a total party kill—comes up very rarely. When the game system provides an advantage like this to the heroes, what truly constitutes success?

In most situations, the characters measure success by weighing how many daily or consumable resources they expended in the battle: healing surges, daily powers, potions, and so forth. Action points and daily magic item powers used provide another measure, although these regenerate during a day's adventuring, so most players don't worry too much about conserving them.

The faster you go through resources that can't be regained without an extended rest (or by spending gold, in the case of consumables), the sooner your characters must consider ending the day's activities. Sometimes this doesn't matter, but if your characters face a deadline (or if you expect vanquished enemies to be reinforced while you sleep), every extended rest makes the next day tougher.

A successful encounter, then, is one that expends as few of your most valuable resources as possible. No matter the strategies that you pursue, this should always be your ultimate goal.

COMMON MISTAKES

In addition to using the basic tactics described above, be aware of these common tactical errors.

Overextending: When you stray from your teammates, you not only make yourself a target for enemy attacks, you also make it difficult for your allies to support you.

This mistake occurs most often when a melee striker—often a rogue—rolls a high initiative and rushes into battle on his or her first turn before the defender can establish a front line. Even after their characters are dropped time after time, some players attribute the result to a killer DM or lack of backup rather than to their own poor tactics. Players who have the instigator motivation (see page 11) also fall into this trap, regardless of the characters they play.

If you must move away from the front line, try to stay near the edge of battle. Minimize enemy flanking opportunities, and keep an escape route in mind.

Disorganized Retreat: D&D players hate to back down from a fight. Even when the battle starts looking grim, they dawdle and vacillate, unable to fully commit either to staying or fleeing. This inability to settle on a plan of retreat has led to more total party kills than any other lapse of judgment.

Put someone in charge of calling for a retreat. Choosing the player of a leader or a defender character is a strong option, since this player likely has the best idea of how much longer the group can expect to survive. More important than role, however, is the player's ability to assess the gravity of the situation and know when it's time to run. Although anyone can call for a retreat, this is the person you all trust to make the final call.

Once you agree on this duty, respect that character's decision without question. When the warlord says, "Delvers, we are leaving!" you'd better get moving. Don't argue that you only need one lucky round to drop that dragon: Head for the exit and live to fight another day.

When retreating from battle, make judicious use of readying and delaying tactics to ensure that the right characters leave last. Sometimes this means sending the fragile characters out first while the defenders hold the line. In other cases, though, speed matters more than durability; give the heavily armored characters a head start and let the quick ones catch up.

Taking Unnecessary Damage: Any time your character takes damage he or she didn't have to, you give away valuable hit points. Make sure you spend these hit points to gain a useful advantage.

This situation comes up most often when you provoke opportunity attacks. Against high-defense monsters, provoking an opportunity attack to move into a flanking position might be the right answer. But provoking two opportunity attacks to chase down a runaway minion is dumb.

KNOW THE NUMBERS

The D&D combat system rests upon a framework of expected attack bonuses, defenses, damage, and hit points, both for characters and for monsters. Knowing these baseline numbers and how your characters measure up to them helps you understand what the game expects you to accomplish.

The attack bonuses and defenses of monsters are based on a monster's level, modified slightly based on the creature's role and the designer or Dungeon Master's whim. See "Creating Monsters" in Chapter 10 of the *Dungeon Master's Guide* for a more detailed description.

Characters are much more varied than monsters, since their accuracy and defenses depend greatly on their choice of class, race, feats, and equipment. That said, the game expects character accuracy and defenses to average slightly above that of monsters, as shown in the table here. An average character facing an average monster can expect to hit on roughly 60 to 65 percent of his or her attacks, but that monster should hit only about half the time.

Don't worry if your character doesn't measure up to this expectation. Accuracy and defenses rarely increase along a perfect line; more often you see intermittent jumps and plateaus in your accuracy and defenses, as your ability scores and equipment improve. In fact, unless you carefully track all the attack rolls made in the game, you probably can't even notice a difference of 1 or 2 points from the baseline. That said, if your typical attack bonus or defense score falls more than 3 points behind these expectations, you should consider options to make up that shortfall.

Your DM isn't obligated to use only monsters of your own level. Many encounters feature monsters of a higher level (and thus higher accuracy and defenses). A monster's numbers also vary by creature role. Brutes have lower defenses, but deal more damage and have more hit points. Soldiers have higher ACs. Controllers are a little better at attacking non-AC defenses, and use those attacks more often.

Attack and Defense	Character	Monster
Attack vs. AC	6 + level	5 + level
Attack vs. other defenses	4 + level	3 + level
AC	15 + level	14 + level
Other defenses	13 + level	12 + level

Dungeons & Dragons combat encounters are designed to use up the party's resources. The more encounters your heroes have, the more resources you must spend. Of all the resources you use to get through encounters, none is more precious than your supply of hit points. A character without daily attack powers can still provide monsters with a formidable opponent. A character without hit points only provides the monsters with food.

Each character manages hit points in two ways: during an encounter, and over the course of a day. Within an individual encounter, you usually only care about the number of hit points that stand between you and unconsciousness. Many players don't care how many healing surges they have to spend to stay above 0 hit points, because once their characters are unconscious, things get worse in a hurry.

On the other hand, your healing surges measure how many fights you can take before you run out of endurance. More than any other resource, healing surges determine whether your character—and by extension, the party—can afford to risk another battle.

The best groups understand that managing hit points and healing surges is a task for the entire group, not just for individual characters or the party's leader. This section explains how to use those resources for maximum effect.

HEALING OUTSIDE COMBAT

If you have a leader in the party, use his or her encounter healing powers when taking a short rest. This might mean that a single short rest turns into two or three (or more) short rests, but in most cases the difference between 5 minutes of downtime and 20 minutes of downtime is minimal.

To speed play, ask your DM if you can forego rolling dice normally used for such healing powers in place of the average value of the die rolls, rounding fractions up. Most DMs recognize the value of getting back to the action quickly and would much rather say, "Each healing surge spent during this short rest is worth an extra 8 points" than require the player of the cleric to roll 1d6 for every surge spent. The Restful Healing feat is an even better answer, maximizing all such dice rolls.

HIT POINTS AND HEALING SURGES

Aside from your class, your Constitution score has the greatest effect on your hit points and healing surges. For that reason, many players see Constitution as a default third-best ability score (after their class's primary and secondary ability scores). Sometimes, 1 hit point or an extra healing surge makes the difference between life and death.

Most characters start with seven to ten healing surges per day. Defenders (and characters for whom Constitution is a primary or a secondary ability score) tend toward the high end of that range. But the sheer number of your healing surges doesn't tell the whole story; the lower your healing surge value, the higher the cost in healing surges to negate damage. Since a monster's attacks don't differentiate their effect between targets with high surge values and those with low surge values, an attack against a high-value character (such as a fighter) is easier to heal than one against a low-value character (such as a wizard). A big hit on a wizard might take two of his or her surges to heal, but the same attack on a fighter might barely exceed a single surge's value.

USING HEALING SURGES

If you're lucky—or very good—you might have to spend healing surges only during a short or an extended rest. The rest of us, however, rely on healing surges to keep us alive during combat.

Some characters call for healing as soon as they take damage. (We sometimes call those characters "wizards.") In truth, however, you usually shouldn't worry about spending one of your precious healing surges until you're bloodied (or very close to it). Few monsters can reliably deal more than 20 to 25 percent of your full normal hit points with a single attack, so an unbloodied character can expect to survive a couple of hits before even nearing unconsciousness.

If you use tokens or battlefield markers for nothing else, use them to indicate which characters are currently bloodied. It's a great signal to everyone that you could use some help, and it saves a lot of time-wasting questions.

WHEN TO USE SECOND WIND

Your second wind gives you the ability to take care of your own wounds. Maybe you wrap a hasty bandage over the gash left by the dragon's claw, or perhaps you get a sudden rush of adrenaline that lets you ignore the pain. Whatever your character's explanation, the effect is the same: heal some damage (and get a handy bonus to defenses).

In groups that include a leader, most characters view their second wind as a last resort. Unless you play a dwarf, using second wind means you give up a chance to attack the monster, and that's a hard trade-off even when it's a good idea. Rather than ignoring your second wind, though, keep an eye out for either of these two situations.

Bloodied and Under Fire: An unbloodied character rarely needs healing. But if you're bloodied on your turn and you can expect to take at least two attacks before another healing opportunity arises, consider using your second wind. The fewer encounter attack powers you have left, the less offensive output you give up by using your standard action for something other than attacking. The monsters will still be there on your next turn (and if they're not, you're winning).

Surrounded: Even if you aren't bloodied, when the monsters greatly outnumber you it can be a good idea to use your second wind. Not only can those monsters pile on damage quickly, but the number of incoming attacks makes second wind's bonus to defenses even more valuable than the hit points you gain.

LEADERS AND SURGES

Every leader class has its own version of a twice-per-encounter healing power that uses surges to restore health. These powers are drastically more efficient than most other forms of healing surge use, since they typically add extra healing on top of your surge value. Leaders who specialize in these powers can often double the value of each healing surge used. Not only does this let characters bounce back from injury quickly, it also increases the number of encounters you can face each day (because you spend fewer surges to regain the same number of hit points).

Save your leader's healing powers for situations when you need a lot of healing in a hurry or when you can't wait for another option. These powers also provide the best method of getting an unconscious character back in the fight.

LEADER HEALING TACTICS

Each leader's basic healing powers encourage and reward slightly different tactics in combat. Knowing how your leader's healing powers work should guide the party's decisions on positioning, teamwork, and the proper timing of those healing powers.

Ardent: This leader's ardent surge power provides the same healing you'd expect from a warlord, and slightly less than a cleric provides. However, depending on your ardent's build choice, the target also gains an additional bonus lasting for a round. Not only does the timing of your ardent surge depend on when the ally can best utilize the bonus you grant—whether to attack rolls or defenses—but using the ardent surge itself influences the target's actions on its next turn.

EMPTY ROOM STUDIO · PETER LAZARSKI

For example, a newly healed character who has a +1 bonus to attack rolls should turn to a high-impact power, perhaps even spending an action point to gain the bonus to two different attacks.

Artificer: Unlike other leader classes, the artificer actually has two distinctly different healing options. *Curative admixture* provides a good baseline choice, supplying almost as much healing as the cleric's *healing word*. *Resistive formula*, by comparison, puts the decision-making into the hands of the target, who can choose when to gain the temporary hit points granted by the power.

In both cases, the target of a Healing Infusion power need not be the one spending the surge. Instead, the artificer recharges his or her infusions during a short rest by taking healing surges from any willing donor.

During each short rest, use the character who has the highest remaining number of healing surges as the fuel tank for the artificer's Healing Infusion powers. As soon as the encounter begins (or just before, if you can get the timing right), your artificer character should use *resistive formula* on the character most likely to take attacks. The target should leave the power's AC bonus in place until he or she become bloodied, then trade it for a boost of temporary hit points. Avoid relying too heavily on *resistive formula*, since its temporary hit points last only until the end of the encounter.

Bard: If your group doesn't use good tactical positioning, the bard's *majestic word* looks weak compared to the cleric's *healing word*. But if you can take advantage of the timely slide it provides, sacrificing that extra 1d6 of healing doesn't feel too bad.

Use *majestic word* when your bard character can slide an injured ally either away from combat or into a flanking position right before he or she attacks.

Cleric: No class heals more efficiently than the cleric. Coupled with the Healer's Lore class feature, *healing word* restores more hit points per surge than any other class-based healing power. Other cleric healing powers follow a similar pattern, from *beacon of hope* and *life transference* to the ever-popular *cure light wounds* (which doesn't even cost a healing surge).

This efficiency makes the timing of your cleric character's healing powers even more important. For instance, don't waste healing by using *healing word* on a character who isn't bloodied.

Shaman: This primal leader shares the healing provided by his or her signature power between two targets. This reduces the potency normally expected of leader healing powers, but provides more flexibility. A shaman who has Protector Spirit also gets to add his or her Constitution modifier to the healing provided to each target of *healing spirit*, which means the total output of the power rivals or even exceeds that of *healing word*.

Like other healing powers, your shaman character should usually save *healing spirit* for use on a bloodied target. Make sure that another ally is adjacent to your spirit companion before using the power to avoid losing the secondary healing provided. You can't grant this secondary healing to yourself, since you're not an "ally."

Runepriest: *Rune of mending* offers slightly less healing than that provided by an average leader. In exchange, though, the runepriest grants a bonus to himself or herself as well as to all allies within the burst (5 squares). This bonus depends on the runepriest's current rune state (either a damage bonus or a defense bonus), effectively giving the runepriest two slightly different powers.

Your runepriest character should share the bonus to defenses when the party needs a breather. Use the bonus to damage rolls to turn the tables or finish off a tenacious foe. Since the damage bonus applies to all damage rolls, the party members should choose that round to spend their multiattack powers, perhaps adding extra attacks with action points.

Warlord: The warlord comes in right behind the cleric when it comes to basic healing potency (and nearly equals that class once you add the Improved Inspiring Word feat). Like the cleric, the warlord should save *inspiring word* for use on bloodied allies.

The warlord's hidden healing prowess, however, shows up in the Inspiring Presence class feature, which heals a small amount of damage each time an ally spends an action point. Over the course of several battles, these few points add up significantly, and they also give each ally a bit of control over his or her own healing.

HEALING FROM OTHER CLASSES

Sometimes you can't rely on a leader for healing. Maybe your leader has fallen in battle, and someone else must revive him or her. Perhaps your leader is too far away to provide healing, or maybe he or she is out of healing powers. Fortunately, many other characters have options that heal damage or allow the use of healing surges.

Spending Healing Surges: Nearly every class has at least one encounter power that allows the user or an ally to spend a healing surge. Use these powers whenever leader healing isn't handy, or when you don't need all the healing that a leader's power would grant.

Daily powers that grant healing surges are more valuable. Save them to use when the leader has run out of better options, but don't hold on to such powers too long—if the target's out of surges, your power becomes useless.

Trading Surges: Everybody knows that the paladin can use *lay on hands* to heal an ally, but many players forget about the cost to the paladin: one healing surge. A paladin who has a high Charisma who also serves as the primary defender can quickly deplete his or her healing surges. A *belt of sacrifice* offers an even less efficient trade: The wielder loses two surges and the target gains one.

Trading healing surges between characters can balance an uneven distribution of damage. If your rogue unwisely charges into battle a couple of times, he or she might run out of surges well before the defenders. That said, weigh carefully the cost and benefit of a surge trade. Even if the rogue cries out for healing, the paladin with only one surge left might need to save it to avoid falling to the monster's attacks.

Temporary Hit Points: As long as the target is still conscious, temporary hit points are as good as real hit points. In fact, for an uninjured character they're even better, since they can allow that character to exceed his or her normal maximum hit point total.

Temporary hit points typically are granted by at-will or encounter powers. Since temporary hit points go away at the end of the encounter, use them early; ending with temporary hit points still in your tank means you lost more real hit points than you should have.

True Healing: Many players use this phrase to refer to healing that comes without the cost of healing surges. The cleric's *cure light wounds* is the most well-known example, but plenty of nonleader classes offer such powers, such as the paladin's *glorious charge* and the druid's *fires of life*.

Save such powers for real emergencies. Powers that provide true healing are almost always daily powers, which indicates how unusual and valuable they are.

Regeneration: The rarest of healing, regeneration works like ongoing damage in reverse: At the start of the target's turn, he or she regains a certain number of hit points.

Regeneration's advantages over other forms of healing include its ease of use (once activated, it automatically applies every round without need for additional actions) and its efficiency. Regeneration costs no healing surges, but it can easily add up to a huge amount of healing over the course of an encounter and the ensuing short rest.

Regeneration has drawbacks, as well. The healing it provides comes slowly, adding only a few points per round, compared to the burst of healing provided by a surge. Many regeneration effects function only while the target is bloodied and so provide more limited benefits.

Use regeneration effects when you believe the battle will last a while, and when you don't think the target needs a lot of healing right away. A defender who has regeneration can keep an enemy busy with defensive options while slowly regenerating back to health.

MAXIMIZING YOUR HEALING SURGES

To make the healing in your party as efficient as possible, your characters should work toward two goals.

Increase healing surge values. The higher your healing surge value, the more efficient your healing will be. After all, would you rather use second wind to regain 16 hit points or 22 hit points?

Anything that increases your hit points can boost your healing surge value, so the Toughness feat and items such as a *brooch of vitality* provide an immediate boost, as does a higher Constitution. Aim to get your hit points to a multiple of four, so that your surge value doesn't get rounded down.

You can also increase your healing surge value directly with items such as an *amulet of vigor*, a *belt of vigor*, and a *belt of blood*. Consuming a feybread biscuit or a flask of astral mead increases your surge value for 12 hours in addition to feeding you for an entire day. A *belt of sacrifice* adds a bonus to each ally's healing surge value. Enduring Mountain is a solid feat on its own, but it gets even better when your allies also take it.

Manage healing surges as a party. Ideally, everyone in the party should run out of healing surges at about the same time. Most groups stop adventuring as soon as one character runs out of surges. If one character routinely exhausts his or her supply of healing surges before everyone else—or alternatively, if one character always has a few left when everyone else is empty—your party is wasting healing surges that could have helped you fight another encounter.

Explore options to equalize healing surge use among the party's characters. Some classes include this versatility through features such as the paladin's *lay on hands* and the artificer's Healing Infusion powers. Look for magic items that let one character spend a healing surge to provide healing for an ally, such as *gloves of the healer* and *armor of sacrifice*. If all else fails, use the Durable feat to boost the supply of the character who runs out first.

B-BUT... THAT WAS *MY* LAST HEALING POTION...

Also, look at your tactics in combat. If you are the defender and you perform your job too well, you might take so many hits that you run out of healing surges early. Consider letting your mark lapse to allow the monster to spread its damage out to another target. Yes, your defender typically has the best healing surge value, so you lose a bit of healing efficiency this way. However, this lost efficiency is worth it if it means you can take on another encounter before you need an extended rest.

Consumable Healing

Don't rely on consumable items for a significant portion of your healing. Not only does the cost add up quickly (see "Consumable Resources," page 111), but these items usually don't provide enough healing to keep you going for long. They also typically cost healing surges, and the healing provided rarely proves as efficient as a healing power.

That said, every character in the party—even the leader—should carry around at least one *potion of healing* or the level-appropriate equivalent (see below). These potions often function as literal life-savers, bringing an unconscious character back to the land of positive hit points and into the fight. Drinking a potion also doesn't cost you a standard action, unlike second wind.

By the time you reach the paragon tier, the 10 hit points restored by a *potion of healing* can't keep up with your own healing surge value (or the damage the monsters dish out). Start collecting *potions of*

vitality instead; not only does each potion grant more hit points than a *potion of healing*, it also allows you to make a saving throw. As you enter the epic tier, upgrade your purchasing to *potions of recovery*. Having a couple of *potions of healing* isn't a bad idea at any level—having 10 hit points is better than having 0 hit points.

In addition to the ubiquitous healing potions, consider other consumable options that enhance your healing. A woundpatch boosts your surge value for the next surge spent during the encounter, and the herbal poultice works similarly during a rest. Feybread biscuits and astral mead increase your surge value for 12 hours. A *potion of regeneration* provides a cheap way of getting your badly injured character back to half his or her hit points—just drink one after a fight and wait.

TELL US ABOUT YOUR CHARACTER

From about 1985 until 1999, I never played a character.

Don't get me wrong: I played plenty of D&D, but I vastly preferred acting as the Dungeon Master, and my groups all seemed happy to let me.

Then, a few months before the release of 3rd Edition D&D, I joined Monte Cook's new campaign as the elf sorcerer named Vexander. I didn't realize it at the time, but playing Vexander would open my eyes about many facets of the game. Most notably, he represented the first in a long line of characters who, when viewed in the right light, appear identical.

I'm not saying that I've been playing elf sorcerers for the last 10 years. In fact, I don't think I've played the same class twice since I started splitting my time between the two sides of the DM screen.

Instead, what I've come to realize is that all my characters reflect my primary player motivation: to make trouble. In D&D terms, I'm the instigator.

I don't know why this motivation comes so naturally to me. I was never the kid who poked anthills with a stick. (Okay, maybe once or twice.) I didn't show off with bike stunts or mouth off in class. (Much.) Perhaps after long years in charge of running the action, I now grow bored too quickly waiting my turn. Maybe I'm paying other DMs back for the years of defeats I've had at the hands of my group. Whatever the reason, every one of my characters shares a predilection for—and a talent set appropriate to—getting into trouble.

Here are some of the characters I've played:

Vexander, the aforementioned sorcerer. He relied on *fly* and *haste* to move around the battlefield and on *mage armor* and *cat's grace* to keep his AC high enough to avoid taking too much damage, and he blasted monsters with an endless supply of *magic missiles* and *lightning bolts*. His favorite tactic? Opening the next door before we finished off the last enemy, because what's the use of wasting a *lightning bolt* on only one target?

Kalar, shifter ranger/psychic warrior. Trying desperately to play against type, I built this character as a quiet, mysterious fellow who let others do the talking. Well, that didn't last long. Soon he was running all over the battlefield with various psionic powers, slicing up foes with his greatsword or filling them with arrows from his longbow. I didn't realize it at the time, but Kalar's failure to dramatically alter my play style clearly foreshadowed my one-track mind.

Nat Mason, human drunken master. He started as a barbarian, multiclassed as a rogue, and soon learned martial arts, but Nat's uniqueness didn't end with his class array. On a small island that represented the entire known world, Nat claimed that he "wasn't from around here." He never hesitated to punch someone in the face if he thought they deserved it, and despite the party's horror he was always right. Even that time he hit an old lady with a chair turned out okay. If you can't quite picture him yet, think about Jack Burton from *Big Trouble in Little China*. Yeah, now you're getting it.

Antheric, half-elf crusader. Once again, this character seemed to represent a new direction for me. As a heavily armored defender, I wasn't skipping around the battlefield willy-nilly. I was, however, the first guy into the fight pretty much every time. I had the AC and hit points to back up my boldness, and I relished how each hit made my character stronger. *"Come on, hit me! Is that the best you've got?"*

Tyrellius Vex, half-elf warlord. By the time I crafted my first character for 4th Edition, I'd read all about the instigator motivation in the *Dungeon Master's Guide*. These paragraphs made me recognize the thread of similarity that ran through all my characters: I like to leap before I look. In imagining Tyrellius, I embraced that tendency and built a bold leader who directed the party by charging headlong into battle. Once again, I turned to pop culture for inspiration. I needed a strong, charismatic character who believed in himself wholeheartedly, but didn't have a lot else going on in the brains department. A few days before the campaign started, it hit me: I would play a D&D version of everyone's favorite blue-suited superhero, the Tick! The party's fighter quickly became my sidekick—at least from Tyrellius's point of view—and I committed entirely to playing a character who just didn't believe in defeat. The fact that he died in the first session didn't sway him; upon his resurrection in a nearby magic pool, Tyrellius concluded that he'd been sent back to the world by Kord to serve that god as an immortal avenging angel. Tyrellius now believes he can't be killed . . . and so far, he's been right!

Talerron, eladrin swordmage. My latest creation is the D&D version of a hard-bitten gunfighter: the swordmage-with-a-past who's arrived in town to atone for past misdeeds by working on the side of justice. He dives into battle with as much frenzy as any of my previous characters, but uses his many teleportation powers to get out of the worst scrapes.

• • •

In role terms, this list features characters who functioned as strikers, defenders, or leaders. It includes five power sources and at least eight different classes. You probably couldn't put together a more disparate list of characters if you tried.

But to me, they're all the same guy poking the anthill.

ANDY COLLINS taught himself to play D&D in 1981. He joined Wizards of the Coast in 1996, and later he helped write some of the Player's Handbooks sitting on your shelf. Today, he manages the Development and Editing teams for Wizards of the Coast Roleplaying R&D.

To make an informed tactical decision, you first need information. This doesn't mean that you must memorize the *Monster Manual* or the entire D&D Compendium. On the contrary, you can glean much of the information you need using observation and in-game tools.

As soon as possible after seeing your enemy, make a Monster Knowledge check as described on page 180 of the *Player's Handbook*. Since this doesn't cost an action, there's no reason why every character shouldn't give it a try until you've rolled the best possible result (or everyone's had one chance).

A result of 15 or higher (20 at paragon tier, 25 at epic tier) gains you the monster's name, type, and keywords. This doesn't seem like much, but it can hint at potential good or bad tactics. Monsters that have the fire keyword, for instance, often have fire resistance and nearly always deal fire damage; avoid using fire attacks and break out the fire resistance. The *Player's Handbook* doesn't specifically list a monster's role among the elements learned from a Monster Knowledge check, but ask your DM if that's reasonable to add to this list (or if not, to the results of a check at a higher DC). See "Monster Roles" below for more on this important characteristic.

With a result of 20 or higher (25 at paragon tier, 30 at epic tier), you also learn information about a monster's powers. Most DMs won't recite the monster's powers verbatim, but you could reasonably expect to learn power names, defenses targeted by the powers, frequency of use (at-will, standard, or recharge), and special effects or conditions applied by the powers. Use this information to choose the right opponent for the monster; if a monster controller targets Will, your fighter might not be the best one to face it. Find out if any of the monster's powers involves a situational trigger or a recharge; if you can avoid that circumstance coming up, you drastically improve your odds of success.

A result of 25 or higher (30 at paragon tier, 35 at epic tier) gives you the most valuable information of all: resistances (including immunities) and vulnerabilities. This data tells you which of your powers to ignore and which to focus on. Picking the right damage type against a creature that has a resistance or a vulnerability can shave a hit (or more) from the number needed to drop it.

In addition to game knowledge, ask the DM about any particular lore your check result grants you. Most monster entries include information about a monster's habits, lairs, tactics, or allies. Even if this lore doesn't give you an edge in combat, it helps immerse you in the world and might hint at plot points. "I hear that kobolds often live near dragons' lairs, so maybe those rumors of a great winged beast seen around here have some truth to them."

Regardless of the result of your Monster Knowledge check, pay close attention during combat to learn each monster's preferred tactics and potential weaknesses. Pay attention to any hints dropped by the DM. Did your Dungeon Master suggest that the monster didn't seem fazed by your scorching burst? That might indicate fire resistance. Is it readying an attack for an ally to move into a flank? It might deal extra damage when it has combat advantage. Feel free to ask the DM when you think he or she has dropped a hint. Offer to make an Insight or a Perception check to notice a clue, but don't badger—this sort of query can get tedious fast.

Assign a player—a watcher or a thinker is a good choice—to track your party's attack rolls and results against each monster's defenses. Record the lowest attack result that hit each defense and the highest result that missed. Use this information to identify a monster's best and worst defense and choose your attacks accordingly. Even if you find this too tedious (or unhelpful) in battles against standard monsters, fights with elite or solo monsters often last long enough that such information can prove quite useful.

MONSTER ROLES

Just like player characters, each monster fills a role in combat, employing a specific set of tactics to cause as much trouble as possible. The roles appear on page 54 of the *Dungeon Master's Guide*, along with a quick look at how the DM should use monsters with those roles against the players. What follows in this section are guidelines about how those different roles can be countered by the players. (Although the *Dungeon Master's Guide* also includes information about minions, elites, and solos, those words say more about monsters' potency in combat than their tactics, and so those terms aren't discussed here.)

These roles aren't set in stone, though. Part of what makes D&D interesting is how enemies can combine in new and different ways to create more engaging encounters. Soldiers typically function primarily as meat shields to protect a more important monster, but an elite soldier such as a spirit devourer can easily serve as the focus of an encounter. This fantasy world holds a lot of variety, and what exactly you face fluctuates dramatically from one combat to the next. You

A brute looks for something to smash with its high-damage attacks. It prefers low-AC characters due to its lower than normal attack bonus, so keep it away from your controller. Whenever possible, pit your defender against an enemy brute; the combination of high character AC and low monster attack bonus means a lot of missed attacks for the brute. If your defender keeps it locked down well enough, you can even afford to ignore the brute for a few rounds while you take out more pressing threats (such as artillery or controllers). Once you decide to focus on the brute, pour on the damage from your strikers—favoring high-damage attacks, even at the cost of accuracy—if you want to drop it fast. The brute's high hit point total means a lone defender can take forever to reduce it to 0 hit points.

The soldier acts much like the defender in your party, aiming to lock down a character with a mark or a similar control effect. Soldiers often go after strikers and controllers to prevent those characters from benefiting from mobility or ranged attacks. Just as with brutes, matching a soldier with a defender keeps the monster from harassing the characters who need to stay on the move. Soldiers rely on higher-than-average defenses, especially Armor Class, so save your most accurate attacks for these enemies (or use combat advantage to even the odds). Pushing, pulling, or sliding a soldier away from a locked-down ally can allow your ally a timely retreat.

Whether you're fighting brutes or soldiers, consider evading their attacks with mobility and a barrage of ranged and area attacks while you take out other foes. These monsters usually have a poor selection of ranged attack options, so if you can keep these enemies at a distance, you can often negate them entirely. Alternatively, slow or immobilize them to keep them at bay. These monsters want to keep you busy while their allies pepper you with deadly ranged attacks from safety, so the more time you spend fighting brutes and soldiers, the more attacks you allow the enemy to make.

SKIRMISHERS AND LURKERS

Monsters of these roles use movement, trickery, and stealth to gain advantageous position and deal devastating attacks. These creatures favor melee, but many have other combat options as well.

Skirmishers use superior mobility to bypass your front line and attack the most vulnerable characters they can reach. A well-designed skirmisher is the defender's nemesis, often ignoring marks and scoffing at your opportunity attacks. Sometimes a skirmisher goes for the fragile controller, but other times it wants to flank a leader or a striker. Don't let skirmishers gang up on a single character, particularly if they can

and your fellow party members must learn to read the situation and adapt accordingly.

Furthermore, your party should have battle plans of your own, and these plans might include direct contradictions of some of the advice here. If that's the case, your own tactics take precedence.

BRUTES AND SOLDIERS

These melee-based enemies make up the rank and file of most encounters. Both categories of monsters want to get up in your character's face and hit you. But although they share this basic similarity, they have different focuses.

EMPTY ROOM STUDIO · PETER LAZARSKI

flank the character. Many skirmishers deal significantly more damage with combat advantage, so they can quickly reduce an otherwise healthy character to 0 hit points.

Lurkers don't penetrate your defense by being faster; rather, they like to remain undetected and spring into action from hiding. At lower levels, this often relies on the Stealth skill. More powerful lurkers add disguise, invisibility, or other trickery to their repertoire. This deception helps them elude party defenses and gain combat advantage, which often means extra damage dice. After a lurker attacks, it often spends its next turn hiding or otherwise making itself difficult to target (sometimes called "going into lurk mode"). If you don't attack it right away, the lurker becomes much harder to find . . . until it attacks again.

Do your best to pin down a skirmisher or a lurker with control effects. No creature is immune to every condition that would slow it down, so use your knowledge skills and combat experience to find the right answer. Dazing these creatures might not eliminate their ability to attack, but it prevents them from moving into the right position, which can drastically reduce their damage output. Once you get this edge, pour on the damage as quickly as possible before the enemy escapes. Skirmishers have average defenses and hit points, but lurkers can be very fragile once pinned down.

Artillery and Controllers

Unlike most of the monsters already mentioned, artillery and controllers prefer to stand back from battle. These are among the most dangerous enemies because they can either deal massive damage or cause crippling conditions to your entire party through area or close attacks. Their attacks are more accurate than most monsters' attacks, meaning they pose a threat even to high-defense characters.

When you think artillery, think cannons—glass cannons. Although they bring powerful attacks to bear, artillery monsters are very vulnerable. Their defenses and hit points are both lower than average, so if you can bring a striker to bear, these monsters won't last long. However, artillery monsters typically use terrain or a line of brutes or soldiers to ward off attacks. Anybody who can get in an artillery monster's face—pay attention, teleporters—can make its life difficult, so send a mobile party member into the enemy's back ranks.

Controllers use their attacks to neutralize your frontline combatants with hindering conditions, allowing their allies to go after your back row. Characters who get or who can pass out extra saving throws (such as wardens or virtuous paladins) can

dramatically improve your party's odds against controllers. Use those knowledge skills to figure out what you face and what tactics might work best. Unlike artillery, many controllers can operate equally well at range or up close. Despite this versatility, these enemies don't have the defenses of a soldier or the hit points of a brute, so concentrated attacks can take them down quickly.

More than any other kind of monster, controllers and artillery can make your combat miserable if left unchecked. Focus attacks on such enemies as early as you can. It's easier to heal the damage dealt by a brute or a lurker than to erase the conditions applied by a controller, and the artillery can easily focus its attacks on your most wounded character. If you can't address these threats directly, spread out and take cover. Ranged attacks need line of sight, and blasts and bursts need grouped characters to have maximum impact. Even if you can't get to the controllers and artillery, maybe you can make them come to you.

Leaders

Leader is actually a subtype of monster role. A leader has one of the roles noted above, which dictates its tactics and statistics, but it also has one or more abilities that significantly augment, protect, or manipulate the other monsters in the encounter (much like the leader in your party). You can tell that you are facing a leader when it grants an ally an extra attack or move, or when it heals a big chunk of the damage you just dealt. A leader's abilities can be quite powerful, particularly when they apply to all its allies. Taking out an enemy leader should be a high priority.

Brute and soldier leaders fight from the front, often boosting the offense or defense of their nearby allies. These leaders simplify your tactics: Attack the leader with everything you have, then rout its suddenly less potent allies.

Skirmisher or lurker leaders are rare, but a few exist. Focusing fire on such creatures poses a greater challenge than when facing brutes or soldiers, which makes it all the more crucial to take advantage of any such opportunity. Spreading your party out can make it more difficult for such creatures to effectively pair attacks with leader benefits.

Leaders that have the artillery or controller role command their allies from the back ranks. As with any such monster, pressure it with a melee character when possible. Keep it isolated from its allies to reduce the efficacy of its leader abilities.

Fictional D&D characters have it easy.

When the floor gives way and dumps the heroes into a watery pit full of aboleths, they know instinctively how to respond. You, on the other hand, must carefully track your character's powers and other resources to know what he or she can do next. This can be quite a job, even when you're not the one covered in aboleth slime.

Fortunately, the *Player's Strategy Guide* is here to help. When you finish reading this section, you'll be ready to choose the method of keeping track of your powers that works for you. Your character can tread water that long, right?

There are three aspects to using your powers efficiently: knowledge, organization, and customization.

KNOW YOUR POWERS

Some players write down the names of their powers as they select them. When such a player's turn comes up, everyone waits while he or she flips through the books to figure out what power to use. This player does not make the game more fun. Don't be this kind of player.

Yes, your character sheet probably has a box to write down all the powers you've selected. This list can't adequately represent the range of options and details contained in the full power write-ups. Most power entries are brief enough that writing them onto cards (such as the ones that come with the Character Record Sheets products, but index cards work well, too) doesn't take much work.

Depending on your class, you can also pick up a pack of power cards designed specifically for you. Preprinted power cards are available for the powers published in the *Player's Handbook*, *Player's Handbook 2*, *Martial Power*, *Arcane Power*, *Divine Power*, and the FORGOTTEN REALMS *Player's Guide*. Each pack includes a few blank cards to record powers you've picked up from other sources.

The D&D Character Builder provides the best solution for knowing your power options. This program includes every power published for D&D and generates a color-coded card for each of your powers.

If you have a power that has an unusual usage—such as the cleric's *healing word*—consider making extra or different cards for it. For example, the player of a cleric should put two *healing word* power cards into his or her stack (or three at epic levels), rather than trying to remember how often he or she has used the power in each encounter.

Consider making cards for activated effects that aren't class or item powers. Some players like to have a basic attack power card to remind them of that option. If you often bull rush or grab, make a card that keeps the relevant information handy.

ORGANIZE YOUR POWERS

Even though power cards are a great time saver, it can take you a while to sort through a big stack of them to find the one you want to use on your turn. This is especially true at the higher levels of paragon tier and at epic tier, when in addition to three daily and three encounter powers, you've accumulated a lot of utility and item powers. To avoid this, keep your cards organized. Here are some methods that might help; you can use any or all of these organizational schemes.

Effect: Keep your attack powers separate from your utility powers. When you need to know what options you have for killing the monster, utility powers can distract you.

Usage: Group your at-will, encounter, and daily powers separately in the stack. Color coding also helps you easily identify which powers to use early and which to save until you really need them.

Action: Splitting up your power cards by the action required to use them—standard, move, immediate, etc.—can help you fill your turn more effectively. It's easy to forget about minor-action powers, and if you leave triggered powers in the middle of your stack you probably won't remember to use them.

If you have room to spread out, you can put each of these groupings into a different stack on the table. For portability and compactness, try using binder clips to attach each category of cards to the edge of something like your character folder or the container you bring to carry your pencils, minis, and dice.

CUSTOMIZE YOUR POWERS

Knowing which powers you have to choose from saves time, but taking another step can prove even more valuable. Make sure each card includes all the relevant numbers associated with your power: the total attack bonus, the damage it deals (including all modifiers for feats and other effects), and so forth. If you have to stop the game to remember every last bit of damage your power deals, not only do you add tedium to the game, but you also risk forgetting a key bonus. The power cards generated by the D&D Character Builder do most of this work for you, but even they benefit from a little extra attention before the game starts.

Don't forget situational bonuses. If an item you wear allows you to deal 1 extra damage when you have combat advantage, jot that down on each power card. If you have a feat that increases the forced movement of your push powers, record that on all the relevant cards. Situational benefits are the easiest

to forget in play, and optimizing your tactics means remembering every last bonus.

Another calculation that speeds the game is noting the damage each of your powers deals on a critical hit. Why bring the room down after rolling that natural 20 with a laborious calculation of your maximum damage? Do the math ahead of time and write it down on each power card. Don't forget to note how many extra dice of damage your magic weapon or implement deals on a crit, as well as any extra effects created when you score a critical hit.

Consider using your own symbols or color choices to further customize your cards for easy identification. Use an orange highlighter to mark all your attack powers that have the fire keyword, and a blue pen to note your cold powers. Draw a sword on your melee power cards or a bow on your ranged power cards. Snip three corners off your cards, with the remaining corner indicating which defense it targets. Anything that helps you quickly pick out the right power for the situation (but not by overloading you with too much to remember) can speed the game and contribute to your success on the battlefield.

Everyone knows how to keep track of damage—just subtract it from your current hit point total, note the new number, and move on. (Players who instead add up the damage dealt until that number equals or exceeds their characters' hit point total are weird, but we still love them.) But the game has so many more effects than simple damage that efficiently tracking these effects marks a key difference between the casual player and the expert player.

Tracking effects on your enemies provides essential information for making good tactical decisions. If the wizard blinds a cyclops, your rogue character should remember that the cyclops now grants combat advantage. You should also recognize that using a power that turns you invisible to the cyclops would be a waste. If your ally dazes the soldier locking down your wizard character's escape, you should realize that you can now safely move away without allowing the monster to make an opportunity attack.

Similarly, knowing which conditions are currently in place on your allies guides your decision-making. If your paladin character forgets that the wizard is taking ongoing poison damage, you won't use your power that grants the wizard an extra saving throw.

Inventive gamers have devised many different ways to track the various effects that come up in play. This section will help you find the one that works best for your group.

WHY TOKENS?

The biggest advantage of using tokens to mark effects is that it puts the tracking information right onto the battlefield, where you are already looking when you make tactical decisions in a fight. The biggest problem is that it's not immediately obvious how to interpret each of the different tokens on the board, and this problem tends to increase at higher levels as lasting effects proliferate. One way to address this problem is for your group to decide beforehand what tokens will be used for what effects and to record that information, either on a whiteboard that the entire group can see, or individually on each player's character sheet.

Several companies sell tokens for use in gaming. Do a little online research to find the tokens that best fit your group's preferences: color options, magnetic or nonmagnetic, size and thickness, 2D or 3D, and so forth.

WHAT TO TRACK, AND HOW TO DO IT

By now we hope that we've convinced you of the importance of tracking effects that occur during combat. But what exactly merits tracking?

The short answer is, track as many details as your group can handle without turning the game into a bookkeeping nightmare. The following section starts with basic options, then moves on to more advanced tracking options. In each case, suggestions are included for how you can keep track of the details given.

Bloodied: Every group should keep track of which characters and monsters are bloodied. Not only do some characters gain extra benefits against bloodied enemies, but knowing which monsters are bloodied also tells you where to focus your fire. Knowing which allies are bloodied helps your party know who needs healing and who could benefit from effects such as a repositioning slide. Even if you don't track anything else described here, find a way that everyone can remember who's bloodied.

We recommend placing tokens directly on or under the minis of bloodied characters or creatures. Use red markers for their intuitive connection with blood and gore. You can instead use a whiteboard to track which combatants are bloodied, but this doesn't provide as clear a view of the state of battle as a bunch of red markers mixed in among the miniatures.

Conditions: Most of the conditions that appear on page 277 of the *Player's Handbook* merit being tracked in a public and/or visual manner. A few conditions either don't merit remembering—such as deafened— or are obvious to everyone at the table. You don't need to track which creatures are surprised: They're the ones you just snuck up on.

Many players use the same kind of tokens for tracking conditions as they do for noting bloodied monsters and characters. Make sure to have a good variety of bright colors on hand—black or brown tokens often blend in too well when placed underneath miniatures. If you can, assign each color to a different common condition. Rare conditions, such as stunned or petrified, can share a color. Keep a list handy so that players can remember which color translates into each condition.

Other groups prefer to use a whiteboard and erasable markers to track conditions. This can prove easier than remembering that a light green token means weakened and a light blue token means dazed.

3

Even if you use tokens, some conditions merit alternative methods of tracking. Turn a mini on its side to indicate that the creature is prone. Use a token replace an unconscious or dying character to make it easier for other miniatures to occupy the same space. Conditions that last longer than one encounter don't merit visible tracking; you can just note them on your character record sheet.

Target Designation: Plenty of character powers (and some monster powers) incent others to attack a target by applying a defense penalty to the target or by offering a bonus to attack rolls against the target. (These powers are often described as "target designation" powers.) For example, *lead the attack* grants the warlord and his or her allies a power bonus to attack rolls against the target until the end of the encounter. You certainly don't want anyone forgetting that!

Because of the wide variety of effects falling into the category of target designation, most groups need help remembering what's going on. Write out a note card for each of your target designation powers that describes its game effect. (If you fold the note card in half to create a table tent, it's even easier for players to see it in the heat of battle.) When you use the power, place the note card on the table near the combat so everyone can see it. Jot the name of the target on the card each time you use the power so that everyone remembers which creature is affected.

Tokens on or under the designated target's miniature provide a good reminder that something special is affecting that target, but you still need some way of remembering the exact effect. If you have enough of these target designation powers in the game, you can't hope to assign specific colors to each. Instead, pick

one or two colors for the entire category and then use note cards as described above to associate the token and the creature with a specific effect: "Yellow (Fire Giant) = Grants Combat Advantage" tells you all you need to know.

Instead of note cards, you could use the power card that created the effect, but this has a lot of text that the other players don't need to know (and you probably don't want to fold your power cards into table tents).

Zones and Terrain: Any area of the battlefield meaningfully altered by a power or another effect should be represented in some way so that the players and the DM remember its presence. This includes zone powers such as *swarming locusts* as well as battlefield alterations such as a pile of books dumped off a shelf to create difficult terrain.

Two-dimensional tokens make the best markers for zones, though if you use an erasable battlemat you could draw the effect right onto the battlefield. Movable zones make the drawing option more cumbersome, since they require a lot of erasing and redrawing. You don't need a token in every square of the zone. Just mark the corners of the effect, and record somewhere what effect corresponds to those tokens (just like you did with target designation effects).

Certain types of area, such as a blast 3 or burst 2, come up often enough that you might want to prepare a more easily reusable and removable solution. Make your own by bending some reasonably stiff wire or twisting together the ends of some pipe-cleaners. Less craft-minded players can cut out cardstock or plastic in the right shape, but using an outline rather than a solid square makes it easier to lay the area down around minis.

Ally Benefits: Many powers grant one or more of your allies a temporary or a lasting benefit, such as the bonus to attack rolls and damage rolls from *war of attrition*. Keeping track of which benefits are in effect helps everyone maximize their value.

Tokens don't work very well for tracking these effects. Most benefits don't last long enough to merit token use, and there are enough of them that no one can remember from just a token what the effect is. Instead, use note cards as described under "Target Designation," above, handing the appropriate card to each player whose character is affected.

Ongoing Damage: Tracking ongoing damage on the battlefield doesn't help players or DMs remember to apply that damage at the start of the affected creature's turn. Instead, note this on your character sheet, near the monster's stat block.

Saving Throws: Players frequently forget to roll saving throws at the end of their turns. Whenever your character receives an effect that can be ended by a saving throw, use some physical reminder of the saving throw to place in front of you on the table. You can use table tents, oversized tokens, fluorescent note cards, or anything else that calls attention to its presence on the table. (If the object includes a reminder of the effect, so much the better.)

USING A WHITEBOARD

If your gaming area has room for an easel, consider setting up a large whiteboard—or chalkboard, if you're feeling 19th-century—to track various conditions and effects. (Some groups are fortunate enough to play in rooms with permanently mounted whiteboards. If you have the means, we highly recommend it.)

A whiteboard has the advantage of immense flexibility. You can write anything at all, including which characters are bloodied and how much damage you've dealt to various monsters, without worrying about elaborate color-coding or memory tricks. In combat, it can be used to track conditions, hit points, initiative order, or other effects. Outside combat, it's great to list your current quests, adventure leads, NPC names, or any other information everyone needs to see. It's also visible to everyone at the table, even the guy sitting way down at the end who can't see the battlefield very well.

One disadvantage to a whiteboard is that it can make it tougher to know which effects correspond to particular figures on the battlefield. Looking at the miniatures, then to the whiteboard to figure out which conditions are affecting the ogre, then back to the battlemat takes time and loses some of the simplicity of tokens.

One DM we know uses coaster-sized discs with a small pad of sticky notes affixed to each disc. When a monster deals a save-ends effect to a character, the DM writes the effect on the top sticky note and hands the disc to the player. When the player saves, he or she discards the top sticky note and hands the disc back to the DM.

ALTERNATIVES TO TOKENS

Some players don't like sliding 2D tokens underneath miniatures. Repeatedly picking up miniatures can easily mess up the battlefield, particularly any of the players suffer from fumble-fingers. Try one of these alternatives instead.

Loops: Any small, colorful loop—such as a rubber band, a twist-tie, or the ring left behind when you open a plastic bottle—can dangle off a miniature's arm or weapon, removing the need to pick the miniature up and put it down every time you place a token. Some players find these detract from the verisimilitude of the game; seeing an ogre with a half-dozen differently hued loops hanging around its neck can definitely break that suspension of disbelief.

Clips: Paper clips can usually be attached to minis, but binder clips or alligator clips are better. Use colorful clips that show up on the battlefield. Clips have all the same advantages and drawbacks as loops, however, they can damage painted minis.

Stickers: Particularly enterprising players craft specialized stickers to denote conditions and effects, placing these directly on the miniatures. Check out http://www.penny-arcade.com/2009/3/9/ to see an example. For painted miniatures, small sticky notes can do the trick as well and without damaging the paint.

WHO DOES THE WORK?

Too many players assume that it's the DM's job to remember everything going on at the table. Not only is this assumption lazy, but it also encourages players to ignore the details of combat.

Don't rely entirely on your DM to keep track of the effects in place on characters and monsters. Even the best-organized DM won't remind every character on his or her turn which monsters are dazed, which are bloodied, and which are immobilized, and repeatedly stopping the game to ask such questions grinds combat to a halt.

Help the DM out by assigning a specific player to place condition tokens on the battlemat, or to keep the whiteboard up to date.

Having problems in combat? Relax; it happens to all of us once in a while, even the experts.

This section provides advice on some of the most common issues encountered by even the most experienced D&D players.

You Can't Hit

No party is immune to occasional bad luck, but if you're having miss-fests night after night, it's time for a tune-up.

First, check your party optimization. The problem might be that you aren't achieving the attack bonuses that the system expects from characters of your level, as outlined in "Tactics 101," page 104. If that's true, try to invest in more accurate weapons and in better magic weapons or implements right away. Check "Level Up!," page 44 for information on retraining feats and powers for a better batting average as soon as you can.

If your attack modifiers are in the right range, ask your DM if he or she has been using an unusually high number of soldiers, or monsters significantly above your level (all of which have higher than expected defenses). Even with the right attack modifier, a 5th-level character fighting 8th-level soldiers will miss more often than he or she hits.

Once you've ruled that out (or if your DM prefers not to share that information), consider tracking your natural attack rolls for a few encounters. Some players experience long strings of low attack rolls, and even whole parties can have off nights. Just because you've rolled three natural 1s in a row doesn't mean you're guaranteed to get a good result on the next roll.

Let's assume you've eliminated all these possibilities, and you still feel the need to improve your accuracy. Now you must turn to smarter tactical play to solve your problem. Start by maximizing the frequency of your attacks made with combat advantage. The +2 bonus to attack rolls it provides makes a big difference, so work with the other players to set up flanks, and collect powers that create combat advantage by dazing, restraining, and knocking down enemies. Find powers that grant temporary bonuses to attack rolls and penalties to enemy defenses. (Leaders have plenty of these, but every class has a few.) Grab feats, items, and other options that provide circumstantial bonuses to attack rolls. Stacking up these buffs and debuffs can quickly and dramatically improve your party's accuracy.

Even the most accuracy-optimized party can't guarantee high attack bonuses every round, so take advantage of these bonuses by using your best powers

TELL US ABOUT YOUR CHARACTER

During the Armageddon Wars of the Orsus Empire, no greater builder of warforged existed than Thom Widdershins.

Model 33 was to be his crowning achievement, a tribute to the god he loved, Kord. The fates, and an assassin from the Bronzeshell clan, had other plans and Thom was killed before he could perform the activation ritual on Model 33.

The assassin took the warforged as a trophy and hid it away in a cave with the rest of his prizes. The wars soon ended, and several years later the assassin's cave was taken by a young black dragon named Arithemius. The assassin's treasure, including Model 33, became the start of the dragon's hoard.

Five thousand years passed. A great apocalypse destroyed seventy percent of the surface world, driving most of the surviving population into the Underdark. The knowledge of how to create warforged was lost; even their existence was forgotten.

Arithemius, now ancient, was found by a group of adventurers searching for a way out of the Underdark. The group parleyed with the dragon and received a single gift from his hoard. Following the dragon's instructions, the party activates the warforged. Etched into its breastplate is

the cryptic code "(t.w.) 33-K" written in a dead language. The warforged does not know its name, only its purpose, and so the adventurers call it Tweek.

When Widdershins created Tweek, he implanted memories of a time and a kingdom that no longer exists, even in the oldest tales. Tweek the invoker lives to bring the word and glory of Kord to those around it. It tells the stories of the greatness of the Orsus Empire and the massive battles that took place during the Armageddon Wars.

Tweek stands a full three feet tall (Thom Widdershins was a gnome, after all). It wears blood-red raiments emblazoned with the fist, bolt, and sword of Kord. Calling upon its angelic powers, Tweek spreads a shining set of metal wings with which it can slash all those who surround it. All those who see it in battle marvel at the wonder and glory of such a perfect creation and can only cower in fear at the might of Kord.

DON FRAZIER dreamed of one day becoming a prophet to the stars, an astronaut, and a game designer for TSR. Even though he started playing D&D thirty-two years ago and has enjoyed every edition of the game, he is NOT a grognard. He gleefully spends his days as a code monkey working in the Wizards of the Coast Digital Studio on D&D Insider.

in those rounds. Save your at-will attack powers for rounds without bonuses; even if you miss, you don't lose as much as if you'd missed with an encounter power.

NOT ENOUGH HEALING SURGES

If you routinely run out of healing surges after only a couple of encounters, finishing adventures in a timely manner can prove difficult.

Once again, your first step is to check the numbers. If your defenses lag behind the expected values described in "Tactics 101," you're probably taking more hits than you should. More hits means more damage, which means more surges spent per battle. To bridge any gap you find, add better armor to your wish list and retrain some feats to boost defenses. Consider using your next ability score increase to improve an odd-numbered score to an even-numbered score if that will increase a defense.

Maybe you've been facing particularly deadly monsters. Ask your DM if he or she has been favoring high-level foes, or if he or she feels that the brutes and lurkers—traditionally high-damage enemies—have been unusually effective lately.

Even with appropriate defense scores and enemies, however, inefficient use of healing surges can drastically increase the number you need to bounce back after a fight. Review "Maximizing Your Healing

Surges," page 116, to see if you can make each surge worth more. Adding a leader to your party—either by replacing an existing character or through multiclassing or the hybrid rules—can kick up your healing surge efficiency. Temporary hit points, regeneration, and so-called "true healing" (page 116) can also lessen your reliance on healing surges.

Don't overlook the value of improving your group's tactics to reduce the number of attacks the enemies make each round. Look for ways to use tactical positioning and features of the battlefield such as walls and bottlenecks to restrict how many enemies can pile on you at once. Even if you can't entirely deny attacks, at least make the enemy work hard to hit you by adding penalties. See "Cover and Concealment" and "Using Terrain," page 108, for suggestions.

Last, remember the immortal advice: "The best defense is a good offense." Killing monsters faster reduces the number of attacks you take. Boosting your damage output and concentrating attacks on individual enemies (see "Focusing Fire," page 105) often provides the best way of conserving healing surges. A dead monster—with a few exceptions—can't hurt you.

COMBAT GETS BORING

Sometimes a fight lasts so long that none of the combatants have anything but at-will powers left. The outcome might even be a foregone conclusion, and

DISCUSSING PROBLEMS WITH YOUR GROUP

Some basic advice applies to many problems you might encounter while playing the game.

Say something. Each player has a responsibility to help everyone at the table have fun, and that everyone includes you. If something makes you unhappy, you're not doing your fellow players, your DM, or yourself any favors by suffering in silence. If you speak up, you might find that others share your concern and are grateful you initiated an opportunity to fix it together.

Use personal conversations. Complaints through email or instant messenger often come off poorly, and even a phone call can't replace a face-to-face chat. Whenever possible, discuss problems in person.

Include the right people. Sometimes everyone needs to be present when you discuss a problem. But if you're concerned about a particular person at the table, bringing that up with the whole group puts that person on the defensive. When in doubt, always start with a one-on-one chat with your DM. That said, avoid making one person feel left out of the discussion. If four of the five players get together to talk about a campaign problem, that fifth player might feel frustrated and ostracized.

Be polite and tactful. Don't yell, don't be rude, and don't accuse other players of causing problems. Your dis-

cussion will go better if you take care to talk only about your own feelings and experiences and avoid making generalizations, assigning blame, or bringing in other unrelated issues from the past.

Be open to opinions. Maybe other players don't agree with your observations, or aren't concerned about the issue you raise. Recognize that some of the problem might be your fault. It is possible that your behavior, expectations, or approach is helping create the situation you dislike. If you're ready to own up to and address the ways in which you're not perfect, you'll find that others are a lot more likely to do the same.

Be realistic. Even if you take the most reasonable approach, you might discover that others aren't willing to listen to your feelings or to cooperate in finding a resolution that makes everyone happy. Don't give up right away, but don't be afraid to walk away and find a new group. If you've made a reasonable effort but aren't getting support in addressing the things that are making you unhappy, there's nothing wrong with finding other players who enjoy the same things you do. When you say good-bye, let everyone know it's nothing personal, and see if you can find nongaming opportunities to spend time with your friends from your old group.

yet you still slog on trading attacks. This problem can have many causes, each with its own solution. We'll examine a few of the most common reasons for long, drawn-out battles.

Poor Accuracy: As the number of hits scored each round drops, the length of battle increases. We've already covered accuracy problems above (see "You Can't Hit"), so look there for tips. Monsters with high defenses create the same problem, so ask your DM to compare the average enemy's defenses to the expected numbers on page 112.

Not Enough Damage: If you lack strikers, or if you've optimized your party for defense, fights can drag even when your accuracy is on target. Pick up some feats or items to boost your damage output, and ask your DM to go easy on the brutes, elites, and solo monsters.

Foregone Conclusion: A party that focuses its fire effectively can find that the last couple of rounds of combat—with five characters facing a single foe—lack tension. Everyone knows that the heroes will win, and nobody expects the monster to deal much more damage before it drops. Offer the monster the option of surrender, or suggest to your DM that you fast-forward to the inevitable end. If he or she balks, offer to measure the resources expended in those last couple of rounds and report back on their insignificance. Consider a compromise, in which one character gives up a healing surge to represent the damage you would have taken finishing the fight.

Combat Lasts Too Long

The "Combat Gets Boring" section describes the boredom of combat with too many rounds, but just playing slowly can make a five-round battle feel like ten. If you routinely spend more than 10 minutes waiting between your character's turns, your group needs a timing tune-up. Figure out what takes players so long to finish their turns, and then find the right solution.

Does your wizard dither over her power cards, never able to find the right spell to cast? Check out "Know Your Powers," page 122, for organizational assistance.

Does the fighter take forever to roll and add up his damage? Try rolling your attack and damage simultaneously. "Customize Your Powers," page 123, also provides useful tips to speed damage calculation.

Do you argue over which monster got dazed last round? Go back and reread "Tracking Effects," page 124.

Maybe some of the players have selected powers or feats that offer too many options or complications. It's easy to accumulate a plethora of feats and items that offer situational benefits, complex attack powers, and other elements that overwhelm you with

information. Politely suggest to such a player that he or she might consider retraining to simpler but no less effective choices.

Your Teammates Don't Use Tactics

Some players can't help but see every missed opportunity to take a flanking position or use exactly the right power as a failure to play the game properly. But the game aims to entertain many different types of players. Remember that quiz on page 12 about player motivations? It's a good bet that not everyone scored the same way that you did.

Don't sacrifice your own ability to have fun so that other players can swap stories about the fascinating diplomat you just met. After the battle, ask the other players if they're willing to listen to a couple of small, helpful suggestions aimed at improving the group's tactics. Assuming they agree, keep your proposals to a minimum: At this point, one or two new tactics is plenty to offer. If these ideas take hold, point out sections of this book that they can review for more. (Better yet, buy them their own copies!)

As part of this discussion, ask for some tips from them on how you can improve your own performance in the areas they care about. D&D is about cooperation, so you shouldn't ask for others to change if you're not willing to accept similar feedback.

When offering tactical advice during a battle, use it as an opportunity to get into character. If you're frustrated by seeing poor tactics, think about how your character feels; after all, his or her life is at risk. Expressing your frustration in your character's voice can help the other players to not take it personally, and it also builds the image of your character as someone who's knowledgeable about tactics and driven to secure success in battle. Don't overdo it, though; a character who constantly complains about bad tactics tends to get left at the inn when the next adventure starts.

If none of this advice raises the party's tactical sophistication to the level you desire, approach your DM to see if you could run a few games. Playing the monsters is satisfying because you have sole control over the tactics for their entire side, and it's challenging to take a team of underdogs against an opponent who's the odds-on favorite to win. After you demonstrate the importance of sound teamwork by making the heroes sweat to defeat a clearly inferior but well-coordinated force, they might be inspired to step up their own game.

Originally released in May 2008 (and now available as a free download at www.wizards.com/dnd), *Keep on the Shadowfell*™ by Mike Mearls and Bruce R. Cordell not only demonstrates a classic dungeon-crawl-style adventure but also provides a great primer in the fundamentals of the game. One encounter in particular, the notoriously difficult fight against the goblin chieftain Irontooth, taught many unprepared parties the lesson, "Run away from a superior force," or for those who were slow to pick up on that one, "The game is still fun even when your character dies." The Irontooth encounter can also demonstrate how even a 1st-level party can win against seemingly impossible odds by using cooperative tactics.

If you've never enjoyed this archetypical modern gaming experience, why not ask your DM to run it for your group before reading this section? If you've already experienced it as a player, read pages 26-29 of the adventure to appreciate it from the DM's perspective. What follows is a guide to how you might approach the Irontooth encounter, using the sample party of the Spellblades (see page 94) as an example.

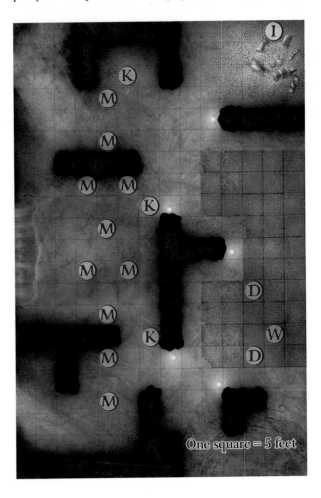

One square = 5 feet

Good tactics begin before you roll initiative. To improve your chances against Irontooth, you need to catch him by surprise. That means making sure the kobolds outside his cave don't warn him of your presence. Sure, if you rush in and attack, you might get lucky and kill the kobold slinger before he can sound the alarm. But trusting to luck is never the best strategy.

The encounter setup signals that you're about to bump into some monsters by the waterfall. Most well-designed parties include a character who can succeed on the Perception check to get that warning, so why not use him or her to sneak up and observe the kobolds' comings and goings? It shouldn't take long to figure out that even more of the lair is a cave beyond the waterfall. That information defines your strategic goal of keeping the inner group from learning that you're wiping out their brethren, so that you can afford to take a short rest before crossing swords with the second group.

Unfortunately, none of the Spellblades are good at Stealth, so they choose a different approach that plays to their strengths. When they hear the kobolds ahead, they fade back into the woods to discuss options. Taellaen and Ruel argue over tales of kobold hunting practices (making History checks). After Raskel and Taellaen use Perception to find a frequently used kobold trail, Delaia uses Nature to set up an ambush site. Then the party lies in wait for a small group of kobolds to wander past. After springing the trap, it leaves one kobold alive and uses Intimidate to learn more about the kobold forces guarding the lair. Whether the captive cravenly tells all about Irontooth's gang or blusters about how he'll be avenged by all his friends in the caves, the Spellblades have learned what they need to know.

Don't be afraid to go on the defensive. Sometimes you need to rush in and take the fight to the foe hard and fast. Time might be critical because of a strategic goal, such as preventing a looming threat or preempting special enemy abilities that make them stronger the longer you delay. And if the battlefield offers a positional advantage such as cover, you voluntarily accept the short end of the stick each round that you put off taking it over for your own use.

The kobold caves, however, reward the opposite behavior. The faster you advance into Irontooth's lair, the more ways his forces can surround you. The kobold advantage comes from their numbers. You can't remove this advantage right away, so you must play a defensive game. Deny them the weight of numbers by staying together and occupying choke points. Hold steady until enemy attrition evens the odds.

Also, because you are a 1st-level party, Irontooth and his friends are just plain tougher than you are. Be ready to make a clean exit if the dice turn against you. By advancing cautiously, you can maintain your line of retreat.

Once they enter the inner lair, the Spellblades decide the entry chamber south of the waterfall offers the most defensible position. Ruel stands in one entrance, while Taellaen occupies the other. They can even stand adjacent to one another, reducing enemy flanking opportunities.

Meanwhile, Delaia and Zulot can stand safely back and launch their spells at the enemies massing behind the warriors. Kobolds moving past the front line to get to these party members provoke opportunity attacks, and Raskel can clean up anything that causes too much trouble. If things get bad quickly, the heroes can fall back through the secondary exit behind them.

This chamber will get claustrophobic if kobolds circle around the outside and start coming in the exit, but by that point the Spellblades should have thinned out the initial mob enough to break through into the chambers to the north, where they can establish a new line of defense.

Deny enemy strengths and capitalize on weaknesses. No single strategy can prevail in every encounter. You must adapt your tactics to the specific capabilities of your enemy, and to do that you need to know what those capabilities are. Use monster knowledge checks and previous experiences to build your strategy.

Once the battle begins, keep your eyes and ears open. Notice how the enemies are armed, where they position themselves, and what they do. Whenever something unusual occurs, ask your DM if your character noticed any details about what just happened. Clues in the way the DM describes things can help you figure out what situation the monster needs to use that special ability and allows you to work to keep it from happening.

From previous encounters in *Keep on the Shadowfell*, the Spellblades have learned that kobolds are shifty. Delaia can shut this down briefly with *icy terrain*, and she might even consider including an ally in the burst if it can keep kobolds from shifting past the front line. The Spellblades know that minions are plentiful among kobolds, so blasts and bursts such as Zulot's *dragon breath* should prove useful.

Questions about the enemy's gear reveal that the denizens of the inner cave lack plentiful ranged attacks, so kobolds not engaged in melee offer little to

no threat. The dragonshields must stay close to make their marking ability meaningful, and there's no easy way for the skirmishers to get combat advantage with ranged attacks. The party's defensive strategy takes advantage of this weakness. Knowing that the kobolds' powers work best up close reinforces the characters' decision to stand fast and force the enemy to bring the battle to them.

The inner caves include some foes new to the Spellblades—the wyrmpriest and Irontooth himself— so the players quickly call for monster knowledge checks as soon as they see these enemies. Once they bloody Irontooth, his change in tactics should be evident, and the players should adjust their own tactics to take advantage of this.

Spread it around. Victory comes when many jobs are performed well. Characters might specialize in a few different jobs, but in a party that works well together, everyone contributes whatever they can to getting each job done. This teamwork isn't as important in an easy encounter, but when powerful enemies such as Irontooth turn up the heat, they make survival so challenging that every job needs all the extra hands it can get.

Good tactics don't stop the Irontooth encounter from being an extremely difficult fight, and during the course of the long battle, every Spellblade relies on assistance from the rest of the party. For example, as the defender it falls to Ruel to soak up as many hits as possible. But if he performs this job too well, the party might lack the healing powers to keep him up and fighting. During the encounter, both Taellaen and Raskel make sure to take an attack that might otherwise have gone against Ruel, spreading the damage more evenly across the party. Even Zulot and Delaia can afford to get hit a couple of times, particularly by the minions.

It was early 2008 when Mike Krahulik and Jerry Holkins of Penny Arcade fame joined Scott Kurtz, the creator of the Player Versus Player web comic, to play some D&D, founding the group that would come to be known as Acquisitions Incorporated. The podcasts of their adventures were so well received that a sequel series came out the following February, adding author and actor Wil Wheaton to the team. The adventure they played for this second session was *Storm Tower*, written by Dungeon-Master-for-the-Stars Chris Perkins just for this occasion. If you weren't lucky enough to listen the first time, don't fret. These podcasts are available for free on iTunes and from www.wizards.com, so check them out! The full adventure is also now part of the *D&D Insider* archives, so Insiders can download a copy and follow along.

In this section, the Guardians of Eastfall, the sample party described on page 96, take on Encounter 2: The Dungeon from *Storm Tower*. Although the encounter against Irontooth in *Keep on the Shadowfell* provides many harsh lessons, this one is more forgiving. Instead of just surviving, the party must end the encounter as quickly and efficiently as possible, attacking immediately instead of holing up against a superior force until the time comes to strike. If successful, the characters need expend only minimal resources, leaving everyone better equipped to continue for later encounters. If they fail, the Guardians will find themselves drained and have to head home early.

WHEN AREAS ATTACK

Some of the most nefarious encounters combine both monsters and traps or hazards. It's hard enough defending yourself against swords and arrows, but when the trees or the building turn against you, things can get pretty difficult. But thankfully, these encounter add-ons can usually be avoided by a savvy adventuring party that knows how to avoid triggering them. For instance, although the snapjaw in this encounter is not technically a trap, it still relies on short-range tremorsense. Staying outside that range buys valuable rounds to deal with other problems.

When beginning an encounter in a new area, make note of the features of the area. Published adventures even devote a section to describing these, so your DM has the information if you ask for it. Good Perception and knowledge checks can help identify and avoid or mitigate these features, or even turn them to your advantage, which makes your encounter that much easier. Failing that, use common sense. If something looks dangerous, it probably is, so don't provoke it!

Know what you're getting into. Like many dungeon-style encounters, the single entrance to this encounter doesn't offer much chance to scout the competition. It is possible to use Perception to listen before descending into the hole, and Sherran's high modifier means the party can glean a few bits of information: Several more bandits wait below, and their leader is not with them. Knowing that other enemies, including the boss, are elsewhere, the Guardians determine that the best course of action is to end the encounter quickly before other foes might arrive to join the battle.

Upon descending into the room, a quick survey accounts for most of the enemies. Tregger, the bandit berserker, stands right in front waiting to face one of the heroes, and the bandits on the scaffolds prepare to take shots at anyone in the middle of the room. As the defenders, Kaliria and Brugar are the first party members down the ladder, and they happily engage Tregger while the ranger Sherran loops around to the southwest, heading for the southern scaffold. When Krizz finally gets down, he can help Brugar take down Tregger while Kaliria fends off Lurash, the bandit cutthroat, (if he's still in the fight) or the snapjaw (if it has found the party; see the sidebar "When Areas Attack").

Knowledge checks are in order when any fight begins, but what you've learned from previous fights can be invaluable. Context and firsthand experience tell you a lot more about your foes than a few lines out of the *Monster Manual*. In this encounter, Sherran definitely wants to take down the crossbowmen quickly; the party remembers their *dazing strike* power from the previous encounter, and being peppered with those is nobody's idea of a good time. Every hit costs the party actions and extra damage from combat advantage. The bandits must be taken out, and as a striker, Sherran is the elf for the job.

Sadly, even the perceptive Sherran isn't likely to notice Lurash beneath the northern scaffold. Unless Sherran thinks to use Dungeoneering, the specifics of "Chomper" must be figured out on the fly. Even without inside information, though, the Guardians should deduce that being far away from the scary iron jaws is vastly superior to being close, so Sherran chooses to go for the stairs *opposite* the snapjaw.

Make yourself at home. This area contains a few terrain features that the Guardians should use to their advantage. Other than the snapjaw, which is purely threatening, a savvy player can turn almost any object into a benefit; anyone who has listened to Acquisitions Incorporated make their way through this room can probably guess a few of them.

The first is the first thing you see: the rope ladder used to enter the room from above. As Jim Darkmagic discovered, when all you have to hold is a one-handed implement, there's not much reason to get down on the ground, and Hobor likes that way of thinking. From a perch on the ladder, the invoker can back up Sherran's attack on the crossbowmen without being in danger from Tregger, Lurash, or Chomper.

The scaffolds themselves offer an open-minded party both defensive and offensive possibilities. They can function as cover, as a tactical position, or as kindling. If Brugar and Krizz can pull the fight on the floor back beneath the southern scaffold, it makes it nearly impossible for the crossbowmen above them to get a clean shot, and the pillars in the middle of the room can even cause problems for the crossbowmen across the room. After its inhabitants have been cleared off, Sherran can use the scaffold as a platform for her own ranged attacks.

A well-placed shot at the brazier on the north side of the room can activate its fire attack property and make the other scaffold an uncomfortable place to stand. Although the fire spreads slowly, it eventually forces the other bandits to abandon their position, likely taking either fire or falling damage and making them easier to get to in the middle stages of the fight. Combining two terrain elements in this way is the mark of a party that's on the ball.

Play to your strengths . . . even unusual ones. Every character does certain things well, but sometimes your talents end up being useful in an unexpected way. In this encounter, the snapjaw is a major threat once provoked. With one hit, it can grab a target (which it immobilizes for the bandits to attack freely) and apply ongoing automatic damage. Even a character who has a good Athletics or Acrobatics skisl takes 10 extra damage from a hit before he or she has the opportunity to escape. But the Guardians have an ace in the hole for a situation such as this: Kaliria.

Kaliria's aegis of ensnarement has an unusual interaction with the snapjaw. If the snapjaw attacks a party member and hits, it grabs its target just before being teleported away by the swordmage. This teleportation breaks the grab before the target can take any ongoing damage. This wasn't exactly what Kaliria had in mind when selecting this build, but it's quite effective nonetheless, and the Guardians will adapt to it. Because the aegis is such a potent counter to the snapjaw's attack, Kaliria is more valuable when she is not being attacked and when she has at least one unoccupied space adjacent to her, so she actually stays away from this enemy. This forces it to either trigger the teleport or to take opportunity attacks to get to her (an unlikely tactic for a mindless construct).

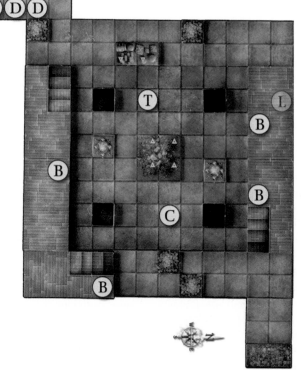

Protect your weaknesses . . . even unusual ones. The dazed condition isn't fun for anyone, but it can be especially painful for the Guardians. For one thing, having only one action makes it difficult for Krizz to use *healing word* efficiently. Every leader faces this problem, but Krizz likes to get in the thick of things, so it bothers him more than most. Dazing also takes away a character's immediate actions, which make Kaliria unable to use her *aegis* or other immediate attacks, making her a lot less effective.

A dazed Kaliria doesn't want to get hit by anyone, and a defender that doesn't want to get hit creates an awkward situation. Brugar can step up to take some extra hits, but it's also important for Kaliria to play defensively. Avoiding attacks altogether isn't practical or advisable, so she uses defensive powers, even second wind, to stay healthy and active on other creatures' turns. Daily attack and utility powers are there to be used, and using them proactively when the situation demands it means you get the most out of them, and it makes things easier in the long run.

CHAPTER 4

PLAYING THE GAME

THERE'S MORE to playing D&D than combat tactics and rolling dice. Even if your group spends most of its time gathered around a layout of Dungeon Tiles, you inevitably encounter situations that can't be solved with *cleave* or *fireball*.

The final chapter of this book covers a range of those situations, from navigating skill challenges to sorting through treasure. Even when you have a perfectly optimized character, poor decisions made in these areas can wreck the game as fast as a total party kill.

This chapter includes the following sections.

+ **Storytelling:** How to cooperate with the DM and the other players to create a compelling story.
+ **Being Part of the Party:** How to build a stronger party through the group's story.
+ **Rising to the (Skill) Challenge:** How to tackle this tricky part of the game.
+ **Knowing When to Rest:** Learn when to say when.
+ **The Campaign Journal:** How and why to track the important details of the campaign.
+ **Treasure and Rewards:** Tips on acquiring loot, dividing it between the characters, and customizing your stuff.
+ **Don't Be a Jerk:** Our closing words, and the most important message of the book.

I TELL THE BARON THAT WE ACCEPT HIS QUEST BUT THE REWARD SEEMS A LITTLE SMALL...

VICTORIA MADERNA

After three chapters full of advice on character creation, party building, and game tactics, you might need to brace yourself before reading this: D&D is all about stories.

Sure, you can play D&D as a tabletop game of tactical combat, but that overlooks the singular opportunity that roleplaying games offer players, to collaborate in the creation of a story that stars you and your friends. In the long run, the impact of these shared stories outweighs any memories you might have of rules, tactics, or treasure.

Stories are weird. They manage to crop up everywhere, even when people try their best to prevent them from doing so. A story can sneak in under the radar, and you can't prevent it.

When you start playing D&D, storytelling might be the farthest thing from your mind. You play the game to kill monsters and save villages, not to create a story arc that follows a hero from humble beginnings to a position of power and importance.

Except, oddly enough, you're doing exactly that. You might not mean to, but you can't help it. It's impossible to play a game like D&D without a story creeping in somewhere. In fact, the very rules of the game subtly nudge you towards a loose version of the classic heroic story as early as character creation. Your character begins adventuring with a handful of abilities, but those talents don't compare with what the character will possess at the end of the campaign. The character might begin a campaign with a group of friends, but it isn't until the game moves forward that you will begin to understand the nature of those friendships. As the game progresses, the character gains strength and knowledge, gradually evolving. That evolution becomes the story arc, and not only do the choices you make and the actions you take drive the story forward, in fact, they *are* the story.

Fortunately, you don't have to construct this narrative alone. The DM, your fellow players, and even the random fall of the dice all contribute to the story as a whole. Each person who participates in the game brings new threads to the story, and like any other project, the more the group works together, the better the end result will be. When the group sets out to tell a story together, each member is like a gear in a complicated machine that, working together, can better complete a task.

DRIVING THE STORY

"Storytelling is the DM's job!"

Although this is a commonly held belief, it could not be more wrong. Everyone at the table has a hand in storytelling, whether he or she is aware of it or not. As a player, you don't have the most obvious role in telling the story, but at the end of the day, the story is about *you*.

Unlike the classic form of storytelling, in which an individual author forges a tale from his or her own vision, D&D players create stories collaboratively, through the choices that you and your friends make. These stories can vary widely, from a twisted multi-stage plot to overthrow an evil lord, to something as simple as "Today we met some orcs, and then we killed them." Either way, you've worked together with the other folks at the table to tell a story.

As a player, you should recognize the power at your disposal. Everyone who plays D&D knows about the power of the DM. The DM is the arbitrator, the narrator, and your eyes and ears into the game world. In contrast, the power of the player is more subtle and often overlooked. The DM is in charge of what you see, but only you get to decide what you're looking at. Although this might not sound like much, it's a fantastic and somewhat tricky way of influencing the story.

Suppose your party finds itself in a village of a hundred people but interacts with only five of them. In the context of the story, only those five villagers matter. Even though you can see a hundred, you only look at five. By focusing on specific elements of the game world, you force the DM to give them significance. When you ask the blacksmith about his family, the DM's response—whether off the cuff or preplanned—has some effect on the campaign. If the family doesn't live in the village, why not? If the family died years ago, what killed them? Any of these answers might present adventure hooks, but even if they don't, they make the world feel more alive.

By showing the DM what parts of the world interest you, you also help direct him or her to flesh out the appropriate details. Don't ask about the blacksmith's family if you don't care; that wastes time and annoys the DM by continually forcing him or her to make up unwanted minutiae. Instead, use this technique to indicate your character's priorities within the ongoing story you're telling together. The more time you spend interacting with a part of the world, the more important that piece becomes to the story.

No matter what choices you make, you and your fellow party members are the protagonists of the story. Even if your characters are not most important people in the world, they are the most important

Stan!

people in the story, around whom the rest of the world revolves. Without them, there is no story.

Question: If a tree falls in the forest and none of the party is there to roll Perception checks, does it make a sound?

Answer: It's a trick question: In the absence of the party, *there is no tree.*

Taking the Bait

Whether the adventure hooks dangled by the DM come from your story interactions or out of the clear blue, find a reason to take the bait. Too many players make excuses for ignoring adventure opportunities offered by the DM. "My character wouldn't do that," they say, and then they wonder why no one appreciates their roleplaying talents. If you're that player, here's a hint: Nothing stops the fun faster than a player saying "no." Find a reason—any reason at all—to say "yes."

Adventure hooks lead to adventures, and adventures lead to action, experience points, treasure, and great stories to tell afterward. A DM dangling an adventure hook usually has an adventure attached to the other end, which means that he or she is ready for the game to proceed in that direction. Ignoring a hook and heading off in a different direction risks wasting the DM's hard work crafting that adventure, not to mention leaving you with an unpolished, off-the-cuff collection of thrown-together encounters in its place. Taking the bait leads to better adventures and more fun for everyone.

Usually, an adventure hook is obvious: A merchant offers gold for the safe return of his missing caravan, or a mysterious stranger warns of orcs massing on the border. But sometimes your DM can be too subtle

with his or her hooks, or maybe he or she runs a game that relies on the characters to come up with their own adventure hooks. If you and the other players can't tell in which direction to head for adventure, make sure the DM knows. He or she might be used to groups that prefer digging a little harder to find their adventures, so a gentle push for clearer hooks could solve the problem.

Creating Your Own Hooks

You don't have to wait for the DM to come up with your reason for going on an adventure. Many players fall into the trap of assuming that only the DM can point the characters toward the action. Yes, the DM tends to set the pace and direction of the campaign, but when the players get involved in this process, everything feels more important.

Some characters thrive in environments full of intrigue and politics. If that's your character, come up with a reason for the group to visit the duke's court. Maybe you've heard about a spy ring infiltrating the city, or perhaps you're the spies. Either way, sharing this hook with the DM is a more pointed method of focusing your attention on a particular part of the world. Let your DM know that not only do you want the court to become more important, you want to go there and have an adventure.

Your suggested adventure hook doesn't have to be complicated. In fact, it shouldn't be: The more details you insist on, the harder it becomes for your DM to inject it into the campaign. Don't tell the DM that your character wants to track down a missing half-orc fugitive suspected of stealing the fabled Amulet of Aundair from Duchess Elaine during her lightning rail trip from Sharn to Flamekeep last Tuesday and then escaping with the help of a pack of tamed black dragons under the command of a warforged archmage named Anvil. All that detail hinders the DM's creative impulses, making him or her less interested in adding your idea to the world. Start with, "I'd like to track down a criminal, and it'd be cool if the trail led into the Mournlands." If the DM bites, you can suggest additional details or let him or her figure out the rest.

Simple, character-driven adventure hooks are plentiful:

✦ Hunt an exotic or legendary monster. Haven't you always wanted to fight a dragon or a beholder?

✦ Find a particular magic item or artifact. It's hard for the DM to say no to your wish list request (see page 150) when you go through a whole adventure to get it.

✦ Join an organization. It stands to reason that powerful groups in the world of DUNGEONS & DRAGONS would ask prospective members to prove their worth in fantastic ways.

✦ Retrieve a rare component or ingredient. Maybe you need this for your own rituals or research, or perhaps you're just a courier.

✦ Locate someone who can train you in an unusual talent. This can be an in-world excuse for learning a new feat or ritual, multiclassing, or taking a paragon path, or it might be a way to get that grandmaster training you want–see "Other Rewards," page 157, for details about that option.

✦ Track down an old friend or rival. This provides a great opportunity to dust off your backgrounds and make them relevant again.

Whatever you decide is right for your character, make sure you give the DM some notice. That way, you have an effect on the game, and you show that characters can indeed change and influence things, but you also show respect to the DM by giving him or her time to prepare.

NARRATING POWERS

Player's Handbook 2 introduced the concept of narrating powers in the sidebar "Your Part in the Story," page 4. In brief, this involves describing your character's actions in combat, using the flavor text found in each power as a starting point. This method puts another aspect of storytelling into the hands of the players, letting them describe not just what their characters do, but how.

When you narrate a power, instead of naming the power and rolling a die, inject a bit of personality into the attack. A player can declare that his or her fighter is using *sure strike* against an enemy, or the player could describe how the character shifts her grip on the sword and deftly thrusts it toward the foe. Although the first gets the point across, the second is more compelling and is more likely to keep the attention of everyone at the table.

Although the descriptive text appearing in the power description provides a starting point, you can use as much or as little of it as you want and vary it

KALMAN ANDRASOFSZKY

however you choose. As long as the rules of the power stay the same, it doesn't matter how you describe it. Maybe your half-elf paladin learned *sure strike* by hearing it described, and thus uses a completely different grip and swing from what fighters use.

Until you learn the success or failure of your attack, don't include the outcome of a power's use in your narration. Saying "My ranger hammers off two arrows in quick succession" is a fine way of narrating *twin strike*, but describing how these missiles bury themselves into your target's throat should be left until you see the target drop to 0 hit points.

Narration is also helpful in keeping your character distinctive. In the case of two otherwise identical wizards, how each player chooses to narrate the use of *magic missile* can provide insight into their backgrounds and personalities. A wizard whose spell

STORY TROUBLESHOOTING

It happens at some point in every player's life. An ordinarily good DM has a bad session, a series of dull adventures, or an uninspiring campaign overall. This difficulty can be painful to watch, especially if you're a good friend.

Rather than sit through it quietly, be a proactive player and figure out what's going on. If the games are listless, is it because no one knows where to go next? If the players commonly forget or ignore important world details, is it because the DM didn't draw attention to them, or because the DM doesn't even remember what he or she has said before? Maybe late starts, frequent absences, or canceled sessions have ruined your sense of story continuity.

After taking time to think about it, talk to the other players, and share your concerns with the Dungeon Master. Maybe the DM is having a rough time at home or at work and can't focus on giving you a high-quality game, but still feels obligated to show up every week nonetheless.

Sometimes, just talking about the issues suggests a solution. Maybe the players need to help the DM with some adventure hooks of their own (see "Creating Your Own Hooks," page 137). Perhaps one of the players should take responsibility for recording key people and events in the game (see "The Campaign Journal," page 148). You're smart folks, so put your heads together and find out how to get the game on track.

If no solutions present themselves, consider taking a break from the campaign for a month or two. Even if you love D&D, you can get burned out, particularly when outside stresses mount up. A little time away from the battlemat can leave everyone more excited and involved when you regather later.

You could also try shaking up the game a bit. Maybe someone else steps in as DM, or you play something else on your weekly D&D night. (Yes, there are other games besides DUNGEONS & DRAGONS.)

resembles a twisting spear of thorny darkness evokes a very different feel from one who strikes with a ray of golden energy. The first wizard probably isn't invited to a lot of royal balls, and the second might be comically out of place when dealing with the criminal underworld. Tailoring the descriptions of your various powers can help you create a visual theme for your character.

Don't be afraid to go even further with power narration. If you keep actual game effects the same, you can alter the flavor of a power as much as you like. Going further with the *magic missile* example, perhaps your wizard doesn't even cast a bolt of energy. You could depict it as an arc of power that leaps between the eyes of the wizard and the target, a cloud of ghostly birds that rip at the target with beak and claw, or a fountain of arcane energy that erupts from beneath the target's feet. As long as you don't ask your DM for different effects or keywords for a power as a result of how you choose to portray it, anything goes.

This kind of narration need not stop with powers. Everything your character does can be described in a way that conveys personality, including actions as mundane as drinking a potion. An aristocratic eladrin might sip delicately, and a barbarian could noisily gulp it and wipe his mouth with the back of his hand. How your character does something can be more evocative than the action itself.

Whether you're fighting, searching for traps, or hobnobbing in the court of a king, if you can perform an action, you can narrate it in a way that makes it interesting. If you can grab the attention of everyone at the table, then they'll look forward to your turns almost as much as their own.

As with all things, there is a danger of overdoing it. You should use narration to breathe life into a character, not to overinflate one. If you deliver a monologue every time your ranger shoots an arrow, odds are you're going too far. You want to engage your fellow players' interest, not encourage them to go grab a snack. A sentence or two should suffice for even the most detailed, elaborate actions.

Steer clear of repetition. The first time your barbarian "leaps into the fray, hacking with his axe" is interesting. After the 57th time he does it, the other players might have to stifle their yawns.

If you're not naturally inclined to spontaneous storytelling, jot down a few ideas for your powers and keep them at hand. Also, listen to how the other players use narration; sometimes a minor tweak to what they say can be all the inspiration you need.

What is the party, really?

At the simplest level, the party is a group of adventurers brought together through fate, fortune, or a common foe, who work together to achieve a mutual goal. This goal can be as straightforward as ridding a village of feral animals that threaten it, or as complicated as saving the world. No matter what it sets out to do, though, a party is what happens when a group of adventurers come together.

In the heat of battle, the concept of the party is easy to grasp. Each character fills a specific role that benefits the group. Defenders hold back a flood of enemies from attacking their vulnerable allies, leaders provide bonuses and assistance to those around them, controllers shift the tide of a battle in the party's favor, and strikers mete out horrible punishment. In battle, the party is a fistful of heroes bringing together the might of their unique abilities to overcome all difficulties set before them.

Membership in the party isn't hemmed in by the borders of the battlefield, however. After the fighting is over, the last enemy vanquished, and the last body looted, the *story* of the party begins. In the same way you wouldn't sit back in silence when your turn to act in battle comes around, you shouldn't fall into the background when there's nothing in front of you to kill. Whether the party is going toe-to-talon with a dragon or trying to figure out whose turn it is to pay for lunch, your character is an important part of the unfolding story.

Don't let your character's combat role dictate which element of the group's story the character will be a part of. Even if you play a solitary ranger who snipes at enemies from the back ranks of the battlefield, your character might be the most personable member of the party, passing around flagons of ale and sharing stories by campfire light. An imposing warlord who bellows orders in combat might be the most quiet, introspective member of the party, listening first and speaking last outside battle. The personality you've crafted for your character is a great place to start when you're trying to determine what part of the story you will fill when the party isn't in the middle of a fight.

No matter what you decide your character will be, always work to be a member of the group. Even if you're not in the spotlight of a roleplaying encounter, you can still provide a voice in the background. Just as when you're in a fight, everyone in the group can work together, bringing the depth of their characters' attitudes and personalities to enrich the story of your games.

Although you might be the starring character of the story from your own point of view, to everyone else, you're a member of the supporting cast. Try to become more involved with everyone else's concepts and stories. The more you entwine yourself in all the stories that unfurl during a game, the bigger a part of those stories you'll become.

As a player, you're also a member of a party made up of everyone else playing the game. In the same way that the different characters in the game bring their own talents and abilities to the challenges they fight to surmount, each person participating in the game brings a wealth of possibilities to the story. When a fellow player introduces a new idea to the table, think of ways you could help reinforce that idea. When another player mentions the small kingdom his character's family hails from, perhaps you decide your character has a distant relative who married a traveler from that kingdom, or remembers being entertained as a child by one of the kingdom's wandering bards.

When your fellow players reveal their characters' backstories, pay attention, because those stories are as important to your gaming experience as the monsters you will defeat, the dungeons you will crawl through, and the tyrants you will depose. You're playing one member of a group of heroes who all have their own unique histories, personalities, and goals. Although the difficulties your DM puts before you are temporary setbacks designed to be overcome, what the other players bring to the story are the friends and allies your character will suffer and strive with, who work together in both victory and defeat. Ignoring the stories the other players have to share closes off many chances to deepen and enrich the entire game. Whether your party is a fractious, bickering affair barely held together by a common enemy, or a group of lifelong friends who have set out together on an adventure, be involved with the other characters—and players—around you.

TELL US ABOUT YOUR CHARACTER

"Aeofel!" Binwin called. "GO GET HIM!"

Aeofel already knew he would stop at nothing until Leer—the target of his *oath of enmity*—was captured or dead, but his friend's pleading voice only strengthened his resolve. He left his comrades locked in combat with impossibly large metal beasts to pursue his chosen enemy.

"Your death will not be swift," Aeofel said, drawing a dagger from his boot and throwing it squarely at Leer's throat. The dagger flew through the air and . . . stopped! More magic?

No—Aeofel saw the shimmering outline of a gelatinous cube as it slowly engulfed the dagger. Leer grinned and fled from view. "*Rhachon Le!*" Aeofel cursed as he leapt around the cube and ran after his foe.

Now Leer stood near the front door of Ambershard Manor, a trail of blood behind him. He drew a dagger from his belt. Aeofel's eladrin senses sharpened in anticipation, but when the blade left Leer's hand, it flew not toward the avenger, but across the room to strike a large gong.

Leer shouted something at Aeofel and limped out the door, but the gong's echo was all the avenger could hear. *No matter,* Aeofel thought, *he is mine. I shall strike him down, for Binwin, for Clan Bronzebottom, and for Melora.* Aeofel flew after Leer with singular purpose, his hand gripping the hilt of his sword as he prepared for the death blow.

Suddenly, the ground gave way, and a sickening weightless sensation quickly turned to dread. Aeofel looked down and saw the bright green acid just before he fell in.

"BINWIN! *No diriel!* Help me!" Aeofel cried as he struggled in vain to find purchase on the smooth walls of the pit. Acid burned through his armor and began to eat away his flesh. Acrid smoke joined his agonized screams, filling the air around him to herald Death's arrival.

With his final breath, Aeofel prayed, "*Melora le suilon,*" as the world around him faded to blackness.

In the third series of the popular Penny Arcade D&D podcasts, my character, Aeofel Elhromnnë, met a decidedly nonheroic death, succumbing to a nasty trap in Ambershard Manor. Though I'd only played him a few times, I felt a sense of loss that lingered for days after the session was over. (And some people say that D&D is "just a game." I pity those foolish mortals.)

Aeofel isn't the first character to die because the players split the party, and he won't be the last, but his death was a very public example of character mortality. When that episode of the podcast aired, I received hundreds—maybe even thousands—of messages on Twitter, through e-mail, and on my blog. Many were consoling, and greatly appreciated, but a substantial number of them were some variation of "that's what you get for splitting the party, dumbass."

Part of me agreed, but when I really thought about it, I couldn't *disagree* more. Yes, Aeofel died in part because I split the party. But more than that, he died because I was committed to *roleplaying* the character I'd created, doing what he would have done in the story, rather than performing the optimal tactical move.

Aeofel was an avenger: in common language, a zealot. Whereas a paladin brings comfort to the afflicted, the avenger brings vengeance and fury to the afflicters. When I created Aeofel, I decided that, once he chose a target and swore his *oath of enmity*, he would stop at *nothing* until that target fell.

If I'd adhered to the second rule of RPGs (the first being "Never pick up a duck in a dungeon"), I wouldn't have split the party and Aeofel never would have chased after Leer. But Aeofel had sworn an *oath of enmity*. He had Leer on the run. Leer was bloodied *and* had offended Melora. And lastly, Binwin had implored Aeofel to "get him." Binwin was the only dwarf in the world whom Aeofel could call his friend, and Aeofel was intensely loyal to those who were close to him. Aeofel had no choice but to chase Leer and end up in that acid pit.

When our characters find themselves in real danger of dying, we can forget that the RP in RPG stands for "roleplaying." It's understandable that we want to keep our characters alive. They spend their entire lives with us, after all, so we're pretty attached to them. We do whatever it takes to protect them, like all good parents should.

But for our characters to become more than numbers on a piece of paper, for the battles we recount to our friends and our patient nongaming partners to become more than just moving minis around and rolling dice, and for us to realize the true potential of RPGs as collaborative storytelling, we gamers *must* engage our imaginations, commit to our characters, and break the unbreakable rules to better serve the story.

I haven't had a character die in . . . I'm not exactly sure how long. Not since I was a teenager, certainly, and even then, characters weren't *dead* dead, because we all kept locks of our hair in special jars labeled "In case of death, break glass and resurrect, y'all." But Aeofel is really, truly, I'm-totally-serious-about-this dead. He might find a way to come back as a revenant, but if he does, he will be *changed* by the experience. If it's possible, and 30 years of acting experience tells me it is, Aeofel will be even *more* serious, *more* overly dramatic.

Regrets? Well, obviously. My character is *dead*, but he died doing what he loved—what he *had* to do. I'm happy that I stayed true to Aeofel's beliefs and played him the way I wrote him.

So remember, kids: Never split the party . . . except for those times when you must.

WIL WHEATON is an actor, an author, a publisher, and a champion of geek culture. A lifelong gamer, he was introduced to D&D at the age of 10 when his great-aunt gave him the Red Box Set in 1982. Currently, he is best known to his fellow D&D players as the eladrin avenger Aeofel, in the wildly popular series of Acquisitions, Incorporated podcasts with Mike Krahulik, Jerry Holkins, and Scott Kurtz. He lives and games in Los Angeles.

A well-designed skill challenge codifies complex situations into easy-to-follow rules and allows you to draw on a deeper range of your character's talents than just those needed to slay monsters. Instead of passively watching an encounter unfold around you, when you participate in a skill challenge, you actively shape the course of events. The outcome of a skill challenge can influence not only the course of the current encounter, but the shape of the adventure still to come.

Skill challenges give you a chance to reinforce your character's individuality. Your character's skills reflect his or her background; the way your character employs those skills reflects his or her personality. A barbarian born into the leadership of the tribe is likely to utilize Diplomacy when interacting in social situations, and a berserker raised on combat is likely to try Intimidate. A rogue who is a dashing rebel uses vastly different skills from one who is an angry cutthroat.

Although skill challenges vary widely, they all have a few things in common. No matter what shape a skill challenge takes, the party needs to work together to make a specified number of successful checks before failing a given number of checks. Success at certain skills (called primary skills) adds to the overall total of successes, and success at other skills (secondary skills) applies other benefits to the challenge, such as giving bonuses to particular primary skills or opening up new options within the challenge.

PRIMARY SKILLS

In some skill challenges, you can tell which skill checks will contribute successes toward your eventual victory. When negotiating with the duke, you expect Bluff, Diplomacy, and Insight to come into play as you maneuver for social advantage. Maybe the DM even tells you which skills will start off the challenge.

A well-designed skill challenge, however, typically includes a couple of primary skills that might not be obvious. Perhaps the duke appreciates tales of ancient warfare, and a History check would raise your standing in his eyes. Maybe he's easily distracted, allowing you to stand in the back and juggle knives (with a successful Acrobatics check) to keep him from focusing on the negotiation.

When presented with a skill challenge, listen for subtle clues that a DM might drop. Whether he or she is aware of it or not, how a DM presents the information relevant to a skill challenge often provides insight into the best way to approach it. For instance, if the characters are trying to persuade an NPC to hear them out, listen to the voice and choice of words that the DM uses for him. If the NPC speaks in a haughty or self-important manner, then attempting to sway him by intimidation probably won't work, but appealing to his ego with flattery might. Listen for these cues when facing a skill challenge; the DM usually has a plan of how to approach the challenge, and the way that the pertinent details are delivered to you is often the quickest way of figuring it out.

Whenever possible, send your experts up against these primary skill tasks. If you aren't trained (or don't have a high key ability score) in a skill, you shouldn't risk failure by making that primary skill check.

SECONDARY SKILLS

The same advice applies to determining what might be appropriate secondary skills in the challenge. Even if you don't think you can contribute with a primary skill check, look for ways in which your character could use his or her other skills to help.

If your character is a terrible sneak, can she fast-talk a guard long enough to let others slip past? If he doesn't have the diplomatic ability to broker a deal, can he stand back as an intimidating show of strength? It's unlikely that your character won't possess at least one useful secondary skill, so take a moment to find it.

WHAT WOULD MY CHARACTER DO?

Some players get caught up in scanning their characters' skill lists for the right option, losing sight of the fact that a skill challenge represents characters interacting with the world. Don't limit yourself to the seventeen skills on your character sheet. Instead, ask what actions a character in the world might take to overcome the difficulty represented by the skill challenge.

If your characters have to get across town without being spotted by the guards, you could assume that a series of Stealth checks is required. But if you instead imagined it as a scene from a movie, you might see your characters leaping across rooftops, using contacts to plant false rumors about your movements, and remembering tales about infamous criminals who used forgotten underground tunnels to escape the law. Once you bring up these ideas, the DM can decide that they represent Athletics checks, Streetwise checks, and History checks, respectively. Even if he or she didn't anticipate your actions, the fact that you've described them in terms of what your character might reasonably attempt makes it more likely that the DM will agree.

As a player, you're responsible for finding a way to actively take part in every encounter. Don't just roll the same skill checks over and over; think of all of the ways in which your character can use his or her skills to help the party succeed.

4

You don't necessarily need to be an expert, or even trained, in a skill to try one of these options. Secondary skill checks often don't impose a failure on an unsuccessful result, so don't be afraid to give it a shot.

OTHER OPTIONS

Don't let the name "skill challenge" fool you; skill checks aren't the only way to contribute toward a skill challenge. If you can't fast-talk a guard, you could still try old-fashioned bribery. Just because you're incapable of disarming the complex mechanism of a booby-trap doesn't mean that you can't try jamming a sword in the gears to keep it from going off.

DMs respond best to these outside-the-box solutions if they include the expenditure of a resource—gold, consumable equipment, action points, and daily powers all get the DM's attention, they demonstrate your commitment to the idea. These small sacrifices are well worth the reward of aiding your party members in victory rather than watching from the sidelines. Always be on the lookout for ways you can help the group effort, even if the path you take isn't an obvious one.

GUIDING THE CHALLENGE

Don't hesitate to drop hints during skill challenges. Even the best DM can't imagine every possible angle of approach when designing a skill challenge, and you might think of one that the DM hadn't considered.

Here's a great tool for subtly guiding the DM's thinking. Rather than just taking the action you're considering, float it as a suggestion among the group. This lets the DM hear your idea and process it without feeling under pressure to make a judgment right away. When you finally decide to take the action a few minutes later, the DM is more prepared to say yes.

Sometimes, it's even in your best interest to force a skill challenge. For example, if the party needs to enter a city encircled by a massive enemy army, it would be ridiculous for the characters to fight their way through. Instead, the characters could draw on their skills to sneak, lie, and negotiate their way through the camp. Even if the DM didn't plan for the event to turn into a skill challenge, how the party chooses to approach things could make a skill challenge the simplest, most logical way to handle things. As a player, it can be more rewarding to think your way through a scenario than to charge into the fray.

SKILL CHALLENGES IN COMBAT

Most skill challenges happen outside combat, but under the right circumstances they can be a part of a combat encounter. Unlike a usual skill challenge, this scenario applies an action cost for participation, depending on the skill you use and the task you attempt.

The objectives of these in-combat challenges vary widely. Your party might be fighting in an arena with slowly closing walls that threaten to crush everyone inside, or it could be trying to convince an opponent to see reason and stop fighting. Regardless, remembering a few guidelines during in-combat skill challenges can help you succeed.

Don't Ignore Other Threats: A party facing a skill challenge during combat also faces enemies trying to kill them. Establish a balance between fighting and contributing to the skill challenge. Avoid the temptation to focus entirely on one or the other, since many in-combat skill challenges include the pressure of a limited time frame, such as disabling an artifact before an enemy can use its power. Focus too much on the monsters, and the evil wizard gains

STAN! BROWN

immortality; focus too much on the artifact; and the wizard's minions cut you in half.

Use Teamwork: Some in-combat skill challenges appear to draw on a single character's skill set, such as a deadly trap that repeats its attacks every round. Even though a character trained in Thievery should expect to spend some time on this challenge, don't leave your rogue or artificer alone to disarm the trap. While that character is out of the fight, the party gains no benefits of his or her combat powers.

Instead, have a few characters take turns dealing with the skill challenge. The rogue might spend most of his or her time disarming the trap, but if the whole party contributes, then no one is left doing all the dirty work (since skill challenges are often less interesting than combat) and the party gets the use of each character's powers for at least part of the fight. Think about the secondary skills or other actions your character could use to help overcome the skill challenge. A well-designed challenge has more than one path to success. Do whatever you can to help the party discover the solution, and don't leave your fellow characters out in the cold during combat.

TELL US ABOUT YOUR CHARACTER

Many years ago, at the end of the Spellplague, the human Joroneen Kaal was a zulkir of some standing among the Red Wizards of Thay. He lived in Nethtabar, a small city on the Plateau of Thay, with his dour wife, Gulca, and their daughter, Parshala.

When Parshala was 6, Joroneen killed Gulca in public after discovering that she had not sufficiently rebuffed the advances of a would-be lover. Parshala learned to fear her father that day, but could not have guessed what he would later become.

Years later, when Parshala was 14, Joroneen brought home a gift for her, a prize from his exploits in Akanul. The gift was a stormsoul genasi infant girl, whose parents he had slain. He thought his daughter would be charmed by the amusing little "doll" with lightning in her eyes.

Parshala accepted the gift, but had no particular love for the infant. She named the genasi child Skeak, a goblin word for lightning. She cut the child's cheek in a vertical line to the jaw: a mark that designated her as the property of the Kaal family. Skeak was raised by Gulca's handmaid, a middle-aged woman named Hegga who bore the same mark.

Joroneen grew distant from his daughter and manor. He had begun working on the walls and buttresses of a fortress that would ring their town of Nethtabar entirely, and as the months and years passed, he seemed to grow increasingly obsessed with the ring-fortress.

In reality the ring-fortress was one of many loci of the infamous ritual of Szass Tam: a Dread Ring. Joroneen was secretly a loyal agent of Szass Tam, the self-proclaimed regent of the Thayan Plateau, and was helping to complete Tam's master ritual, the ritual that would destroy Toril and make Szass Tam a god.

As Joroneen's obsession became madness, Hegga took the adolescent Parshala and the baby Skeak and fled to the city of Nethjet to the west. They never saw Joroneen again. Szass Tam's ritual was thwarted, but not before Thay was transformed into an undead kingdom. Joroneen secured a place in Szass Tam's necrarchy: He became a lich and a prominent tharchion in Tam's service.

Parshala, embittered by the fact that she would never complete her birthright training as a Red Wizard, grew into a shrewd young woman and eventually turned to mercantilism to make a living. The Red Wizards had been chased off and dispersed, but Parshala, clinging to her ill-fated lineage as one of them, was desperate to be part of the group, even if that group was now nothing more than an association of merchants.

When Parshala was 26, she abandoned Hegga and left Nethjet. She headed to the city of Undumor to build her career as a merchant. She took 12-year-old Skeak with her to do chores and errands. Skeak was traumatized by the loss of her adoptive mother. She came to daydream of becoming a mighty warrior, using her lightning-quick blade to rescue Hegga from the brigands and rats of Nethjet.

Six years later, Parshala was an important merchant of Undumor, conducting trade in the Sea of Fallen Stars. She had even created a strategic partnership with Mariss Bez, the leader of Company Bez and the captain of the sky-ship *Storm of Vengeance*. Skeak had grown into a stunning young woman (except for the scar on her cheek), but she was a mere handmaid with virtually no interaction with the wider world.

One night after a failed negotiation with rival merchants, Parshala and Skeak sailed back to Undumor aboard a Company Bez galleon. Parshala grew increasingly drunk and angry until she was violent. She beat Skeak savagely. At first, Skeak didn't fight back; she never did. But Parshala didn't relent. Skeak panicked and grabbed a scullery knife to defend herself. Parshala, indignant and furious, charged at the girl, and Skeak blindly swung, lightning roping from her hands and around the knife blade. The blade cut Parshala's cheek and the lightning cauterized it, leaving a jagged, ugly wound unlike the simple scar Skeak bore. Parshala, bewildered, froze. Skeak dashed from the galley and dove overboard, knowing that Parshala would kill her if she remained.

Four years have passed since that night. Skeak chose the name Eska and resolved to make a new start. She learned to wield a blade in case Parshala tracked her down. She dreams of finding Hegga again but doesn't know whether the woman who raised her still lives.

BRADY DOMMERMUTH is senior creative designer for Magic: The Gathering. He has played D&D since 1982, has played Magic since 1995, and has worked at Wizards continuously in various capacities since 1997.

Usually, being a hero means knowing how to use all the resources at your disposal to vanquish evil. Heroes push themselves to the breaking point—using every last power, spending every last healing surge, and drinking every last potion—to win the day.

That said, successful heroes know when to put their feet up and take a breather.

Short and extended rests, described on page 263 of the *Player's Handbook*, allow characters to regain resources spent during encounters. Understanding how best to manage your rests is part of the resource management of D&D.

SHORT RESTS

Representing about 5 minutes of in-game time, a short rest gives your character a chance to stop and catch his or her breath, to regain strength and wipe the blood off his or her blade, to tend to injuries, and to ready mind and body for the next difficulty. In game terms, you renew your encounter powers and spend any number of healing surges you want.

Typically, a character needs only a single short rest to be ready for another encounter, but there's no reason you can't take multiple short rests one after another. In fact, if you have a leader in the party, multiple short rests are the most efficient way to heal damage. Unless you have time pressure keeping you from waiting around, a party that has a leader should never spend a healing surge during a short rest except as a result of that leader's class-based healing powers. Those powers can easily double the hit points provided by each healing surge, so take as many short rests as you need to renew those powers over and over

again. See the sidebar "Healing Outside Combat," page 113, for more on this topic.

Taking a short rest doesn't mean the party can't accomplish other tasks. You can't perform strenuous activity while resting, but you can keep watch, sort through treasure, and plan your next move. You can even rest while traveling, as long as you aren't the one walking or flying. Some DMs might frown at riding a mount during a short rest, but sitting in a wagon is perfectly restful, at least as far as D&D is concerned.

The entire party need not rest simultaneously. If the cleric needs to perform a ritual or the fighter wants to clear rubble from the collapsed tunnel, your rogue could take a short rest while you wait. Because the nonresting character doesn't get any of the benefits of that short rest, your party might need to take another one when he or she finishes.

EXTENDED RESTS

An extended rest accomplishes everything a short rest does as well as renewing daily powers and replenishing your hit points and healing surges to their full values. An extended rest also resets your milestone progression, starting you once again with 1 action point and one magic item daily power use (or more at higher levels). It is the most potent method of recharging your character's capabilities in the game.

However, the extended rest comes with a substantial cost of time: 6 hours of enforced inactivity (nonstrenuous activity is acceptable), and you can't take another extended rest for another 12 hours after that. This means your characters can't take an extended rest any time they want, and each extended

KALMAN ANDRASOFSZKY

rest comes with the knowledge that the campaign's storyline advances another day.

In many adventures, an extra day spent overcoming difficulties might not prove meaningful. You should never assume this to be true, though; DMs have a fiendish way of making you regret the overuse of extended rests by adding reinforcements to later encounters, planning ambushes to catch your characters unaware, or even letting the villain finish his or her master plan before you get there.

A hidden cost of the extended rest is a loss of tension around the table. Taking an extended rest means every player becomes a little less worried about how his or her character can make it through the next fight. Sometimes, pushing on with low resources is the right decision because it gets everyone at the table more excited about upcoming events.

All this means that your decision to take an extended rest shouldn't be made lightly. Make sure the payoff is worth not only the downtime for the characters, but also the lost excitement. Avoid the

temptation to take an extended rest just because the party has used all its daily attack powers. Yes, these are exciting and powerful, but ultimately they're only attacks, and every character has plenty of those even without daily options. Heading back to camp because one or two characters are out of daily attack powers encourages everyone to use them all up early in the day to avoid being the character who doesn't get to use his or her best powers.

The more important resource you must manage with extended rests is your supply of healing surges. Without healing surges, you can't regain hit points in most of the usual ways. A character without healing surges can probably survive a single encounter (if he or she is careful), but a tough fight, bad tactics, or unlucky rolls could prove disastrous.

As soon as a character has one or no healing surges left, the group should talk about the possibility of taking an extended rest. You might have other options, such as powers that swap or restore healing surges, or new tactics that would protect that character from

TELL US ABOUT YOUR CHARACTER

When we started a weekly DUNGEONS & DRAGONS night two years ago, I knew it was going to be fun, but I also knew that we were a crazy bunch of idiots who wanted to make each other laugh just as much as we wanted to kill exotic monsters for their pocket change. I had to create a character that would let me do both and with such a sense of self-righteousness that I could blame everything on my character's devotion to god, to justice, to his backstory, or some other such umbrella. In other words, I would be an obnoxious paladin.

Ptah Trakken swung a bastard sword because it was the biggest sword I could find and it was the only weapon with a curse word in it. I wasn't in the mood to play a character with finesse or subtlety. I wasn't showing up to pick pockets or talk to plants. I can do that stuff in real life. Here, I wanted to run in sword-first and remove chunks of things: a great way to get out stress and relax.

Of course, I wanted to be a wiseass while doing it. We're a creative bunch of Hollywood writers, artists, and prop guys, so we all created snarky or humorous characters and played to make each other laugh as much as to get experience points. Often, Ptah would slam his sword against a goblin's shield while yelling, "I mean you no harm!" or shout at the biggest baddie in the crowd, "Don't you dare die before you fight ME!" I was one crazy nut of many, but I'd never play this way if I weren't playing with friends.

But even among friends, a character like this can grow a little tiresome. Ptah tended to give away our position with ill-timed battle cries (after all, my deity rewarded bravery), and there was that one little disagreement about splitting up treasure. Hey, when the rogue tried to pocket some treasure for herself, I don't see that I had any option other

than throwing her across the room and threatening to kill her.

The other players eventually tried teaching me lessons aimed at changing Ptah's behavior. Running headlong into battle and provoking opportunity attacks garnered less and less sympathy. They even argued that Ptah should give up some of his goodies to help the weaker characters. "Wouldn't a paladin want me to have a higher Armor Class?" the dwarf asked. Yeah, I thought, why don't I give you a massage after each battle, too? You're not getting my ring of +1 AC.

Sadly, Ptah's self-confidence would get him killed, but not at the hands of a horde of monsters like you'd expect. Instead, he overheard some werewolves warn each other that the last thing they should do was pull a certain lever. Of course, what the villain says don't do, the hero does. That was quite the jolt of electricity that fried Ptah to beef jerky. Everyone was upset—you might even say shocked—that such a fun character died.

Of course, that didn't mean they lifted a finger to stop the zombies from carrying off his corpse. Ha ha, guys.

After all those months of playing Ptah, I think I got enough stress out of my system to play a character who was a little less disruptive. Turns out my catfolk ranger/scout can stay in the background and shoot arrows with enough damage to blow monsters away just fine. The only controversy left is my friends' disbelief that a single arrow can bring that much pain!

DOUGLAS GOLDSTEIN is a television writer and points to being co-head writer of Robot Chicken to prove it. He forgives, but he does not forget.

taking damage, that can keep you going. But if those options don't exist, a character out of healing surges becomes a liability. He or she can't stay in combat long, can't be healed by normal methods, and could easily fall unconscious or even die in the next encounter.

Though most DMs don't ambush characters on their way out of the dungeon, always keep in mind the possibility that even after you fight what you believe to be your last battle, you aren't safe until you're back at the tavern (and sometimes not even then). Pushing forward until everyone's tank is empty leaves you terribly vulnerable to even a low-level encounter on the way home.

Another time to consider taking an extended rest is before an encounter you expect to be very challenging. Time or story constraints might not allow this decision—you can't exactly take a 6-hour time-out

when the dragon shows up to eat you—but if those aren't a factor, think about facing the big fight with a full tank of resources.

Sometimes, the right time for an extended rest comes because of the timing of your sessions. When you reach the end of a game session, taking an extended rest before the next session starts makes record-keeping easier for everyone. Otherwise, each player must record his character's current healing surges, which daily powers he or she has expended, and how many action points and magic item daily power uses he or she has remaining. Taking an extended rest resets all these values, so even when it's not entirely intuitive, it can be the right choice.

With very rare exceptions, an extended rest is a group activity: Everyone finds a place to bed down, perhaps with someone keeping watch, and you all gain the benefits of resting. Having some characters take an extended rest while others stay active leads to a confusing mix of milestones and resource tracking, so avoid having the characters rest at different times except in dire circumstances.

That doesn't mean that someone shouldn't keep watch; such nonstrenuous activity is allowed during an extended rest. Choose a character who has a good Perception check or who can see well in dim light or darkness. Even better is a guard with those qualities who doesn't need to sleep, such as an eladrin, a revenant, or a warforged. If you don't have a good night guardian, invest in a Warding ritual such as Eye of Alarm. For 25 gp each night, the watchful eyes of this ritual let everyone get a good night's sleep.

SERIOUSLY . . . GET SOME SLEEP

Some players can't stand the idea of taking a rest when monsters remain to be slain. These players are convinced that every minute wasted somehow makes the rest of the adventure that much harder.

In reality, the reverse is true. Ignoring opportunities to rest is perhaps the best way to get characters killed. Pushing ahead for one more fight when you're out of healing surges often feels thrilling, but that doesn't make it smart.

It might seem unusual that not taking action is vital to a character, but it makes sense if you take a moment to think about it. Imagine your character, weighed down by armor, arms aching from swinging a weapon, or drained from ripping apart an enemy with powerful magical forces. Being a hero takes its toll, and the toughest champion needs to take a break from time to time. Like every vital reserve at your character's disposal, make sure that when you decide to take advantage of a rest, it benefits not only your character but the entire party.

DM: *". . . and the note is signed, 'The Emissary.'"*

Joe: *"I wonder who that is."*

Kevin: *"Wasn't that the guy we fought last month?"*

DM: *"No, that was the Adversary."*

Viet: *"It still sounds familiar. Didn't we see that name on another note three sessions ago?"*

Joe: *"Don't look at me, I missed that session."*

Viet: *"Yeah, I swore I wrote it down on my character sheet, but I don't see it here."*

Kevin: *"Remember, we leveled up last time. You probably just threw away your old sheet."*

Joe: *"If it's important, I'm sure the DM will tell us again later."*

If this conversation sounds like the players at your table, consider starting a campaign journal. By recording the notable people, places, objects, and events of each session, you create an archive that preserves your shared story and provides a reference for later sessions.

Like any new habit, the first and most difficult hurdle of keeping a campaign journal is starting it. Early on, this record-keeping can seem onerous, and its value doesn't always become apparent right away. After a few sessions, however, maintaining the journal turns into a normal part of your gaming routine, and your group begins to reap its rewards.

THE JOURNAL

Your campaign journal can take a variety of forms. The simplest and most familiar method for many groups is to use a three-ring binder with one section full of blank pages for keeping notes and another with transcribed versions of those notes. A hard copy has the benefit of being readable anywhere and at any time, but unless you make multiple copies, it limits accessibility to one player at a time.

You can also use a host of online document sharing services to craft a journal that any player can reference or even edit from the comfort of home. A wide range of different web-based services are available, and many are free. A digital campaign log can be as complicated as a link-embedded encyclopedia, or as simple as a thread in a forum. No matter what method you plan to use, find one that your group can agree on and use it.

THE JOURNAL KEEPER

Some fortunate groups have a member not only willing to keep notes and transcribe them into a journal, but talented at doing so. If you find yourself in such a group, consider yourself blessed, and make sure that the writer knows how much you appreciate his or her hard work.

Most often, no one looks forward to the extra responsibility of maintaining your group's campaign journal. In that case, find ways to share the work.

For instance, one person can keep notes, passing them to a second player to turn into journal entries. Just make sure everyone can read the first person's writing. Alternatively, players can take turns as journal-keeper. This method gives up some continuity of style, but it ensures that nobody feels too burdened by the task.

You can also take advantage of technology to spread the work around. By using a wiki or a similar format for your campaign journal, every player can contribute. Even in this situation, however, it pays to have one person in charge of setting up the wiki and keeping it tidy.

If you take on any portion of the responsibility for tracking campaign events, keep your end of the bargain. When it is your turn to write, don't slack off. If one person in the group doesn't keep it up, it puts that much more work on everyone else, and there's no faster way to kill a campaign journal.

WHAT TO WRITE

Another challenge to keeping a good campaign journal involves deciding how much to write down. Your journal should be more than a list of monsters killed and treasure obtained, although that's a good place to start. The world of your campaign brims with interesting details that you could include, from the NPCs you meet to the exotic locations you visit. Puzzles, conspiracies, and clues serve as the mile markers along your group's path of adventure, and all deserve mention. Prioritize the information you believe most significant to the session, but don't forget to add the details that help you remember the events of the session. Mentioning the verbal tic of an NPC instantly brings that character to everyone's mind. If you describe the city you visited as "Gruenveldt, a trading capital built upon bridges across the Khyler River," even the players who don't remember the city's name might still recall its unique architecture. And who knows? Some of those details might end up being crucial to the story later.

Whenever possible, include the "why" of events in your log. It's easy for a group to forget what was so important about meeting with a cleric, but if the log mentions "we met with a bombastic cleric of Pelor to discuss the undead plaguing his village," then everyone not only remembers that you met the cleric, but a brief detail about him and why you were there in the first place.

Avoid too much complexity, or keeping the journal becomes a chore. You can reduce even the most convoluted game sessions down to a few brief paragraphs. The important thing is that the details are there for you to reference when you read the log later.

As you play and use your journal, pay attention to the entries that come in most useful. Knowing the kinds of details that pay off later can help you focus on those things at the table.

Other Benefits

A campaign journal can be crucial if your group includes one or more members who don't regularly attend. Without up-to-date game notes, the group either spends time bringing the absentee player up to speed on current events or leaves the player in the dark, struggling to understand the significance of the names and places that pop up in conversation.

The same goes for new players joining a long-running game. You'd be surprised how much assumed knowledge builds up in a game after only a few months; trying to explain it all to a new player in one sitting can leave him or her feeling overwhelmed.

Even if your group doesn't suffer from either of these issues, sometimes real-life responsibilities or emergencies arise that prevent a group from meeting regularly. Missed or intermittent sessions can leave everyone struggling to recall current quests, key relationships, and other game details. Without a clear record of your objectives, a game facing these circumstances can stumble or even fall apart. A campaign journal solves this problem by functioning much like a "saved game" file, reminding you exactly where you were when you last played.

In any case, a campaign journal—especially one that can be read online or distributed electronically—lets any player catch up on a wealth of detail away from the table at his or her own pace. A new player can even use the journal to help build a character that fits into the events of the campaign.

The journal also provides the DM with a measure of which elements of the campaign have resonated with the players. Because the players write the journal, it gives the DM a perspective on how much of the plot the players actually pick up, understand, and stay interested in.

Last, your completed journals provide a wonderful way to recap a campaign, whether just after finishing or even years later. Just like logging a great trek, keeping a journal of your campaign provides you with a permanent version of the story you told together with your friends. You might discover clues or story threads that you didn't notice earlier. It brings back memories of momentous occasions, both the climactic battle and the ludicrous interaction between the gnome and the archvillain.

Your journal can also inspire new campaigns and new characters. Perhaps one of the players wants to run a short game based in a city you visited, or the group decides that it wants to build a new set of characters belonging to an organization it encountered. Sometimes, reading about the places you have been can show you where you would like to go next.

No aspect of slaying a dragon is more anticipated than claiming its treasure: mounds of silver and gold dotted with scepters, swords, scrolls, and gems, but also guarded by deadly traps. Some players find sorting through a treasure hoard the most enjoyable moment of any adventure.

Unfortunately, dealing with loot can get ugly. How do you decide who gets the magic amulet? How should you split up the gold and gems? How do you keep your collection of magic items from becoming useless, annoying, or (worst of all) boring? When you bring a character into a game above 1st level, how should you equip yourself?

This section walks you through the treasure-gathering process, from getting it, to dividing it up, to deciding what to do with your share.

Acquiring Treasure

D&D characters gain treasure in two basic ways. Either the DM gives it to them—whether as part of a treasure hoard or as a reward for a completed quest— or they obtain it through their own means (such as by buying or making magic items).

Creating a Wish List

The *Dungeon Master's Guide* suggests to DMs that asking players for wish lists of magic items can help ensure that treasure hoards hold items that players want for their characters. If your DM uses this idea, don't ignore the opportunity to help customize the contents of the next treasure chest you find.

To create your wish list, review the lists of magic items ranging from one to four levels above your own. Start with the lists for armor, neck slot items, and weapons or implements (depending on what your character uses). For your first draft, jot down each item that sounds exciting. After you finish, cut the list down to no more than two or three items of each level. This should give you a list of about ten magic items.

Including more than one item at each level gives your DM extra flexibility to place items that fit the encounters, the adventure, or the campaign's overall storyline (and to leave out items that he or she doesn't feel comfortable including).

As a low-level character, don't worry about including items from other slots or categories on your first wish list. You need a good magic weapon or implement, a suit of armor, and a neck slot item to keep your attacks and defenses up to par. You can always go back and buy low-level bracers or boots later (see "Filling the Gaps," below).

Once you have an item in each of those three categories, which should happen by 4th or 5th level, extend your wish-list search to other slots, and eventually to wondrous items. Even with this expanded range of options, try to keep your wish list to around ten items. Not only does this prevent your DM from becoming overwhelmed—remember, he or she has to read through a wish list from every player at the table—but it also helps you remember which items you wrote down when one of them shows up.

Each time you gain a new level, review your magic item wish list to ensure it still represents what you'd like for your character. If you found a new magic weapon in the last session, consider crossing off any weapons appearing on your list—your DM might not remember that you just found a +3 *jagged greataxe* when he or she places the +3 *adamantine greataxe* that you forgot to take off your wish list. Conversely, if your paragon tier wizard is still running around with a measly +2 *magic wand*, it might be time to ask the DM for an upgrade. You should also add a new level of magic items to your wish list.

Just because you've written a wish list, the DM isn't limited to placing only those items. Part of the fun of D&D is finding unexpected treasure, so don't get mad because you haven't found that fabulous cloak you wanted. See "Filling the Gaps" for advice on how to address your need for magic items that aren't included in the DM's treasure hoards.

Unexpected Windfalls

You've slain the dragon, found its hidden treasure chamber, deactivated the traps, picked the locks, and sorted through the loot. When the DM announces that you've discovered a +3 *rod of the pyre*, you look at each other blankly. Then somebody says, "Uh . . . did anybody want one of those?"

Even if you use the wish list method described above, some DMs love to drop seemingly random items into treasure hoards. They say it makes the world feel more realistic or mysterious, but players often conclude that the DM likes to mess with them. Before you start whining about never finding the gear your character needs to keep up with the monsters, let's explore some questions that can help you deal with those unexpected discoveries.

Can you use it? First, figure out if anyone at the table could reasonably use the item. If you don't have a divine character, even the coolest holy symbol probably doesn't do much, but even your wand-wielding wizard could use a magic staff. Most DMs know better than to place an item that no character can use, so don't immediately jump to the conclusion that you've found something useless. That said, if your DM has done this, it might be time for a friendly chat. Maybe he or she doesn't know your characters very well, or maybe your DM has a different idea of how random treasure should be.

Does it come with a story? Some DMs place magic items as adventure hooks or to help describe their campaign worlds. Ask to make an Arcana check or a History check to learn more about the item. Maybe it's linked to the villain you're pursuing, or its presence here provides a clue to the current mystery you face. It might be part of an item set, leading you to seek out the rest of the set in future adventures. Or maybe it provides a little more insight into the world that the DM has crafted for the campaign.

Can you adjust the item? Many DMs would prefer to tweak an item than have the characters sell it for gold (or disenchant it for *residuum*). If you find *+1 sylvan hide armor*, but your rogue doesn't want to spend the feat for proficiency with that armor, ask yourself if you could use *+1 sylvan leather armor* instead. The Transfer Enchantment ritual accomplishes this nicely for a mere 25 gp, but some DMs will agree to retroactively change the item: "Did I say hide armor? I meant leather armor."

Can you adjust to use the item? Even if your barbarian prefers to wield a greataxe, maybe it's worth changing a feat choice to use that shiny new greatsword you just discovered. The retraining rules allow you to swap out one option the next time you gain a level (see "Retraining," page 47). If you have more than one feat or power invested in your old weapon, ask your DM if you can retrain them all when you level up. Come up with a story about the intense training your character undergoes to

THE PARTY WISH LIST

Many time-crunched DMs rely on party wish lists to place most magic items. This makes players happy because they get the gear they want, but it can leave out many useful and iconic magic items that aren't designed to benefit individual characters. For instance, every party likes to have a *bag of holding*, but who's going to put it on a wish list in place of a 5th-level magic weapon?

To address this issue, some DMs ask players to add a party wish list to their character wish lists. This list includes items designed to help the entire group, such as *everlasting provisions* or a *rope of climbing*. Ask your DM if you can make a party wish list like this. Keep the list short, and make sure that each player gets a say in what goes on the list.

master his or her new acquisition to help explain the sudden change.

Can you trade the item? Depending on your DM's campaign, you might have the option of swapping the item with an NPC for another item of similar value. This can be a much better deal than selling it, depending on how accommodating your DM is willing to be. If you can trade the item for something no more than four levels lower, that's more efficient than selling it.

Can you sell the item? Your last resort for dealing with an unwanted item is to sell it for gold (or to use the Disenchant Magic Item ritual to turn it into *residuum*). This nets you only 20 percent of the item's value, which is the equivalent of an item five levels lower than the one you're getting rid of. But if you can't find a use for it, even a little gold is better than cluttering up your character sheet or your hand of power cards with something you·won't use.

Filling the Gaps

In most campaigns, you can't rely on your DM to place all the magic items you want or need. Even the best wish list can't fill every slot or stock your bag with the right collection of consumable items. Use the gold you find to round out your gear, following the guidelines below.

THAT GUY HAS MORE STUFF THAN ME!

No matter how carefully your DM places treasure, no two characters will ever have an equal store of magic items. That's a good thing—if every character's list of item levels was identical, finding treasure would start feeling predictable.

Accept that sometimes your character will have fewer items or lower-level items than another character. After all, there's always another treasure chest waiting to be opened. If you think a real problem exists—for instance, the wizard got the last three magic items, and you haven't seen a new weapon in eight levels—talk to your DM. Maybe he or she doesn't realize that you've gotten left out of the magic item lottery.

This disparity can be even more apparent when a character joins an existing group. If you've paid attention to how magic items get passed out normally, you can see that the items handed to a new character doesn't quite match up to what a normal character would have at the same level. After all, treasure parcels include items up to four levels above the party, so most other characters have at least one item that is more than a level higher than the characters' level.

This disparity is intentional. It keeps new characters who join an existing party from outshining their comrades right away, and it also gives your new character a reason to go adventuring: You want better gear.

On the other hand, you have an advantage of flexibility that the other characters don't necessarily possess. Getting a big chunk of gold to spend on rituals, consumables, and cheap items gives you a unique opportunity to customize your equipment. Characters who grow organically over many levels tend not to have that flexibility, so you will likely end up with a more focused selection of items than your new companions.

No matter what the cause of a perceived disparity in loot, don't worry: Within a couple of levels, the distribution will probably be completely different.

Primary Items: If you're lucky, your DM keeps track of the enhancement bonuses of your armor, neck slot item, and weapon or implement and makes sure you have a reasonable item in each of those categories. Ultimately, though, this responsibility lies with you, and writing *+3 magic longsword* on your wish list doesn't mean you'll find one.

Each time you reach a new tier, check your enhancement bonuses. At paragon tier, you should have a +3 enhancement bonus in at least two (if not three) of these three items. By 21st level, this goes up to +5. If your big three items don't measure up, consider using your gold to buy a basic version of the item in question (*magic armor*, an *amulet of protection*, or a *magic weapon* or *magic implement*). Borrow gold from another character if necessary; remind him or her of how important it is for the whole party that your character remains alive and effective.

Secondary Items: Use your other item slots to improve your strengths, shore up your weaknesses, and add variety to your character. In addition to the needs you identify in play, keep these specific issues in mind when purchasing or making magic items.

Don't focus on items near your level; you probably don't have the gold to afford them. Instead, drop down five or even ten levels and look for bargain purchases. The *battlestrider greaves* (level 12) might have been too pricey when you were at 10th level, but a 21st-level character can easily afford them.

By the paragon tier, you might find your non-AC defenses lagging behind the target numbers (see "Know the Numbers," page 112). Look for items that provide situational or even always-on bonuses to these defenses. For example, a *belt of vim* (level 8 and up) grants you a bonus to Fortitude; by the time you reach paragon tier, it's a pretty inexpensive purchase.

Nobody argues with healing. If you struggle to get through tough or long encounters, pick up an item to keep you (or an ally) alive. *Gloves of healing* (level 12) improve your healing powers and also let you spend a healing surge to heal an adjacent character. These functions are useful even for a 30th-level demigod.

Higher-level monsters commonly rely on frustrating tricks such as flight, teleportation, and invisibility. Make sure someone in the group can deal with such tactics; magic items offer some good options.

Backup Weapon: Even if you love your weapon or implement with the passion of a thousand burning suns, it pays to have a backup available for special circumstances. Fighters don't make many ranged attacks, but when the dragon hovers out of reach, that *+3 distance javelin* might be your only means of keeping it marked. Having a *flaming weapon* in the group comes in very handy when a pack of trolls shows up.

And maybe your DM is the kind of person to set a few rust monsters on your trail right after you sell off that *+1 magic longsword* you weren't using any more.

Consumables: We mentioned in Chapter 3 to beware spending too much gold on potions and the like (see "Consumable Resources," page 111). But "don't spend too much" isn't the same as "don't buy any," and having a few consumable items handy provide another way to keep the party going for another encounter.

Every character needs at least one *potion of healing* (or a higher-level equivalent). Beyond that, spend your gold to grab consumable items that give you an option fundamentally different from what you can already do. A *potion of mimicry* probably doesn't help you win a fight, but who knows when you might need to look like someone else?

If you have the luxury of knowing what you might face in upcoming encounters, pick up some consumables to address those threats. Everyone going into the Hall of the Fire Giant King should have a *potion of resistance (fire)* in hand.

Ritual Components: If you use rituals, make sure you have plenty of *residuum* handy. Don't be bashful about asking for party contributions to the *residuum* fund; these rituals are for everyone, not only for the caster.

At a minimum, you should always carry enough *residuum* to cast your most expensive ritual at least once. If you routinely use any particular ritual multiple times in each adventure, consider keeping a steady supply of *residuum* with you sufficient to cast that ritual at least five times. Who knows when you'll have the opportunity to buy more?

STARTING ABOVE 1ST LEVEL

Before getting into details, it's worth mentioning this up front: Your DM gets the final say on the magic items that your character starts the game with. Your brand-new 18th-level barbarian doesn't have any right to a particular item or group of items. That's why the original guidance on "Starting at Higher Level" appeared in the *Dungeon Master's Guide*, rather than in the *Player's Handbook*. Respect your DM's preferences on this matter.

Now that we have that out of the way, let's talk about the most common method of equipping your higher-level character. The *Dungeon Master's Guide* suggests that you choose one item of your level + 1, one item of your level, and one item of your level - 1. In addition, you have gold pieces equal to the value of one magic item of your level - 1, which you can spend on whatever you need to fill out your character.

Use your three item slots to select a weapon or implement, armor, and a neck slot item (in that

order). Spend about half the gold on a few other magic items that fit your character. Spend about a quarter of the gold on potions, ritual components (if needed), and other consumable equipment. Hold on to the last quarter to deal with unexpected costs that arise in the adventure (or save it for your next item purchase).

DIVIDING TREASURE

We've seen more arguments and more crazy schemes about treasure distribution than about any other part of the game. It's hard to blame players for taking this element seriously.

Agreeing on a method of splitting up the loot you find should be one of the first discussions your group has after building the party. Trust us: The sooner you talk about how you plan to assign ownership of the magic items, gold, and gems you're going to find, the happier everyone will be later.

Every group has its own method of dividing treasure; to be honest, most of these are probably well-intended but flawed systems that unintentionally create inequitable comparisons, bruised egos, and selfish behavior. Here are a few common methods that we've seen used, and their strengths and weaknesses.

THE EVEN SPLIT

This method aims to give each character an equal share of the loot recovered during the session.

Whenever you divide up treasure, each character gets precisely the same amount of gold (or gold-equivalent), right down to the last copper piece. What could be easier?

Good: Nobody complains about an inequitable distribution of wealth. Also, this method seems intuitively fair, particularly to new players. If players can't get along or agree on anything, this method prevents argument over who gets what.

Bad: This method runs into a simple but unfortunate mathematical truth: Once you factor magic item values into the equation, splitting the loot equally becomes impossible without extensive bookkeeping and getting rid of items the party needs.

Let's look at a typical haul for a 1st-level group's first session:

+1 *vicious longsword* (worth 520 gp)
Two pearls (worth 100 gp each)
One *potion of healing* (worth 50 gp)
70 gp in coins

This represents treasure parcels 4, 5, and 7 (see page 126 of the *Dungeon Master's Guide*), which is a reasonable haul for one night of adventuring.

Obviously, giving the longsword to the fighter (thrilled to find an item from his wish list) makes dividing the rest of the loot impossible. The sword's worth more than all the rest put together.

You could sell the longsword and add the resulting gold to the pool, but this decision effectively eliminates all magic items from future treasure hoards. If characters carry only the items they can afford to buy

with their meager split of the gold, the entire party becomes weaker.

Some groups use long-term bookkeeping to achieve an even split, tracking each character's haul from session to session to ensure equality. But isn't that exactly the sort of chore that we play D&D to escape?

Note: Even if you use a different method of distribution for items, we recommend using this one for all the gold, gems, and other currency discovered. Even if one character gets a magic item and another doesn't, both should get the same amount of gold. It makes the game simpler.

THE RANDOM DRAFT

This method relies on the dice to decide the fate of the treasure you find.

When you divide treasure, each player rolls a die. The players then choose one item apiece from the loot list, starting with the highest roll and proceeding down until all items are gone. If there are more items than players, reverse the order after each player has an item, allowing the lowest-rolling player to choose a second time, then the next-lowest-rolling player, and so on.

Good: Like the Even Split method, this process theoretically achieves equity over the long term. Assuming an even distribution of die rolls, everyone eventually gets to pick first, second, third, and so on. After all, how can you complain about unfairness with random die rolls?

Bad: The drawbacks to this method are less obvious than in the Even Split, but they're just as insidious and potentially even more divisive.

First, there's no guarantee your party will achieve an even distribution of rolls. When you get lucky and roll the highest three times in a row, try telling the other players that this method is fair.

Also, who decides how often you roll? If you roll every time you find an item, only the high roll really matters, since you often find single items. But if you save up the rolls until you have a whole level's worth of magic items, that means some items sit around unused for several encounters. How is it a good idea to let the +3 *rod of obliterating wrath* gather dust when the warlock desperately needs a new implement?

The worst part of this system, though, is the greedy, party-destructive behavior it encourages. If you don't see any items appropriate for your character when your turn in the draft comes up, you might reasonably select an item anyway, thinking that you could always sell it or disenchant it. Not only does this waste a newly discovered item, but how does the next player in the order feel when you take his or her ideal item just to trade it in for a 20 percent payout? Trust us, that player won't remember you kindly when he or she gets the same opportunity in the next random selection.

Over time, the Random Draft method can not only create a magic-poor party, like the Even Split method, but it can also easily foster ill will between the players. Use this system only if your group can handle the competitive mindset it creates, or if the players at your table are incapable of cooperation when dividing up treasure.

FIXED DRAFT

This method replaces a random order of selection each time with a fixed order of selection that lasts for the entire campaign.

As with the Random Draft, each player rolls a die at the start of the campaign. The high roller becomes the "active selector" and automatically gets the first item found. The next item goes to the player who has the second-highest roll, and so on down to the last player. Then you reverse the order, as described in the Random Draft method, taking turns up and down

the fixed order you determined at the start of the campaign until your characters retire.

If you find multiple items in the same hoard, you can either determine their order of assignment randomly or let the active selector choose among the available options.

Good: This method improves on the Random Draft by eliminating the chance of any player picking first (or last) more often than another. It also clarifies the frequency of selection: Every time you get an item, the next player takes it.

Bad: You're still stuck with the worst drawback of the Random Draft method: the greed factor.

Variant: Some players give the active selector the right of first refusal for the next item, rather than automatically assigning it. If no one chooses it, the first player in order automatically gets it. This slightly improves the chance that each character will receive a useful item, but it makes every noncrucial item found a potential disappointment.

GET WHAT YOU NEED

This method foregoes any systemic attempt at equality in treasure distribution, instead relying on the players to cooperate in assigning items and gold to the characters who can best use them.

Whenever a magic item shows up, the players take time to discuss which character needs it most. Sometimes, the item itself suggests an obvious solution: if only one character wears hide armor, the *+4 great cat hide armor* probably goes to that character.

More often, however, two or more characters can reasonably lay claim to any item you find. That's when you need calm, reasonable discussion between the players. If both the fighter and the ranger want that *+2 amulet of vigor* you just found, you must weigh the benefits and drawbacks of either choice. Here are some good questions to ask during the discussion.

✦ Does it replace an existing item? If the fighter already has a *+2 amulet of protection*, that should factor into the decision.

✦ Who benefits more? Continuing the example started above, imagine that the ranger has only a *+1 amulet of warding*. Clearly, the increased enhancement bonus makes this quite useful to that character. On the other hand, the fighter's player points out that the ranger hardly ever spends healing surges, so the new item's power and property aren't worth as much to that character.

✦ Who got the last new item? If the fighter just found a *+2 magic longsword* in the last treasure hoard, it might be time for someone else to get a new toy.

✦ Who makes the final call? If the group can't all agree on a decision, you must have a method of

---

THE PARTY FUND

The game includes many expenses that benefit the entire group, from the bribe you pay the city guard to sneak into the armory to the *residuum* the wizard uses for rituals. Sure, you can divide these costs evenly between all the characters every time they come up, but why not establish a central account of gold—a "party fund"—from which to draw such expenses?

The simplest way to set up a party fund is to give it an equal share of the gold and similar currency you find each session. For example, if you have five players, each player gets one-sixth of the gold, and the party fund gets the remainder.

Once established, the party fund covers all costs deemed to be "group expenses." Make sure you set the criteria for this decision early on to avoid arguments. Some groups, for instance, include the costs required to return a dead party member to life, but others put that expense on the dead character instead. You don't need a comprehensive list of everything the party fund covers, as long as you discuss its most likely uses and reach a consensus on the fund's purpose.

If the fund runs low, ask everyone in the group to pitch in an equal amount to refresh it. Alternatively, the fund can take out a loan from one of the characters; just make sure you agree when the loan's due.

As with any house rule or social contract, write down your decision. If you have a campaign blog or wiki, include it there. Make sure new players see it and understand why you're doing it.

making a final decision. Although the classic "cut-the-baby-in-half" method has some appeal—if you can't agree, we'll sell the amulet for gold—it's still a reversion to the Even Split method. A majority vote is a good place to start, with a dice roll or a coin flip to break a tie vote.

✦ What happens to old items? Whether the new amulet goes to the fighter or to the ranger, it will replace an existing neck slot item. Does the character get to keep that old item (perhaps selling it for gold), or does it go back into the party for reassignment to a new character? The former option feels fairer to many players—it's my item, I can do what I want with it—but the latter choice helps the party more. Assume the new amulet goes to the fighter. If the ranger would rather have the fighter's existing +2 *amulet of protection* than the +1 *amulet of warding* he currently wears, it makes little sense to sell off the fighter's old item for gold.

Good: With the right group of players, this system ensures an equitable and effective distribution of magic items. Characters get what they need, the party doesn't waste good items by selling them, and everyone gets a say in what happens with the loot.

Bad: Discussions take time, and an indecisive group can become paralyzed by this method. This method also requires a level of trust and cooperation that often takes a new group many sessions to achieve. A single player can wreck this system by putting a claim on every item or refusing to respect other players' opinions. Also, players uncomfortable with debate tune out of the discussion, and they often end up feeling excluded from the group.

DM Assignment

If all else fails, you could put the responsibility for treasure distribution in the hands of the Dungeon Master.

Instead of letting players decide who gets which item, the DM can assign each found item to a particular character. Perhaps magic items are given to individual characters as rewards, rather than as seemingly random treasure discoveries. Alternatively, magic items in the DM's campaign might have a strange affinity for particular individuals, seeking them out and functioning only for them.

Good: This method avoids the unfortunate consequences of drafts, and no items need to be sold off to equalize treasure distribution. This method also encourages the DM to create a story for every item placed. Why did the ranger get that +2 *amulet of vigor*? Does it have some link to the character's past? Are

such items traditionally linked to members of the organization that the ranger recently befriended?

Best of all, though, this system ensures that every player gets items that he or she wants. Most DMs who use a method like this one use player wish lists (see page 150) to help them make appropriate selections.

Bad: This system can appear arbitrary. Unless all the players trust the DM entirely, some players could feel slighted because another character got a better item than the ones they did.

Some players will miss the old-school feeling of divvying up the loot after a dungeon crawl. Knowing that every item found already has an intended destination takes some of the mystery out of the game.

This method requires a lot more work of the DM. He or she must figure out which character gets each item, taking into account the players' wishes, the characters' needs, and the levels of the items he or she has already given to each character. Using player wish lists is a start, but a DM relying on this method should also record all the items given out as treasure to make sure that no player is accidentally getting better items than everyone else.

Customizing Your Gear

If you ever find yourself complaining that your magic items are nothing more than a list of numerical bonuses, it's time to take matters into your own hands. By taking a few minutes to describe the look of your item and imagining what story lies behind it, you turn a block of game statistics into a part of the campaign world.

Defining the Look

The Thayvian markings on Solandria's vermilion cloak suggest it might have been created by a Zarchion of Illusion. When she walks, the swirling cloak reveals three vertical slashes on the left side of her leather armor, a style once prevalent in the land of Durpar.

She carries a Moonshaevian dirk, honed from obsidian that formed after the explosion of Mount Kasterlak on the Sword Coast during the Spellplague. It sits in a scabbard that bears ancient Impilturan markings, passed down to her from her father. Slung across her back is a yew greatbow, crafted in the style of the half-elf bowyers of the Yuirwood nearly three centuries ago.

After a session in which you find a new magic item, take a few minutes to describe its appearance. What color is it? Does it have a special pattern or texture? Does it look old or new, and is that appearance accurate? Does its look suggest its power or property, or does it conceal its nature? Does it bear any other sensory details, such as an odd hum when used in battle or the smell of brimstone when activated?

Many magic items include a bit of visual description, but you aren't constrained by those. You're the one wearing *hero's gauntlets*, so if you want them to be tight black leather rather than shiny steel, go ahead.

ADDING STORY

Just because your DM hasn't created a story for every item that appears in the campaign doesn't mean those stories don't exist. Writing up a few details for your newly found *+1 pact dagger* turns it from a collection of numbers into a part of the world.

Ask yourself some questions about the item to spark your creativity. Who made the first one of its kind? Are these items still made using a special process or ingredient? If so, who controls the knowledge or supply? Does this item have any connection with a specific person, place, group, or event? Does carrying the item have any social or cultural significance? Does its presence signal the approach of a momentous time in history? Did the item once belong to someone else, and does that someone actively seek it?

Don't try to write a novel for every item. Start with a few details, then share your ideas with the DM. Perhaps he or she has thoughts about the item that aren't apparent yet, or maybe your work suggests a connection that your DM hadn't imagined. Together, you can use the item to add to the story of the campaign setting, integrating it and your character into the overall plot line. Look back at the descriptions of Solandria's items—these hint at story without locking in too many details.

Adventurer's Vault 2 includes many magic items with background information. The description of an *alfsair spear* details the rare trees required to craft these unusual weapons and the druids who harvest the wood, even including a few interesting locations for the DM to place into his or her campaign world. If you need help crafting a story for your magic items, check out these samples for a creative kick-start.

When your DM understands that it's important to you to know the story of items, you might find that he or she responds to the challenge. Rather than just coming across a *+2 dagger* that also can deal poison and acid damage, you want to find the *dagger of Omharia*, which was named for a beautiful maiden in the court of Rarien the Cruel. When Rarien thought Omharia was dallying with his brother, Rarien stabbed her with this dagger, making her hideous. She became a hag, and legend tells of her slashing young maidens with this dirk as she had been cut, dealing poisoned acidic wounds that left horrible scars.

OTHER REWARDS

Gold and magic items aren't the only forms of treasure. (No, really, hear us out.)

If your DM has read *Dungeon Master's Guide 2*, he or she might have noticed the section on "Alternative Rewards," which starts on page 136. It includes three different types of nonitem rewards. Divine boons represent the gratitude of a powerful temple or a deity. Characters might gain legendary boons by fulfilling deeds worthy of myth. A character seeking to learn rare techniques might pursue grandmaster training.

If any of these ideas interest you, don't wait for your DM to use them, suggest the ideas in your regular chats or email conversations about the campaign. (You do have regular chats with your DM, right?) Ask how your dragonborn paladin of the Raven Queen might earn his deity's favor, and you might get an exciting adventure out of it. Better still, your character might end up with something that nobody else in the campaign—or perhaps even the entire world—has.

Although these alternative rewards specifically replace magic items, rewards can come in other, less material forms as well. Building a friendship with a prominent NPC can give your character an edge in social situations. Gaining membership in an elite organization can offer you access to equipment and assistance that others would envy. Learning a well-kept secret can unlock campaign mysteries or provide fodder for blackmail. Even a single clue gleaned from a thorough investigation propels you farther along the plot line. Recognizing the value of these unorthodox rewards not only improves your party's chances of success in future encounters, it allows you to appreciate your past victories even more.

At some point, every group that plays D&D has to deal with "that player." This player stabs allies in the back. He or she kills vital NPCs without provocation. This player monopolizes the DM's attention and ignores other players when they need help. He or she somehow manages singlehandedly to make the entire experience less fun for everyone else.

This player is a jerk.

Worst of all, it's possible to be a jerk without even being aware of it. If you suspect that you could be acting like a jerk, this section provides a few suggestions to alter your behavior and make the game more fun for everyone at the table.

Hogging the Spotlight

One of the worst things the jerk does is hog playing time. It happens to all of us occasionally, and for very understandable reasons. D&D is an exciting game, and while you're imagining your character cleaving through armies of the enemy, it can be easy to forget that while you're taking your turn, everyone else is waiting for theirs.

You can take up more than your fair share of game time in several different ways. One of the most obvious is by taking too long to describe what you're doing. Although you should try to illustrate your character's actions in an interesting way, waxing poetic about the ancestral sword the character uses in combat before performing every attack is unnecessary. No matter how interesting the weapon's pedigree is to you, everyone else wants you to hurry up so they can have a chance to act, too. Save long descriptions for moments of roleplaying and downtime, not when everyone else is itching for their opportunity to attack.

Every time you narrate the specifics of what your character is doing, you walk a fine line between saying enough to be interesting and saying too much. This is a good time to take a cue from your fellow players. If you can see them going glassy-eyed or fidgeting, odds are that you're overdoing your narration. Do your best to be compelling while remaining concise.

Lack of Preparation

Another way that players overextend their turns is by not being prepared when their turn comes up. Lack of preparation takes many different forms, but the result is the same—your turns last longer than they need to. You can refer to "Combat Lasts Too Long," page 129, for some tips on dealing with this problem, but above all else pay attention to the game, even when it isn't your turn to act.

Waiting until your turn comes up to start thinking about what to do frustrates everyone else trying to enjoy the game. Pay attention, so that when you have the opportunity to act, you can take it without hesitation. As your fellow players act around you, you should be loosely sketching a plan of action to execute on your turn. The more attention you pay to the events that lead up to your turn, the easier it will be to adapt and respond to them. As you and the other players master this technique, you might be surprised at how naturally your party begins to work together, and how effective you all become at dispatching the challenges you face.

Interruptions

Another way you can dominate the spotlight doesn't even happen on your turn, but on everyone else's. Avoid interrupting during another player's turn or the DM's turn. If you feel inclined to take action based on what other players do on their turn, wait until your turn to describe your action. If a player or the DM misinterprets a minor aspect of the rules, wait until the end of the encounter or the end of the session to bring it up. No matter what, don't interrupt the flow of the game to quibble over the rules. Doing so slows down the game for everyone and will only frustrate and annoy the entire group. The group has a finite amount of time to play the game, and everyone participating in the game deserves an equal share of it.

Ignoring Your Team

Another thing that a jerk does is ignore the teammates that he or she should be working with. D&D isn't a game about you, singular. D&D is about you, plural: a group of heroes who have come together to defeat everything that the world (or the DM) throws at them. Against the overwhelming odds that a hero is sure to face, a team of heroes who work side by side offers the most certain path to success.

Be there for your group when the other members need you. A good player is ready and willing to lend a helping hand. Whether you attack a monster to draw it away from a vulnerable ally, give a *potion of healing* to a wounded comrade, or loan someone a handful of gold coins for a big purchase, assisting your fellow players helps to guarantee that when you need them, they'll be there for you. When you watch another player's back, it becomes that much harder for someone to stick a knife in yours.

Being there for the party can also be quite literal. Characters who constantly break away from the group to pursue their own agendas hurt the game in several different ways. First, when your character runs off on his or her own, it creates a hole in the party that enemies can exploit. Second, it forces the DM to simultaneously run separate games. If the DM has to split his or her focus between different groups simultaneously, the less detail and attention each group receives.

By keeping the group together, you move the game forward and reduce the number of things that your DM must remember. The fewer extraneous things that a DM has to pay attention to, the more detail he or she can put into the world around you.

ARGUMENTS

No matter how well your party works together, though, the cardinal rule of playing D&D is that although characters can argue, bicker, and fight to their hearts' content, players should not. Arguments between players—or between a player and the DM—are unproductive, divisive, and take up time that you could use playing the game. If you find yourself regularly bickering during games, take a moment to consider why.

If your arguments are over an interpretation of the rules, try to wait until after the session is over to discuss them. The middle of a game is the worst time to get into a debate with the DM or another player. Let the DM's ruling stand, and bring up your analysis of the rules during a break or at another appropriate time.

Arguments within the party can be especially tricky when there is treasure to be had. When the party has one more fighter than the treasure hoard has magic swords, it's easy to imagine an argument ensuing. Head these arguments off by agreeing in advance how to divide up the loot (see" Dividing Treasure," page 154).

CLOSING THOUGHTS

D&D is a game, and we play games to have fun. When you act selfishly rather than as part of a group of friends working together to tell exciting stories, you make the game less enjoyable for everyone else at the table.

If you learn nothing else from this book, remember the golden rule of gaming: Do unto other players as you would have them do unto you.

When it comes right down to it, everything else is secondary.

ADD TO YOUR D&D® EXPERIENCE.

Bring more to your characters and campaigns with a constantly growing source of new and exclusive content, tools, articles, and applications. Whether you're a player, a DM—or both— D&D Insider™ will help you get more out of every game.

D&D
INSIDER
LESS PREP. MORE PLAY.

 LEVEL UP YOUR GAME NOW—AT DungeonsandDragons.com

All trademarks and logos are property of Wizards of the Coast LLC in the U.S.A. and other countries.
©2010 Wizards. Restrictions apply, see site for details.